The End of Advertising As We Know It

SERGIO ZYMAN
with ARMIN BROTT

John Wiley & Sons, Inc.

Published by John Wiley & Sons, Inc., Hoboken, New Jersey.
Published simultaneously in Canada.

For general information on our other products and services please contact our
Customer Care Department within the U.S. at (800) 762-2974, outside the
United States at (317) 572-3993 or fax (317) 572-4002.

Wiley also publishes its books in a variety of electronic formats. Some content
that appears in print may not be available in electronic books.

ISBN 0-471-22581-9

Printed in the United States of America.

10 9 8 7 6 5 4 3 2 1

ACKNOWLEDGMENTS

I'd like to thank the many people without whose help you wouldn't be reading this book: Ric Alvarez and everyone at ZMG who contributed their time, expertise, and suggestions to this project. Terry Aronof for keeping it all legal. Tracy Costen for making sure everything was where it was supposed to be when it was supposed to be there. All my Coke direct reports for showing me the right way. Gene Kummel, who gave me my start in advertising. My agent, Jim Levine of James Levine Communications, Inc., for getting it all started. Chris Malone for his wisdom on sponsorships. Airié Stuart and her team at Wiley for keeping the wheels turning. Kim Nir and her crew of editors and proofreaders, for the fine tuning. David Ogilvy and Lester Wunderman, who really got that advertising is about selling. Dave Singleton for his research assistance. David Wheldon and Ian Rowden for their little books of wisdom. My incredible team at Z-Marketing for their proofreading skills. Armin Brott for not dying in Thailand and for keeping me sane by asking "Why, why, why?" And finally, my mom, Jenny, and Jessy always.

To all the advertising executives and advertising agencies who, after reading this book, will join in the revolution and evolve advertising to its proper place—helping sell.

—SZ

To Lulu, Roodle Pie, Little Zippy, and, of course, Ma and Pa.

—AB

CONTENTS

The End of Advertising As We Know It

INTRODUCTION

Let me start with a warning: If you picked up this book because you thought you were going to get a short course in how to produce killer 30-second television commercials, put it down and consider buying a primer instead. This book is about a lot more than that.

I'm not saying that you won't learn something about 30-second ads here. You will—and hopefully it will change your entire perspective on them forever. But 30-second ads are only a tiny part of this book, and, more important, they're only a tiny part of what advertising today is all about. Unfortunately, not enough people understand that advertising encompasses communication of all kinds, which is the whole reason why **advertising, as you know it, is dead.**

It doesn't work, it's a colossal waste of money, and if you don't wise up, it could end up destroying your company (or your clients' companies) and your brand. This point—that advertising is a lot more than 30-second movies—is critical and needs to be understood whether you're a CEO, a marketing manager, a creative director at an advertising agency, or a brand manager. It may be possible to bring advertising back to life, but the *only* way to do it is to forget everything you know—or at least used to know—about it and start over by learning these definitions:

- Advertising is *a lot* more than just television commercials—it includes branding, packaging, celebrity spokespeople, sponsorships, publicity, customer service, the way you treat your employees, and even the way your secretary answers the phone.
- Advertising is not an art form. It's about selling more stuff more often to more people for more money. Success is the result of a scientific, disciplined process, and absolutely *every single* expenditure must generate a return.
- If you don't keep giving customers reasons to buy from you, they won't. Awareness is absolutely worthless unless it leads to sales.
- Finally, and most important, *everything* communicates—everything you do or don't do or say or don't say.

As important as these definitions are, advertising will never be brought back to life unless everyone who's involved understands that along with advertising itself their roles and responsibilities have changed, too. Traditionally, companies abdicated responsibility for what they called marketing to ad agencies. They let the agency come up with a strategy and then execute it. In the case of a brand-new company or a brand-new product, that approach works fine. Companies want to do what they do best, which is provide a product or service, and it's natural to want to leave the marketing and advertising up to someone else.

After a while, though, the goals of the agency (to produce commercials and increase exposure) start diverging from the goals of the company (to sell products or services and make money). When this happens, it's time to make a major structural change: The company has to regain control of its own marketing and advertising. This is going to mean a lot of adjustment for a lot of people. Internal marketing departments and brand managers will have to broaden their scope beyond promotion. They'll have to start providing strategy—which includes advertising—as well.

The agencies themselves will have to make the biggest shift of all—strategy will now be the sole domain of the company. The role of the agencies will have to change from creating strategy and giving directions to executing strategy and taking direction. The agencies that make this transition will survive. The rest won't.

I should warn you that I'm going to be repeating most of these points over and over throughout this book. Just as businesses have to keep reminding their customers why they should buy from them, I know from lots and lots of experience that if I don't emphasize these points from a variety of angles, you may forget them. Don't be insulted: I do this with my consulting clients all the time.

Some of what you're going to read in the following pages will seem unorthodox, counterintuitive, or even just plain ludicrous. But every single point I make here is based on actual experience. I have an executive MBA from Harvard and I can spew theories and speculation at you all day long. But frankly I don't care about theories. I care about actual results, and what you're going to read about are battle-tested, real-world strategies that work. I've built and maintained some of the biggest brands in the world, and I've helped a number of other companies develop their brands as well, largely through the strategic use of advertising. I know what works and what doesn't because I've been there, which is a claim not many other people can make.

During my years at Coke, I had a chance to work with some of the greatest marketers in the world. And after leaving the company in 1998, I decided to write down the most important lessons I'd learned both from my mentors (who were my peers and subordinates as often as they were my superiors) and from my own experience.

I wish I could say that I had a chance to implement all these ideas while I was with Coke. But I can't. In fact, one of the main reasons I left Coke the first time, back in 1988, was that they absolutely refused to make the kinds of changes they needed to. (I got lured back a few years later, but that's a different story.)

In 1990, I got a call from Joe Roth and Strauss Zelnick, two wonderful guys who were running 20th Century Fox. They offered me a job as marketing president and asked me to meet with Barry Diller, CEO of Fox. Barry and I hit it off right away and he decided to call the president of the Coca-Cola Company, Don Keough, to check my references. As Barry told me afterward, Keough was going on and on about how great I was when Barry interrupted and asked, "If he's so great, how come he's not working for you anymore?" Without missing a beat, Don said, "He's too strong for us. He wants to grow the business too fast and do too many things, and we're a soft organization that does things as a team and does things slower." I guess he never knew how crazy that must have sounded.

I decided not to take the 20th Century Fox job and eventually went back to Coke when Roberto Goizueta, CEO of Coke, promised me that I could have free rein to do what I felt needed to be done—like grow the business. Unfortunately, Roberto died and the guy who took over had the same Neanderthal attitudes as the people who were there before Roberto. So I left again. This time, though, I decided to put my thinking down in writing. The result was my first book, *The End of Marketing As We Know It*, which was published in 2000.

The message of that book was fairly simple: **Marketing isn't about trinkets and trash; it's about selling. It's not an art; it's a science.** And if you're not getting a return on the money you spend on marketing, you're going to have trouble.

Before *The End of Marketing* even hit the stores (some magazine excerpts had come out early), I started getting calls from people who all asked me basically the same question: "I never knew marketing was supposed to be that way—how can I get me some of that?"

The response was so overwhelming (I was getting dozens of emails a week) that I started doing consulting. Eventually, I started a company, Zyman Marketing Group (catchy name, don't you think?), which now has three U.S. offices and employs 45 of the best marketing, advertising, and financial people in the business. We have clients in just about every industry, including banking, aluminum, skiing, video rental, telecommunications, golf, and even politics. Interestingly, we don't do as much work in mass consumer products. I have found that those companies are resistant to reinvention and change. I guess all those years of selling sugar water taught me something about how to take products that are essentially commodities and sell them for their *benefits*, not for the products themselves. Just last year, *Time* magazine agreed and named me one of the three best pitchmen of the 20th century—right up there with David Ogilvy and Lester Wunderman. All of that is the outgrowth of a single book that doesn't do a whole lot more than describe the principles and practices of a guy who *got it* early by learning it firsthand.

A lot of companies were getting my message, but a lot more weren't. Despite all the response I got (and continue to get), the vast majority of businesses out there seemed content to just keep on doing things the same old way. I bumped into a friend who's the CEO of a Fortune 500 company and asked him how business was. "We've got 70 percent awareness," he said. When I said, "That's great, but how are sales?" he suddenly realized he was late for a meeting and had to run. Right.

I was at a meeting at one of the companies whose board I'm on, and I told them that something was drastically wrong with their marketing. The first response I got was "Oh, no, Sergio, everything's working fine. We're just in a transition period." So I asked, "Transition? Transition to what? If everything's working so well, why are sales down 30 percent from last year?" Then came the hemming and hawing and excuses. It's the economy or the weather or whatever. What a load of garbage.

I get basically the same kind of reaction when I give speeches, no matter where I am in the world—to major *koretsus* in Japan, to marketing managers in London, or to professors and students at the school of business in Warsaw. A few people always come up to tell me how much my theories have influenced them, but the majority of the comments I get are "Oh, what you're talking about sounds very interesting, Mr. Zyman, but things are different here."

Hey, guess what. They *aren't* different. I don't care whether you're selling heating oil in Ireland, souvenirs in the Australian outback, or fighter jets in 125 countries. If you want to stay in business, your goals are the same: Maximize your assets and sell more stuff. But if you have no value proposition and no way of differentiating yourself from your competitors, consumers and even your existing (and most loyal) customers will go somewhere else.

The big problem is that most people don't really get that marketing isn't about the ad; it's about communicating the benefits and features of a product or service in a way that will make customers feel that their life is easier or simpler because of it. Advertising just happens to be the way to communicate those benefits. But how do you evaluate your marketing efforts? How do you measure them? What do you keep? What do you dump?

It was obvious that I needed to go deeper into what was still wrong with the way most companies do their marketing. But rather than go over the same territory again, **I decided to focus on the one segment of marketing where the most mistakes are made and where the most money is spent—and wasted. The hands-down winner was advertising.**

In a lot of ways the premise of this book is the same as that of *The End of Marketing:* The way businesses are doing things today not only isn't working; it's actually aggravating the situation. With advertising, though, the situation is even worse. In this book I'm going to tell you in a very hands-on way how advertising died, what killed it, and what we're going to have to do to revive it. I'll show you how to analyze your efforts, chart your results, connect with your consumers, and make your company better than it is now.

If you're in the ad business, consider this book a wake-up call, a warning of sorts: Either change your ways or find another line of work. Advertising is not about winning Effies or Gold Lions. It's about making money for your clients, some of whom will have read this book and who are going to be pretty ticked off to see you up on stage holding your first-prize statuette while their sales are dropping. It may not be easy to make the changes, but rest assured, you'll have plenty of company. In fact, I heard that there's a new organization forming—Ad Execs Anonymous—kind of a 12-step program for getting rid of archaic thinking. Dues are pretty cheap.

WHAT'S IN THIS BOOK

First, I'll tell you where and why advertisers go wrong and I'll show you what you need to do to avoid going down the same path. In Chapter 1, I'll explain why advertising is so much more than television commercials, and I'll tell you why it's not working. I'll also talk about the self-congratulatory nature of the ad business and show you that the pats on the back and the awards that the ad industry gives itself have absolutely nothing to do with how well the ads actually work.

In Chapter 2, I'll show you why it's dangerous to take your brand for granted and I'll try to put an end to one of the oldest—and most idiotic— myths in business: that if people know who you are, they'll buy your product. I'll give you a bunch of examples of companies who rode that myth right out of business.

Next, I'll talk about how to rethink and make the best use of traditional advertising methods. The main point of Chapter 3 is that trying to retain your existing customers is more profitable than trying to attract new ones. I'll show you what you need to do to determine the ideal media mix to best communicate with your customers and your target market. I'll discuss how and when to place—or not place—media buys, and why it's crucial to do all of this *before* hiring an ad agency. Because most agencies are more concerned with building their own businesses than their clients' sales, I'll discuss how to select an agency that will keep *your* business at heart and how to clearly define the agency's role.

Almost every business owner I know fantasizes that having the right spokesperson would make all the difference in his or her company's success. In Chapter 4, I'll talk about whether creating icons or using celebrity endorsers is really the best way to increase sales. I'll discuss and analyze a number of celebrity-driven campaigns and analyze what made them work or not work. Then I'll show you how to find the right personality to represent your product or service.

Last, I'll introduce a number of new elements and strategies that no one has ever considered part of traditional advertising before, but you'll have to master them if you're going to survive in the 21st century, where *everything* communicates. How your product looks on the shelf is the very last point of defense against your competitors. But most companies consider packaging only when they're about to launch a product and then they forget about it—sometimes for years. In Chapter 5, I'll use real examples of successes and failures to show you how everything from the shape of the container to the color of the label communicates to prospective buyers. I'll also encourage you to broaden your definition of *packaging* to include more than just the can or tube or box or bag that a product comes in. Among other things, packaging includes the size and color of the trucks that deliver your products, how many are shrink-wrapped together, the building your offices are in, and even the plain cardboard shipping boxes that come across your loading docks.

It always surprises me how many companies don't realize that they should get a return on their sponsorship dollars. And I'm always amazed by how many companies sponsor events so that they can get free tickets and socialize with pro athletes. By the time you're done with Chapter 6, you'll know why to sponsor, how to do it right, and how to measure your results. You'll never find yourself wondering how all you managed to get for your money was the chance to put your name all over something that no one's paying any attention to.

Chapter 7 will debunk the myth that any publicity is good publicity. The truth is that getting your company's name in the newspaper or on TV isn't all it's cracked up to be. Free media may not cost you any cash, but if you don't manage it properly, the consequences can be incredibly expensive. In this chapter I'll show you how to get free press when you need it and how to make the media—whether it's print, broadcast, or the Internet—an essential part of your company's marketing efforts. I'll also talk about the best ways to manage crises when they happen.

It seems like a simple enough idea, but it stuns me that so many companies completely forget about the people who keep them in business: their customers. In Chapter 8, I'll show you how the way your company interacts with your customers or clients has a huge impact on purchase intent and customer conversion. I'll also show you how to develop a comprehensive customer service and retention strategy. Then I'll talk about how all the best advertising, promotion, and publicity can be undermined by employees who aren't clear on what their jobs are, and I'll show you how to make sure this doesn't happen to you.

In Chapter 9, I'll take you through a detailed look at two companies whose successes and failures are perfect illustrations of all the points I've

CHAPTER 1

The First Casualty: How We Killed Traditional Advertising

The vast majority of people in the advertising business—and by that I mean agencies more than anything else—define an ad as a 30-second commercial. Yes, I know, print ads and outdoor billboards have always been around, but the reality is that when an agency is recognized for outstanding work it's almost always for a television commercial. There are plenty of times when a television commercial is the best thing, but there are also a ton of other ways to advertise that don't involve hiring a frustrated and expensive Hollywood director. Your packaging, the way you treat your employees, the way they treat your customers, how your receptionist answers the phone, how your delivery people are dressed—whether you want to admit it or not, all of those things are advertising. Let me show you what I mean.

About 30 years ago, I got a job working for Procter & Gamble in Mexico. P&G had just introduced a detergent called Ariel, and the challenge was to convince skeptical Mexican housewives—most of whom did their washing by hand and didn't own a washing machine—that a packaged detergent could get their families' clothes as clean as whatever product they were currently using. So we put together some ads that showed a traditional wash bucket that started churning and sudsing when some Ariel was poured into it. The message was simple, straightforward, and very clever: Buy Ariel because it will turn your ordinary wash bucket into a powerful washing machine.

As a young marketing guy, I was nearly in awe of the power of advertising: It was able to change people's minds, and, more important,

it actually got people to go out and buy. **Partly as a result of those ads, Ariel became (and still is) P&G's biggest-selling detergent worldwide— even outselling Tide.**

All excited about advertising, I left P&G and went to work for McCann Erickson, where they assigned me to the Coca-Cola account and I got my first introduction to the world of soft drink advertising. This was the 1970s and Pepsi had just started with their "new generation" approach. McCann's philosophy (which was the same as the rest of the industry's, including Coke's) was "grab their hearts and their wallets will follow." So we kept coming up with ads that made people feel good, made them cry, made them grab their hearts, and won us awards. We just produced our ads, turned them over to the clients, collected our statuettes, and went to work on the next campaign, never thinking for a second about what happened next. We just didn't care. Or maybe we just didn't know any better. Either way, it was a creativity race—no more, no less.

We assumed that because we were creating advertising, Coke's business was growing. But in reality, Pepsi was the leader in Mexico. It was only by using a lot of glass bottles (so that customers could return the bottle instead of having to pay a deposit) and coming up with consumer promotions that we grew the business. **Actually, it was our client who grew the business, not us. We just did great ads, or should I say movies?** And on we went.

At that time, Coke's head of marketing was a simpatico guy named Vicente Fox. Yep, the same guy with the boots and the big smile who now runs a slightly more complex organization: the country of Mexico.

Vicente spent lots of time motivating the bottlers and making them do what was needed to increase their volume, and advertising was part of that motivation. We used to have bottler meetings to introduce the new ads and campaigns, and we judged how effective they were by how hard the bottlers applauded (and, of course, how many awards we won). Boy, was that fun!

Things got a little more complicated in 1973 when McCann started sending me all over the world. My first stop was Japan. Gene Kummel, a fantastic person who was head of the company, was a true pioneer and ad biz visionary. He figured that if I could make it in Japan, I could make it anywhere.

In Japan they didn't get what a Mexican guy was doing there, but Gene had sent me, so there I stayed. They put me to work on the Nescafe account and on the newly formed joint venture between Isuzu and General Motors.

On the Nescafe account, the assignment was actually to try to do something about the dramatic decline in coffee sales that happened like clockwork at the beginning of every summer. The Japanese, who are very orderly people, drink hot things only when it's cold. To make a long story short, we came up with the idea of ice coffee (yep, back in 1973!) as a way to counteract a drop in hot coffee sales. I was thrilled—someone else besides me had finally caught on that advertising was about sales, not movies.

The Isuzu–GM thing, on the other hand, was back to business as usual. All they wanted was to get advertising standardized around the world. "Sales?" they said. "Ha! We can't be bothered with sales, that's for the dealers to do."

Just last year, I met with Jacques Nasser, who was still running Ford, and a bunch of his "marketing" people. (I put marketing people in quotes because they were really ad people in marketing people's clothes.) I immediately started asking questions about Ford's advertising. "What's the DNA of the Explorer brand?" I asked.

The marketing director jumped in and said that Explorer's DNA was "American Spirit." So I said, "American Spirit? That's not Explorer, that's Jeep." But she insisted, so I kept on rolling. **"If it's all about American Spirit, how come there's none of that in your ads? How come they're full of soccer moms and kids in car seats?"** She told me that I just didn't understand, that Ford may have had a few advertising problems, but they were working on them.

My point was that in most people's minds, no car is more American than Jeep—it's freedom, independence, and the great outdoors. For Ford to claim that Explorer captures that same spirit takes a lot of chutzpa—and even more ignorance. Even GM is closer than Ford. But I just couldn't get through to her.

I was challenging the conventional wisdom, which Ford had bought into completely: "Ads advertise, dealers sell cars"—the same conventional wisdom that Isuzu and GM had bought into 30 years before. Nothing had changed! Not surprisingly, the dinner was an absolute disaster and they practically threw me out.

After leaving me in Japan for a while, Gene decided that a bit of New York would do me some good, so I got back to doing ads that entertained—and back to the Coke account. Then it was off to Guatemala, where I did more of the same until I took a job with Pepsi and went to Brazil to be their marketing director (I eventually became president of Pepsi Brazil).

When I got there, I found out that Pepsi Brazil had the same advertising philosophy as Coke, but to make things worse, Coke was outselling us there 10 to 1. Not good. I knew that with the odds so heavily against us and with comparatively no penetration in the market, the only way we could dig ourselves out would be to do an ad campaign that provided contrast between us and Coke. So we came up with the Pepsi Challenge.

I thought it was a great idea, but the bottlers almost lynched me. They were furious that I'd had the audacity to come up with advertising that was supposed to sell. **"Stay the hell away from sales," they said. "Just give us something that's going to make people feel good."** What a mess.

In 1979, I joined the Coca-Cola Company in Atlanta, right at the time when Coke was heavy into entertaining and making emotional love to consumers. That's when I found out exactly what happened after those ads I'd worked on at McCann were sent off to the media and aired 20,000 gazillion times, and I was shocked. Nothing happened. All those beautiful, heart-grabbing, award-winning ads that were supposed to be getting people to buy Coke weren't having much of an effect.

I immediately called up my old buddies at McCann Erickson and the other agencies we had working on various Coke accounts. **It was a simple speech but one they'd never heard before: "Stop entertaining people and start selling Coke. If you can't do that, you're gone."** My bravado wasn't supported by the management of the company, except for Brian Dyson, who was the president of Coke USA. Everyone else immediately went on the defensive. After all, I was just some little Mexican guy, and where the hell did I get off giving crap to the creative geniuses who were hired to make movies about Coke? And now I was demanding that they sell the stuff! Well, it kind of shook up the whole industry.

Until then, the advertising community had looked at me as kind of a golden boy—the ad man who had become the head of marketing at a big company, a fellow traveler, their man on the inside. But as soon as I started demanding measurable results, I was tagged as a traitor. By 1980, the ad agencies were calling me the Ayacola (this was back during the Iran hostage crisis when Ayatollah Khomeini was running the show in Iran and was hated by everyone in America), the guy who tried to turn the ad business upside down by making unreasonable demands. The trades and business publications around the world picked up the term and it stuck. Nearly 25 years later, that's still what they call me. **And nearly 25 years later, I'm still preaching the same message: Traditional advertising that only entertains doesn't work, and companies that don't get wise to this are going to fail. I tell people that awareness—which is what most ads are designed to increase—doesn't get you sales,** and I'm baffled by how many people still don't believe me. Sometimes all I can do is shake my head and laugh. How are Kmart's and Enron's awareness levels now that they're in Chapter 11? **Awareness doesn't sell.** All it does is get you into the consideration set. And then you still have to sell.

SO WHY ISN'T IT WORKING?

Too many people—including most advertising execs and agency heads—don't even know what advertising is. I'm perfectly serious. Think about it for a second. **How do *you* define advertising? I know I've said it before, but the first thing that pops into most people's minds is that advertising is commercials—a 30- or 60-second movie—and that's the problem.** Yes, sometimes television ads are important, but sometimes they're a waste. **Given another minute or so to think about it, some people might add that advertising also includes radio spots and print ads in newspapers or magazines.** A few might throw in billboards and bus-shelter posters. That's about it.

Those definitions form only a small portion of what advertising is all about. **My definition is that advertising is everything.** Yes, it's those television ads that are the darlings of the ad industry. And yes, it's those radio and print ads, too. Plus, it's the way your product is packaged, the spokespeople you use—or don't use—to endorse it, the way you treat your employees and the way they in turn treat your customers, your annual reports, your promotional materials, the articles that get written about you, the events you sponsor, and even the way you handle unexpected business successes and failures. **In short, everything you do communicates something about your brand to your customers and prospective customers.** It all influences the way people view your company and your products, and it all influences whether anyone will buy what you're selling.

An airline can run expensive commercials all day long showing smiling flight attendants walking down the aisle carrying those fluffy pillows and china and crystal. But when you get on board and ask for a pillow and some flight attendant with a lousy attitude says, "They didn't give us any," you're not going to remember those TV ads and the company's claims of dedication to service; you're going to remember waking up after your uncomfortable nap with a stiff neck.

Think about the thousands of companies that rely on consumers to buy their products every day—soft drinks, fast food, coffee, stuff like that. If consumers don't get a reminder every day, they'll forget and become free agents, available to be picked up by whatever advertisement they happened to see last. Trying to reach every potential customer out there with a television ad would be insanely expensive—that's assuming it was even possible. **No matter how much television people watch, they can't possibly see every commercial.**

Advertisers and agencies put the whole industry on life support by refusing to let go of their idiotic belief that television commercials are all there is to advertising. But what *is* advertising all about?

Simply put, the goal of advertising is to sell more stuff to more people more often for more money. Get used to that sentence because you're going to see it a lot in this book.

Now, as much as I'd like to claim that idea as my own, it's not really all that original. When companies first started advertising, the whole purpose was to help them sell more of their products or services. And back in the beginning it did exactly that. Somewhere along the line, though, something went terribly wrong. **Instead of focusing on their clients' consumers, ad agencies and advertising executives at companies fell in love with themselves.** And instead of trying to help their clients increase sales, they hid behind their creativity, shrouding themselves in mystery and concentrating on coming up with award-winning (or simply spectacular) ads that end up more as works of art than works of communication.

THE CULT OF CREATIVITY, OR "THE EMPEROR'S NEW AD AGENCY"

This whole thing reminds me of a story I used to read to my kids when they were little: "The Emperor's New Clothes." You know the story, right? A couple of scam artists come to a country where they've heard that the emperor is obsessed with clothes. They manage to get an audience with the emperor and they convince him that they're the best tailors in the world and that they'll make him the most beautiful set of clothes anyone has ever seen. They get the commission, demand a huge deposit, order tons of gold and silver cloth, and then proceed to do absolutely nothing. When the king's advisors come to see how the new outfit is coming along, the con men show them an empty loom and tell them that the fabric is visible only to people who are qualified to do their job. In other words, stupid people can't see it. Naturally, no one wants to admit that they can't see anything, so they rush back to the king raving about how great the fabric looks.

Well guess what? The same exact thing has been going on in the advertising industry for decades. **Ad agencies and ad execs lure companies in with promises that they'll come up with the best ad campaigns anyone's ever seen.** They collect big fees, and whenever anyone questions what they do, these "creatives" act offended and basically say the same thing that the emperor's con men did: "Advertising is an art and only artists and creative people get it. Stupid people won't be able to understand what we do." And just like the emperor's advisors, the clients don't want to admit that they're ignorant. So they keep sending money and the ad agencies (including in-house ad departments) keep working on some mysterious thing behind closed doors.

Toward the end of the story, the king gives a big bonus to the fake tailors, puts on his nonexistent new suit, and heads a procession through town to show it off. In much the same way, ad execs eventually trot out their finished campaign and announce that it's brilliant. As proof, they show off the Addies and Clios they won for creative genius. Company execs get written up in the trade publications and go on stage to collect their statuettes and pose for pictures, all of which makes them feel brilliant.

In the final scene, a little kid shouts out the obvious, that the emperor is naked. **Well, when it comes to advertising, I guess I'm that kid, shouting out that advertisers are basically being stripped bare by ad agencies whose ads aren't doing what they're supposed to do: Sell more stuff to more people more often and for more money.**

Just as the emperor should have been more than a little suspicious when he didn't see any fabric, advertisers should be suspicious when they don't see any return on their investment. No matter what anyone else says, the truth is that advertising is *not* an art. It may involve some artistry, but in the final analysis it's a science whose results are 100 percent measurable.

If someone in your purchasing department bought a million-dollar machine that looked beautiful but didn't work, you'd boot him and his machine out the door in a heartbeat. Businesses can't afford to have assets sitting around not generating any return. So why isn't it the same when it comes to advertising?

I'm not saying that creative people shouldn't be rewarded. Of course, they should. But only when they come up with something creative that gets people to buy more stuff more often for more money. They should be scared to death to come out of their secret rooms until they're ready to face the music just like everyone else in the company, just like the tailors who scammed the emperor. Hey, David Ogilvy and Dan Weiden got it and so did Jay Chiat. Why doesn't anybody else?

Really and truly, though, the emperor wasn't just a hapless victim. He brought his problems on himself. And the same goes for a lot of advertisers. **Burger King, for example, has changed agencies so many times that consumers have completely lost track of what the company's value proposition is in the first place.** Still, Burger King keeps looking for that silver bullet that will magically make people line up at their restaurants, but there's no such thing. It's about steady communication and establishing a value proposition that appeals to heavy users first and the rest of the consumers second. The agency frenzy is as much the fault of the untrained client as it is the fault of the opportunistic agency.

Remember that country song "Looking for Love in All the Wrong Places"? Well, that's Burger King's story. But it's not about their agency; it's about them. **It's about relevance and giving people reasons to buy, not about ads.**

THE MYTH THAT ADVERTISING DOESN'T WORK TO SELL PRODUCT

Okay, back to the emperor. After the most embarrassing moment of his life, the emperor probably ran back to the palace, put some pants on, and got back to work. But advertisers aren't nearly as willing to accept that they made a mistake. They sit there and watch sales drop. Rather than say, "We've been idiots not to have insisted on measurable results from our advertisements. Let's change things," they decide that the way to stem their losses is to slash their advertising budgets. In fact, advertising is often one of the first expenses that companies cut when they're having tough times. Because they've never looked at advertising expenditures as an investment, they think it's something they can do without. Big mistake. **As Bruce Barton, who founded BBDO, said, "In good times people want to advertise; in bad times they have to."**

But not everyone's as smart as Bruce. Let me give you a bunch of quick examples of companies that were going through tough financial times but made the mistake of not following his advice—and have hurt themselves even more as a result:

- Samsung decided in 2001 to eliminate "unnecessary" costs. A spokesperson said, "The company is seeking ways to reduce travel, traffic, advertising, and miscellaneous expenses." **I'm sorry, but if you're the kind of company that puts *advertising* in the same sentence as *miscellaneous expenses*, you deserve what you get.**

- WorldCom cut ad spending by more than a third, saying they wanted to get more for their money by promoting long-distance and local phone services in the same ads.

- Buy.com cut ad spending, thinking it would save the company. Sales immediately dropped from $70 million to $50 million.

- Worried that earnings might suffer, Bristol-Myers cut advertising by 14 percent and raised R&D by 10 percent. Three of the five top-selling drugs at the company are losing their monopolies.

- Wisconsin Tobacco Quit Line, which helps smokers kick the habit, cut ad spending in July 2001. From May to July, they took 6,200 calls from smokers. From July to October, they took less than half that amount.

Overall, in 2001, when *recession* was probably the most commonly heard word in business circles, ad spending dropped almost 16 percent from the previous year. On the other hand, the handful of major advertisers who bucked the trend and spent more money on ads than the year before were able to increase sales. AOL-Time Warner raised advertising spending by almost 12 percent, while Ford was up 5.4 percent. **When Home Depot increased their ad budget, sales jumped 16 percent and net income rose 10 percent.**

It always strikes me as funny that when agencies pitch a client they start by showing their reel. Wouldn't it be better if they showed results?

And whenever clients make presentations, they always refer to their ads: the Chihuahua, those people singing "I'd like to buy the world a Coke" on a hilltop, Mean Joe Green, the sock puppet. Oh boy . . . We'll talk more about these a little later.

WHAT WORKS AND WHAT DOESN'T

Let me give you a few brief examples of some ad campaigns that have generated lots of awards but haven't produced much in the way of sales. I'll also give you a few examples of ad campaigns that may not have been as glamorous but did exactly what they were supposed to do: drive sales.

"Wassup?"

In 2000, Budweiser introduced a series of commercials featuring four young African American guys who called each other on the phone and greeted each other with some wacky variation on "Wassup?" The ads were incredibly popular and people were running around all over the place sticking out their tongues and asking each other "Wassup?" The campaign won just about every advertising award in 2000, including the 2000 Grand Prix Cannes Lionnes, the 2000 Grand Clio, and the 2000 Grand Award: Best Commercial New York Festival at the Television and Cinema Advertising Awards. **But while the ad execs were on stage, Budweiser's market share dropped 1.5 to 2.5 percentage points and sales in barrels fell by 8.3 percent**—the largest share loss by Budweiser since 1994 and by far the largest drop in sales over the same period. To hear them tell it, it was the weather and the economy and the private labels. Yeah, right.

"Think Different"

Launched in September 1997, the print version of the campaign featured huge billboards of famous people who broke the mold in their fields, such as Albert Einstein, Amelia Earhart, Muhammad Ali, and Pablo Picasso. The television ads presented a series of black-and-white images of the same notable personalities. As they appeared, the narrator (actor Richard Dreyfuss) explained how these people were innovators. The ads ended with the Apple logo and the printed phrase "Think Different." Apple's ad agency collected the 1998 Emmy Award for best commercial, the 1998 Silver Clio, and the 1998 Silver Lion at Cannes. The company's revenues dropped for the next three quarters in a row. The bloodshed finally stopped when they introduced the i-Mac. (Sales were up a tiny bit during the same period, but the increase had more to do with lower prices than effective advertising.) "Think Different" was great positioning for Apple, but it just didn't resonate with consumers until Apple paid off on the promise. **Just goes to show you how well ads can work to sell—or to unsell.**

If you make a promise in your advertising, you have to deliver. It's that simple. "Think Different" was supposed to establish Apple as the insurgent, different brand, but until they actually came up with a specific product that delivered, nothing happened. I've never heard of anyone winning an award for coming up with one of those boring yet highly informative print ads, but I have heard that they make sales go up. What gives?

The Pets.com Hand Puppet

This company is now out of business but when they were alive, they advertised a lot.

In one spot, the puppet sings Blood, Sweat & Tears's "Spinning Wheel" while riding along on a cat food delivery. In another, he watches dogs romp with toys in a park. One of the dogs says, "Look, he's got a stuffed thing. I love stuffed things." In another, set on city streets, the puppet tries to get a doorman to let him make a delivery for a parakeet and asks a tabby cat to "buzz him in." These commercials won a ton of awards, 37 percent of consumers who had seen the ads said they were effective, and company execs were delighted that the sock puppet had "crossed over from advertising icon to pop culture icon." Yeah, whatever. **Icon or not, no one was buying Pets.com's products.** They got so carried away with their own creativity that they forgot they were supposed to be selling pet supplies, not advertising. In my second book, *Building Brandwidth*, I chronicled—in advance—the idiocy of the whole idea. It's one of those great ironies that even though the company is dead, the puppet is alive and well in the advertising hall of fame.

"Dave"

Starting in 1989, Wendy's founder, Dave Thomas, did nearly 800 simple, folksy television commercials. The company's ad agency thought it would be suicide to cast ordinary-looking Dave, but he insisted. Viewers loved him—even more than Clara Peller (the feisty "Where's the beef?" lady). **More important, though, despite the fact that they weren't big award winners, the company's sales trend and market share have been consistently strong.**

"Don" for Hollywood Video

These ads parody those coming-attractions trailers you see in movie theaters. A couple, movie in hand, asks a Hollywood Video sales clerk for a little information about the movie. The clerk looks down, knocks on a cabinet, and says, "Don, we need you up here." Don, who happens to be the same guy who does a lot of voiceovers for theatrical releases, climbs out and starts delivering a typical movie-trailer description in that trademark voice of his. The spots started running in June 1998 and same-store sales have been on the rise ever since, growing faster than the industry average.

The AFLAC Duck

AFLAC is an insurance company that most people hadn't heard of until around July 2000 (the company itself estimates that name recognition was about 2 percent in 1990). But then they ran their first commercial featuring a duck who runs around quacking "AAA-FLACK" at people who need insurance. Sounds like a dopey proposition, but it works. The company estimates that since the duck campaign started, U.S. sales have risen 25 percent, and the trend is continuing.

My company, Zyman Marketing Group, did an exhaustive analysis of the qualities that award-winning ads have in common. We identified 15 categories (if you're interested, see Table 1.1), and what we found basically proves my point: 84 percent of the award winners from 1999 to 2001 incorporated humor—satire, slapstick, whatever. But only 22 percent actually made a call to action—told you to buy the product—which is what any marketing professional will tell you it takes to get people off their couches and into the store. But ad agencies obviously have a different agenda. To them, entertainment is more important than selling.

TABLE 1.1 QUALITIES OF AWARD-WINNING ADS

CATEGORY	CRITERIA USED TO ASSESS AD
Umbrella branding	Was the ad for a brand that covers multiple products or was it an ad for a specific product?
Product description	Did the ad provide a description of the product or brand being advertised either verbally or in on-screen text?
Product use shown	Did the ad demonstrate use of the product being advertised?
Emotional appeal	Did the ad make an emotional appeal as opposed to a purely rational one?
Humor	Did the ad use humor of any kind? Slapstick? Funny, surprise ending? Satire?
Sex appeal	Did the ad use sex appeal (male or female)?
Call to action	Did the ad call the viewer to action? (e.g., "It's time for E*Trade")
Price	Did the ad mention price at all?
Celebrity	Was there a celebrity endorser in the ad?
Text	Did the ad use on-screen text to do more than show the simple brand name and tag?
Animals	Were animals present in the ad?
People	Were people present in the ad?
New product	Was the ad for a new product?
Patriotism	Did the ad make a patriotic appeal?
Pop icon	Did the ad or some part of it become part of pop culture? (e.g., "Wassup?" and the sock puppet)

Ad execs and agencies also have another little problem: They hate to see their hard work go down the drain, so instead of just dropping things that don't work, they try to recycle them. When we first introduced Diet Coke in 1982, we tested a few different campaigns and ended going with "Just for the Taste of It," which was a huge success. A few years later, in 1987, the agency came in and tried to sell me one of the rejects: "Taste It

All." I'd turned it down the first time because our research showed that customers interpreted "Taste It All" as "Go for it, be all you can be, you can do anything," which was much more of a sports drink message and didn't appeal to diet beverage drinkers. So I turned it down—again.

Then, in 1992, I was doing some consulting for Coke and they showed me their new campaign for Diet Coke: "Taste It All." The agency had actually had the audacity to drag that dog out of the dump and present it for the third time. But this time it worked: They found a new brand manager who bought it! Not surprisingly, sales for Diet Coke tanked. Doug Ivester, the president of Coke at the time, called Tony D'Grigorio, the creative chief of the agency, in for a chat. He told Tony that the campaign wasn't working and that he wanted a new one. I'd worked with Tony before and he was always something of a prima donna, but I was amazed at what happened. Tony—this one really gets me—insisted that there was nothing wrong with "Taste It All" and refused to make a change! Eventually Coke wised up and fired Tony and his company, but it was a painful road.

There are a couple of explanations for why this kind of thing happens. **Ad agencies used to get a 17.5 percent commission from the media outlet for every placement. So there's a financial incentive to do as little work as possible and keep ads running as long as possible.** But there's a bigger reason. The truth is that most agency art directors are frustrated movie directors and most agency copywriters are frustrated playwrights—and both consider themselves artists. Asking them to change something they've come up with would have been like going to Michelangelo and telling him that his whole Sistine Chapel thing just wasn't working. Michelangelo would probably have said, "Forget it. I've worked my butt off on this and I want it used." Same with agency creative types (most of whom don't belong in the same paragraph as Michelangelo). They've produced something they think is high art and they want to see it in print or on the air.

A WHOLE NEW SET OF RULES

Part of the reason advertising as we know it today is dead is that the rules of the marketplace and the rules of business have changed. Take a quick look at the following table to get a rough idea of what I'm talking about. Then I'll tell you a little about each of the changes here and explore them in far greater detail in later chapters.

TABLE 1.2   MARKETPLACE RULES

OLD RULE	NEW RULE
1. Give people budgets to spend wisely.	1. Give projects budgets, not people.
2. Awareness is king and assume people get it.	2. Awareness is irrelevant, so overcommunicate.
3. Promote from within, grow organically, and don't train.	3. Teach continuously and get regular transfusions.
4. Expand for success.	4. Maximize your existing assets.
5. Get lots of data.	5. Get relevant data.
6. Marketing is an expense.	6. Marketing is an investment.

1. **"Give people budgets to spend wisely" becomes "give *projects* budgets." Not all that long ago—actually this is still going on in most places—companies didn't allocate money for individual projects.** Instead, they allocated money to individuals—usually division or department heads—to spend any way they wanted to. So you'd have a situation where the department head or division head goes to the budgeting committee and says, "Hey, you need to give me 10 percent more than you did last year because we're going to open up a bunch of stores and grow 10 percent." The committee writes him a check, which he dribbles out to activities as they come in.

And then there's the one about percent of sales. Eh? **The simple rule is spend to make money, spend to sell, and keep doing it until you're not selling anymore.** Reminds me of the guys from Africa who proudly strutted into a meeting in Atlanta and showed us a new idea: a traveling movie theater on the back of a Coke truck. The idea was that they'd drive this truck around from small town to small town and show movies to the locals. I asked the head of the team how much she was planning to charge people for the movies. "You don't understand," she said, "these people are poor!" So I asked her whether these people drink Coke. "Of course!" she said. "So why not charge them the crowns from Coke bottles?" I suggested. She thought it was a great idea but then asked me how many to charge. "Easy," I said. "Start with one per person. If you're filling up all the seats, charge two. If you're still filling the house, go to three, and keep on raising the price till you start seeing empty chairs. That's when you know what price elasticity is." The same thing applies to advertising: Keep spending while your sales are increasing and cut back or stop when they're not. I'm not smart, just practical.

The problem with this whole thing is that if someone's going to give you a check to spend any way you want, it's only natural to try to get as much money as you can, not as much as you need. And if you don't happen to get the blank check you're looking for, the natural thing is to try to hoard your money, which means that when someone comes in the door with a great idea for a new project, you're going to tell her that you can't afford it.

The solution is to give every project a budget and to effectively make each one a separate profit center. But be careful. **It's very tempting to try to save money by not hiring the people you need to do the job right— especially advertising and marketing people. Too many executives (and I've met hundreds of them) think that advertising people are always net spenders instead of people who grow the business.** As a result, they view increasing their employee head count as a sign of weakness.

In case you're wondering where I got these great principles (humor me), it's really a case of necessity being the mother of invention. When you've got a $5 billion budget, it's kind of hard to ask your boss for more. You've got to make do with what you have, which is what we did by applying these rules. Okay, you can stop laughing. I know that pleading poverty when you're sitting on $5 billion is a little hard to accept, but poverty isn't the point. **The point is that no matter how big your budget is, you still have to get a return. If you don't, you're doing something wrong.**

2. **"Awareness is king and assume people get it" becomes "awareness is irrelevant, so overcommunicate." One of the biggest advertising mistakes companies make is to assume that just because _they_ understand what they're talking about or what their strategy is, the consumer will, too.** The other big mistake is to imagine that name recognition and consumer awareness will magically translate into sales.

The assumption that if they know your name, their hearts and wallets will follow is flat-out wrong. Everyone knows McDonald's, but not everyone who eats fast food eats at McDonald's. And everyone knows Honda, but not everyone who's ready to spend $20,000 on a car buys a Honda. Clearly, an awful lot of people aren't finding any utility or relevancy in what McDonald's and Honda are offering.

Companies spend millions to put their name on football stadiums, develop packaging, buy television and radio time, and so on . . . and then they sit back and wait for things to happen. But really and truly, consumers aren't all that bright. If you don't tell them exactly what you're doing, why you're doing it, and why they should buy your product, they'll ignore you and take their wallet (and their heart) to someone who will tell them those things. Dozens of the biggest corporate names in America made the mistake of coasting on their name recognition, and a lot of them have coasted right into bankruptcy. I'll talk about some of these companies in Chapter 2.

The result of blindly assuming that people automatically "get it" (whatever that means to you) is that you end up spending money on things that don't work, you never bother to measure your results, and you spend a lot of time rationalizing what went wrong instead of making the necessary changes.

The best example is the marketing of New York City after the tragic events of September 11, 2001. Clearly New York doesn't need help with awareness—even if you lived in the middle of the Gobi desert, you'd know what New York is. And everyone in the world knows what you can do there: the museums, theater, sports teams, Empire State Building, Statue of Liberty, and so forth. So the goal of advertising shouldn't be to make people aware. **The goal should be to give a bunch of scared consumers reasons to buy the product—to come to New York and spend their money there instead of in some other city.** In effect, the tragedy itself became the advertising manager. So did Ground Zero, the scandals about the mafia having the concession to haul away debris, Giuliani, Bloomberg, the armed cops guarding the entrances to the city's tunnels, the commercials with Woody Allen ice skating and Henry Kissinger sliding into home plate head first, and more. Every single one of these elements communicated something about the city. And every one of these elements contributed in some way to consumers' decisions whether to buy New York.

The same could be said for every other product. In the very beginning of a political campaign the goal of advertising is to make people aware of the candidate and his or her views. But very shortly afterward, everyone knows the candidate, and the goal becomes simply to get consumers to buy the candidate (why should I buy George W. Bush instead of Al Gore?). **Everyone knows Delta airlines, but the goal of their advertising is to get people to buy them instead of United.**

This same "assume they get it" versus "overcommunicate" thing applies internally as well. I'm always surprised by how many of my clients assume that their employees understand the company's strategy. **Employees are a lot like consumers—you can't just assume they'll figure things out for themselves. Employees who don't know your strategy or your mission can't possibly advertise your brand effectively.** Every single person your customers come in contact with—whether it's a receptionist, a cashier, a driver, a manager, or you—is a walking advertisement.

I recently went to Philadelphia to give a speech for one of my clients, Merck, and was staying at the Loews hotel there. My client wanted to get together with me to go over what I was going to talk about, so we met in the hotel lobby bar. We sat there for 20 minutes trying to flag down the waitress but couldn't get her to give us the time of day. Finally, she showed up and I asked her whether she was new. Yep, she'd been there three weeks. I then asked, "Did you get any training?" She leaned forward as if she were telling me a big secret and said, "They tried, but I got out of it." Well, it showed.

So what's the solution? In a word, *overcommunicate*. **You have to explain to your employees what your product is,** which in this case is actually service. **If you want consumers to buy your product, tell them to and tell them why.** Don't spend much time worrying about whether consumers know your name. Instead, worry about whether they intend to buy your product (and if not, why not). And if you want your employees to do their jobs right, tell them where you're going and how you're planning to get there, and they'll follow you anywhere.

3. **"Promote from within and grow organically" becomes "teach continuously and get regular transfusions."** Pay attention because this is absolutely critical: The people who got you where you are right now—no matter how good they are—can't get you where you want to go. They just can't. **If you're going to move ahead, expand your business, or get into new markets, you need to bring in some new people with new ideas. If you can't do that, you at least need to send your old people out to be retrained.** Why *out*? Because there's no room for new thinking inside (if there were, your employees wouldn't need to be retrained!). Before running for president, Bill Bradley announced that he was going to take a year off. When asked why, he said, "Once I start running, I won't have any time to think."

But that's not what most companies do. Instead, they keep promoting the people they have, based almost exclusively on tenure or seniority as opposed to performance and ability. The senior flight attendant who served you the last time you flew is senior because she's been there 30 years, not because she's the most competent flight attendant on board.

You might be able to get by hiring exclusively from within if you are constantly training and educating your employees. But that's incredibly rare. Most companies simply stop training their employees after a certain point, assuming that they'll somehow pick up what they need to know by osmosis. The problem is that if they do end up learning anything, it's going to be how to keep doing things the way they're currently done instead of how to do things the way they need to be done to get to the next level.

Kraft, Procter & Gamble, Coke, and dozens of other big marketers used to have incredible training programs. P&G, for example, gave every new MBA six months of intensive training (on top of the basics they'd already learned in grad school) before sending them into the field. After two years, they'd have learned a tremendous amount and they'd be promoted to assistant product manager.

What happened, though, was that a lot of second tier companies were using Kraft, P&G, Coke, and others as hiring agencies—hey, **why go through the hassle and expense of hiring a wet-behind-the-ears MBA who doesn't have any practical experience when you can hire someone who's had the best possible sales and marketing training in the industry?** Makes sense to me.

As a result, the big guys ended up with so many empty product manager slots that they cut back the time they spent training so that they could fill the pipeline and get managers into the field quicker. So now there are a bunch of people out there doing things they aren't qualified to do. The companies could get these greenhorns some training once they're on the job, but they're really enjoying the millions of dollars they think they've saved by not doing this.

4. **"Expand for success" becomes "maximize your existing assets."** Back in the big expansion of the 1980s and 1990s, companies were growing at astounding rates—20 percent, 30 percent per year—and they were keeping up that pace for years. They'd run all over Wall Street shouting about their growth rates and their earnings per share, and the Street rewarded them by sending their stock price soaring. But the whole thing was a complete fantasy.

Instead of growing their business the old-fashioned way (by increasing same-store sales), they basically bought their increased sales figures

by opening new stores or buying competitors. Conglomerates became
the accepted way of growing a business.

The fall of the Berlin Wall gave lots of companies a huge opportunity to tap into new consumer bases. They opened up stores and built
plants all over Eastern Europe. All of a sudden, they had business that they
hadn't had before. No one—least of all Wall Street—seemed to notice or
care that these rapidly expanding companies weren't generating any kind
of a return on their capital. It wasn't until a year later, when people said,
"So how are your sales compared to last year's?" that Wall Street started
getting suspicious.

Anyone can buy bigger sales numbers. That's not hard at all. The
real challenge is to figure out how to sell more stuff to more people
using the assets you have now. The secret weapon is to do better
advertising.

Another way companies have tried to buy increased sales is by expanding their product lines. Sometimes, of course, that's a good thing. Say, if
your research indicates that there's truly an unmet need out there. But
introducing products for the sake of introducing products is a dumb
idea. Take Saltine crackers. Saltine, as you might expect from the name, is
a salted cracker. That's what it's supposed to be. So what on earth was
Nabisco thinking when they launched a low-sodium Saltine? I could see
them coming up with a new low-sodium cracker, but a low-sodium
Saltine? Come on. People who have sodium problems are probably not
going to line up to buy a product that's designed to be salty.

And is there any real reason why Procter & Gamble manufactures 19
types of Pert shampoo and 72 varieties of Pantene hair treatments? Is there
really a demand for all 19 different kinds of Colgate toothpaste? Why do
Eggo waffles come in 16 flavors? Does Kleenex really need to sell 9 different kinds of tissue?

In most cases, the answer to all these questions is *no*. Rather than
work on keeping their existing products relevant to their customers,
companies decided that they could bump their sales up by introducing
new things. It's as though the philosophy is "we've got a new product
development department and we're going to use it even if it doesn't make
sense." Dumb idea. If you're truly satisfying a need, great. But in most
cases all these new products do is cannibalize sales from the old ones.

5. "Get lots of data" becomes "get relevant data." American businesses are great at market research and we've been collecting data and

crunching numbers for years. We build models, segment markets, fore-
cast, do focus groups, and plot trend lines. You can buy market-share data
from companies such as Nielsen and you can hire others to do U and A
(usage and attitudes) studies to see whether consumers are using your
products and what they think about them. **We're practically drowning
in data.**

**Unfortunately, all those oceans of data don't contain much usable
information.** There is a difference, you know. Data tell you what already
happened, or, at best, where you are right now. **Data don't allow you to
change the way you connect with consumers and customers.** Knowing
your share of your category is great, but how does it help you increase that
share? U and A studies tell you whether anyone's using your product, but
they don't tell you why—or, more important, why not. Focus groups may
help you track changes in how consumers think of your brand, and asking
them to keep diaries may give you some insight into what they're buying.
But none of this gives you the faintest idea of what motivates consumers
to change brands and what you need to tell them to get them to buy.
Unless you do that, you're in deep trouble.

To do business effectively you need to gather only data that are relevant to what you're doing, data that help you understand what consumers
want. And since this is a book on advertising, let's narrow that even
further. Gather only data that allow you to accurately—and quickly—
measure how effective your advertising initiatives are. Anything else is a
total waste of time. I'll talk more about how to do that in Chapter 3 when
I get into results-oriented advertising.

6. **"Advertising is an expense" becomes "advertising is an investment." Conventional wisdom (what a dumb phrase) has it that marketing is a long-term activity, that building brands takes a long time.**
Everyone thought that advertising was a great way to help build that
awareness, but no one felt pressure to actually measure whether the ads
were effective. The assumption was that they'd work eventually.

In today's environment, though, *eventually* might as well be *never*.
Advertising has to sell your product today. When Macy's takes out full-
page ads for underwear in newspapers across the country, you can be
damned sure that they'll be comparing the number of pairs of Jockey
shorts they sold the day after the ads ran with the number the day before.
If there isn't a difference, Macy's will know they've got a problem.

Those used-car dealers that advertise at two in the morning do the same thing. If their customer counts the day after their ads run aren't higher than on the days the ads don't run, things will change.

Unfortunately, Macy's and used-car dealers are exceptions. **Most companies still operate on the *eventually* theory.** I'll give you lots and lots of examples throughout the rest of this book, but let me give you a quick one now.

I was watching the U.S. Open tennis finals in 2000, and, as I always do, I noticed a lot of the television commercials. One, from a company called Tyco, stood out. "Tyco makes winners," their ads said. They also apparently make disposable medical products and undersea communications. According to the ads, Tyco does business in over 80 countries and has more than 160,000 employees.

I pride myself in being pretty up to date on who's doing what in which markets, so I've got to admit that I was a little surprised that I had never heard of that big a company. More than that, though, I was amazed at the stupidity of Tyco's advertising on the U.S. Open. I gather from the ads that Tyco is a B2B (business to business) company, which means that almost no one watching the Open will buy any of their products. So who's their audience, and why is Tyco wasting a ton of money on television commercials? Hard to say. My guess is that their goal is to increase awareness of their brand, and they figured that taking out some television ads would be a great way to get their name in front of millions of people. The fact that 99 percent of them don't care didn't seem to matter—either to the company or to the agency that sold them the ads in the first place.

That kind of outdated attitude will cost Tyco big, and they will never—I mean never—see a return on the money they invested in those U.S. Open ads. For the same money they could have bought a year's worth of full-page glossy ads in trade publications where 99 percent of the readers would have been interested. I don't know that much about Tyco, but I can guarantee you that if they bought a machine that produced some of their disposable medical products, they'd know within days whether that machine was going to be able to generate a return on the investment. And if it wasn't, I can guarantee that Tyco would get rid of the thing in a hurry.

The same should apply to *your* advertising spending. If you treat it like an expense—maybe a fixed cost like your rent or electricity bill—it'll get lumped in with all your other balance sheet expenses and you won't pay much attention to it. But if you treat it like the investment it is, you'll focus on the return.

THE BIGGEST CHANGE OF ALL

By far the biggest difference between the way things used to be and the way they are now is that there's been a huge shift in the way people spend money. In technical terms I might say that cash flows are moving more intracategory. In English, the explanation takes a little longer.

About a decade ago, if you were in the canned tuna business you'd see your competitors as other companies in the tuna business, and you'd assess your market share based on how much of the total canned tuna market you owned. It was sort of a zero tuna game: You gain, someone else loses; they gain, you lose. If your customers weren't buying your tuna, you'd want to know whose they were buying.

That entire model is completely useless in today's economic climate. **People have a nearly unlimited number of products to choose from but a very limited amount of money to spend.** As a result, categories that used to be neatly organized aren't anymore. A shopper who once had a choice between your brand of tuna, Bumble Bee, and Chicken of the Sea, now might consider buying a bag of chips or a package of macaroni and cheese instead. **So, instead of whose tuna are they buying, the question is now more complex: "If they aren't buying my tuna, what are they spending their money on instead?"**

In Russia, we found that Coca-Cola's number one competitor wasn't Pepsi or Fanta or Kvas (a Russian drink). It was the bus. **Money was limited, so a lot of people were faced with the choice of buying a Coke and walking home, or not buying a Coke and having money for the bus.** In this country, people who used to be daily Coke drinkers are now strutting around with a bottle of water because it's cheaper and refillable.

Someone who's watching her weight might go to McDonald's and order a zero-fat, zero-calorie diet drink so that she'll be able to eat the Big Mac and not feel guilty (or at least a little less guilty) about eating a high-fat, high-calorie sandwich. **Obviously, this kind of fundamental change in consumer behavior requires an equally fundamental change in the way products are positioned and advertised.** But advertisers and their agencies keep on using the same old methods that they've used for decades, and they're pouring money down the drain. Are you going to do the same thing?

CHAPTER 2

Success Can Be Deadly—
Don't Take Your Brand
Awareness for Granted

It seems as if you can't open the business section of any magazine or newspaper these days without being bombarded with articles about branding. "It's all about branding," the experts say. And so everyone scrambles around trying to position themselves, trying to differentiate themselves from the competition, trying to capture the public's attention.

Don't get me wrong: Those are all good things to do. But the problem is that most companies don't understand that differentiation for differentiation's sake is a waste of time and that building a brand is only the beginning. In fact, I'm not sure if most companies really know the difference between a name and a brand despite all the focus on brand leadership.

My name is Sergio Zyman, and if you don't know anything about me (which could be a good thing), I am just a guy with a name. But by the time you're done with this book, the Sergio Zyman brand will be made up of my name plus the feelings that I elicited from you and your perception of what I've done to help you out—or piss you off. **If I do a good job, the Sergio Zyman brand will mean something to you and you'll be more likely to buy another one of my books or hire me or my company to consult for you. If I do a rotten job, the Zyman brand will have a negative connotation and you probably wouldn't even buy a used car from me.**

Branding is so misunderstood these days that I really need to spend a few minutes talking about the wrong ways and right ways of doing it.

My company, Zyman Marketing Group, is often invited to come up with proposals for companies that have decided they need a branding project. They usually put us together with design firms, as if creating a

brand involves nothing more than coming up with a series of pictures and jingles to magically change the public's perception of the company or its products or services. I can't get out of meetings like those fast enough. Granted, custom designing a company's "look" is a good thing. It's not unlike grooming yourself—somewhat superficial but still pretty important. But branding is a whole different thing.

A frequent variation on this theme occurs when companies decide that the way to build a brand is to go out and hire an advertising agency to produce some ads. Usually, the ads run a couple of times and then take up a permanent position in the company's boardroom, where everyone sits around waiting for their brand to develop and grow. Yeah, right.

The big issue facing your business today is how to differentiate yourself from your competition in a way that's relevant and meaningful to consumers. The sameness that we see everywhere is simply the result of lazy marketing, of taking brands, products, or services for granted. And let's not forget about Kmart and Enron—the most recent cases of product or product name awareness without relevance.

Sometimes businesses get the crazy idea into their corporate heads that changing the name of the company is going to help create (or redefine) a brand. This is almost always a rotten idea. Back in 1987, United Airlines, which at the time also owned Hertz and Westin hotels, renamed itself Allegis, which had absolutely nothing to do with the one-stop travel empire they were trying to create. It took them about six weeks to figure that out, and when they finally did, they got rid of the name and the CEO who'd signed off on the thing in the first place. And in 2001, Philip Morris decided to change their name to Altria. Did they really think that no one would know they still make cigarettes?

Absolutely no company—even mine—is immune from the need to be different. Since my company isn't the only one out there that specializes in branding, we've had to come up with ways of separating ourselves from the rest of the pack. One of the differences, of course, is the name. There's no question that some companies end up in our reception area because my name is on the door. But getting people through that door isn't the same thing as getting them to sign a contract. So we came up with the chart (shown in Figure 2.1), which highlights the differences between Zyman Marketing's services and everyone else's.

Most of our competitors, for example, do traditional brand consulting, meaning that they gather a bunch of data and leave it up to the client to

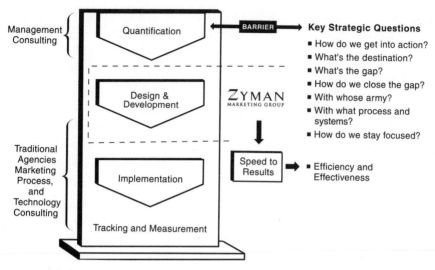

FIGURE 2.1

come up with a way to turn those data into a plan. They'll tell a client that the overall category's sales are off x percent and that the company's share of the market is up, but they don't help the client identify opportunities.

That's where we come in. No question that knowing how the market is changing is important, but we go way beyond that. Branding isn't only about data; it's about understanding how people's lives are changing and why, and reacting to those changes. It's about developing—and implementing—a strategy that's grounded in a deep understanding of consumers and customers, that connects companies with customers, and that helps them sell their products and services in a more efficient way.

Even companies that have built brands that everyone knows often make the mistake of taking them for granted. **Everyone knows Polaroid, right? And everyone knows what a vibrant and meaningful brand it was. And where is Polaroid today? Chapter 11, along with a lot of other big companies that didn't change and didn't keep their brand alive.**

Of course, some people might say that Polaroid died because instant photography is an outdated idea and the world has moved on. That may be true, but think about what Polaroid really offered: a new way to capture moments in pictures. They called it instant photography and built it into a hugely successful brand. But they never evolved and never adapted their basic approach to keep up with people's changing needs. So instead of focusing on new ways to capture moments in pictures—which is a fluid concept—they locked themselves into instant photography, which, in the era of digital cameras, is an idea that's long past its prime.

Take a lesson from Target and Montgomery Ward. Both of these companies had big names that lost a lot of their luster over the years and weren't nearly as vibrant as they could have been. Montgomery Ward took their brand for granted. They assumed that if people knew who they were, people would buy the brand. But Ward never really bothered to redefine what that brand was and what it stood for. And now they're gone. Bye-bye. Target, on the other hand, was able to redefine themselves and what they stood for, and they've remade themselves into a viable retail institution with a loyal following. And as if to rub it in, Target has actually built some of its stores on the very spots where Montgomery Ward's stores once stood.

The message here is pretty simple: Constantly renew and redefine your brand or die. You can have a big name and maybe even a patented, unique product. But your big name won't do you any good if your company's out of business. The solution? Don't take your brand for granted. Look at it. Look at your target market. Look at how you're selling. Who were you selling to before and who are you selling to now? Are your customers the same? If not, have you changed your advertising accordingly? Redefine your positioning and figure out how you can actually get done everything you need to do. And don't make the mistake of thinking that remaking your brand is a one-time thing. It's really an all-the-time thing.

I know you're thinking that this is going to be tough. After all, you work so hard to do what you do and starting all over would just be too painful. But think about it this way. The finish line of one race is the starting block of the next one. It's like a heavyweight fight. You can win one round, but you still have to get back in there and fight the next 14. All you've got is 60 seconds to recover before you have to get out there and fight again. And every new round needs a new strategy.

Consumers want to know that the product or service you're offering is at least as relevant to their lives today as it was yesterday. Our lives change, our needs change, and our values change as consumers, but more important, our values change as people. And any time those values change, our brands have to reposition themselves in front of consumers in slightly different ways, adding relevance to what the brand means. Not only what it means in itself, but, more important, what it means in these terms: "What is this going to do for my life?" and "How is this going to make my life better?"

Is it possible to be successful and never change your approach? I guess so. You could certainly argue that Wisk's "ring-around-the-collar" campaign and positioning has worked well. They're the undisputed kings of the dirty-collar segment of the market. But, really and truly, how big a market is that? **How much bigger could that brand have become if the company had broadened its definition, say to include getting sweat stains out of armpits, too?**

The cemetery of bad branding is so full now that we're going to need more land to bury the new arrivals. In 1989, I did some consulting for Club Med, which was hurting badly. The concept of an all-inclusive village had been copied 100 times, first by the usual upscale resorts, then more successfully by cruise ships and big hotel chains.

The market was saying, "You aren't any different from anyone else," but Club Med kept saying, "You don't understand: We're Club Med and we like us just the way we are." Unfortunately, consumers didn't, which is why the company's still in trouble.

Before we get too much further into this, let's take a step back. **As much as we hear and talk about branding, how confident are you that you know what a brand really is? If you aren't 100 percent sure, don't be embarrassed; you're certainly not alone.** As a matter of fact, you're probably in the majority. Anyway, even if you're sure, bear with me for a minute.

A brand is the original way to scale an idea, to make it grow, to get the word out about your product. The whole idea probably started back in the Wild West. No, I'm not talking about the Wild West mentality of the 1990s dot-com craze; I mean the real Wild West of 150 years ago. It all had to do with cows. Cows and the cowboys who physically wrestled them to the ground and burned a unique mark onto their hide.

It was all about differentiation—brilliant! These early brands gave owners a simple way to identify their cattle and keep them separate from everyone else's. Later on, buyers began to rely on brands, too, to give them more information than the eye could see about the products they were buying.

Say, for example, that the people who owned Brand Z put the word out that their cattle had been fed on organic grains and frolicked happily in the fields (which would make the meat more tender), while Brand A cows ate nothing but tumbleweed and were chained together in uncomfortable pens. From across an auction barn, the cows might look the same, but Brand Z conveyed some essential information that gave the animal-loving cattle buyers a reason to open their wallets. **In the minds of these buyers, Brand Z was very different from Brand A. And, as a result, Brand Z could charge a premium.** It was more than just a symbol that told people whose cows were whose; it was a symbol that made a difference.

In a way, nothing's really changed since the 1800s. **Brands still give buyers a way to tell one nearly generic product from another, and they give buyers a reason to buy.** But even that goes only so far. **Unless you constantly tell people** *why* **your brand is better and** *why* **they should buy it, you'll end up with nothing more than a name.** Pretty package, cutesy symbol, but no meaning.

Take the soft drink business. As much as I love Coca-Cola, I have to admit that most soft drinks are pretty much alike. Sure, some are clear and some are dark, but for the most part, they're all sugar and carbonated water. **The reason people buy Coca-Cola instead of Pepsi or the generic supermarket label is because of what the brand tells them. Coke is it, the real thing. Coke is always. Pepsi is the choice of a new generation. The supermarket brand is cheap.** Just the Coca-Cola or Pepsi name on a label isn't enough to get anyone to buy. The brand has to have meaning; it has to signify something special in the mind of the consumer (not unlike the reasons why Brand A was different from Brand Z in the cow example). The brand that does that best, that resonates most with the customers (in other words, the one that's closest to what they're looking for), is the one they buy.

Okay, let's get back to the cows. Eventually, Brand Z buyers discovered that organic grains and beautiful pastures didn't make the meat taste any better. Oh, everyone still knew about Brand Z and they knew it stood for happy cows, but it didn't take long for buyers to do what they always do when sellers don't give them a clear reason to buy: They dumped Brand Z and switched to a cheaper brand. And why not? **Why pay a premium for a brand that doesn't offer any particular value or that isn't any different from a cheaper brand? In the absence of relevance, consumers always fall back on price.**

This lesson illustrates one of the major misconceptions about brand: that name recognition translates into brand success. The theory is that all you need to do is make sure that everyone (potential and current customers) is aware of your brand, then you can go on vacation. I wish it were that simple. The reality is that unless you redimensionalize your brand and keep it relevant to consumers, awareness won't get you anywhere.

Whenever I go to the grocery store and walk down the juice aisle, I always see V8 prominently displayed on the shelf. And I walk right past it. I'm very aware of V8. I've seen their commercials for years and some of them are very clever. I know all about the eight vegetables and how healthy they are, but I still have no interest in buying V8. They've simply never given me the reason I need.

Of course, not every company can make its products or services appeal to everyone. That's an admirable but completely unrealistic and unachievable goal. The point I'm making is that name recognition by itself isn't enough to sell your product. Get it? I hope so!

Just think about Al Gore, Fuller Brush, Sunbeam appliances, and even Xerox. All of these brands (yes, people can be brands, too) had as close to 100 percent name recognition as you can get, and they still failed. Why? Basically because after they built themselves into national brands, they kicked back, rested on their laurels, and expected everything to take care of itself.

They also forgot one of the most important lessons in business: **If you don't give customers a reason to buy—and keep hitting them over the head with it—they won't.** Don't believe me? We already talked about Polaroid, but what about Singer (sewing machines) and Smith Corona (typewriters)? Remember those? Gone. Their ads? Beautiful! Their sales? Nonexistent. We'll talk about what big companies have done to undermine their own brands a little later in this chapter, but first let's talk about what a brand really is and how to build one the right way.

SO WHAT IS A BRAND, ANYWAY?

Defining what a brand actually is seems like a simple enough task, but it's actually fairly complicated. It's kind of like an impressionist painting: From a distance it looks like a single image, but when you get closer and start analyzing it, you find that it's actually made of a variety of components. Take a look at what's involved:

• **A brand is essentially a container for a customer's complete experience with the product and the company.** The Microsoft brand, for example, projects an image that the company and Bill Gates himself are committed to making their products better, brighter, and more useful.

They even try to involve customers in product development. By continually putting out a product that is not perfect but is on the leading edge, they're giving the impression that Microsoft's technology is so advanced that their products are always in development. The company responds well to suggestions for fixes offered by heavy and light users alike, and people end up feeling almost as if they own the company.

• **A brand is a bundle of functional and emotional benefits, attributes, usage experiences, icons, and symbols.** Who could possibly have guessed that Coke's polar bears would have become so popular? But the fact is that they connected with consumers on an emotional level. People don't think of polar bears as aggressive (even though they're just as dangerous as grizzlies or other bears). Plus, the company made them look sweet and cuddly. Polar bears are slow, lumbering, and consistent, which is pretty much the way millions of Coke drinkers see Coca-Cola: slow, consistent, offering no big surprises, sweet, and cuddly.

• **A brand is the company's link to the likes, wants, and needs of its customers.** For decades, the airline industry didn't give consumers much in the way of expectations. People Express changed that when they started offering their $99 fares. No one seriously expected to leave on time, but they did expect to meet a lot of interesting people while they were waiting. Decades later, when Virgin Atlantic came into the market, they created a bunch of expectations out of nowhere, then set themselves up as the only ones who could deliver. On Virgin it was "upper class" instead of "first class." They would whisk you out to your plane on a motorcycle if they had to, they would give you on-board massages, and their flight attendants were gorgeous. It was all about alternatives and choices. Virgin told consumers that they no longer had to put up with the run-of-the-mill treatment offered by the other airlines.

• **A brand is what keeps a company's loyal users coming back.** Think about Absolut vodka. It's really nothing more than fermented potato juice in a sleek bottle. But the company's ads have gotten across the message that Absolut is everywhere and in everything you know—from golf-course putting greens to cloud formations and everywhere in between. That takes a lot of chutzpah.

• **A brand is a way of conveying the meaning of a company's product or service.** Hertz's #1 Club reflects the Hertz brand and differentiates it from its competitors—even though all those competitors have

BRANDS AND BRANDING DEFINED

What is a Brand?	▪ A brand is a container for a customer's complete experience with a product and company.
	▪ A brand simplifies the buying process by differentiating a product on something besides price.
	▪ A brand is the bundle of functional and emotional benefits, attributes, usage experiences, icons, and symbols that in total comprises the meaning of a product or service.
	▪ A brand is a company's most valuable asset.
What is Branding?	▪ Branding is the conscious strategy and action of turning a product or service offering into a brand.

FIGURE 2.2

"clubs" that offer essentially the same benefits. Who said that we shouldn't have to wait for our car at the airport? And who said we should have our name up in lights and pay through the nose for the privilege? Hertz did. They made us feel special. They defined a brand and they keep on delivering.

Overall, a brand is a company's ultimate asset. It invests an otherwise generic product or service with a meaning that goes beyond the product itself. Managed correctly, a brand provides some wonderful benefits, not the least of which is an ability to charge premium prices; foolishly managed, though, it can kill you.

The Gap managed their brand perfectly, at least in the beginning. They pretty much defined hip, modern, and cool. People were walking around with their Air Jordans, a pair of Gap jeans, and a T-shirt with the Polo or Chanel logo all over it. The problem was that the *product* started becoming the dominating factor, not the brand. It didn't take long for The Gap to be copied by everyone in sight and become irrelevant.

Although I've talked about brands in terms of companies, it's possible to brand just about anything. There was an article in *Foreign Affairs* magazine by a guy named Peter van Ham who made some great points relating to this: "Look at the covers of the brochures in any travel agency and you will see the various ways in which countries present themselves on the world's mental map. Singapore has a smiling, beautiful face offering us tasty appetizers on an airplane, where Ireland is a windy, green island full of freckled, red-haired children." The 15 countries in the European Union are branding themselves, too: They made up a new flag (a circle of stars), and they're out there branding the hell out of their new currency, the euro, positioning it as a convenient alternative to having to change money every time you cross a border.

BUILDING A SUCCESSFUL BRAND

Now that you know what a brand is and what it can do for you, let's talk about what's involved in creating a successful one. Here are the initial components:

- Come up with a strategy through an understanding of your brand's DNA.
- Position yourself.
- Differentiate yourself from the competition.
- Connect to consumers' wants and needs.
- Go back and do it again.

Let's take a look at each one of these in detail.

Strategy

An effective brand strategy starts with a thorough examination of your brand's DNA, the building block that determines how your customers see you and how well your brand meshes with their needs. Keep in mind, though, that since your brand is only one component of your complete advertising initiative, your brand strategy should be a reflection of an overall corporate strategy where *everything* communicates.

I can't emphasize enough how important it is to have a strong strategy. You're not going to be able to set up an effective branding program (or even run your business successfully in the long term) if you don't have a very clear idea of where you want to go and how you're going to get there. Without a destination, you'll never get anywhere.

Most companies tend to try to drive their business by having activities such as promotions and ad campaigns. I have no problem with activities—as long as they're not random. You need to integrate every single activity into a long-term plan that drives you to your destination. So start by asking yourself what your brand is going to stand for, what your goal is, how you're going to fit into people's lives, and how you stand with regard to your competition.

Who's going to run the show? A critical part of your strategy is to put the right people in charge of your brand. **Most companies have one of the following approaches to brand management: (1) Either they close their eyes and hope that the brand will somehow manage itself, or (2) they let the marketing department run the whole thing.**

The first approach is obviously stupid. Nothing takes care of itself. If you think it does, you're going to wake up one morning to find that you've lost all of your customers and you're out of business. The second approach sounds reasonable, but it's not a whole lot better than hoping things will take care of themselves.

As I've already said, managing and building a brand are too important to be left to the marketing people. The person who's in charge of running your brand absolutely must be someone who can recite Sergio's Rule #1 by heart: The purpose of a brand, just like the purpose of any other component of your advertising mix, is to sell stuff. That's it. Anything else is failure.

As influential as a brand manager can be, sometimes your brand may be affected by something that's completely beyond your control. Just think of the George W. Bush brand on September 10, 2001, the day before the terrorist attacks. He had an approval rating of about 45 percent. In marketing terms, we'd say that consumers of the Bush brand were only giving him a 45 percent share of market, based on the criteria Americans had for evaluating presidents, which included things such as leadership, taxes, education, social security, and foreign policy. But the next day all those criteria changed. Before September 11, most people wouldn't have considered rating a president based on his ability to rally the nation, how tough he'd talk if we were attacked by terrorists, whether we thought he could actually protect us from getting killed, or whether he'd have an economic recovery plan to help out thousands of people who suddenly lost their jobs. But after September 11, they became the most important criteria, far overshadowing his tax-cut plans, education reforms, or social security.

It's exactly the same thing with products and services. Folger's coffee, for example, used to be defined by its aroma and the wake-up call of "Folgers in your cup." Then along came Starbucks, changing the criteria to latte, cappuccino, and muffins. All of a sudden people's values changed. George W. responded well to the new criteria for a president, and within days of the terrorist attacks, his approval rating had hit 92 percent. Folger's, on the other hand, hasn't adapted to changing coffee criteria and their business has been hit hard.

The point here is that a brand may be managed by internal efforts, but it's also affected by things that may be completely out of your control. So it's essential that you have someone you can trust to analyze everything that could possibly impact the brand and position the brand properly. Even more important is that whoever is running your brand absolutely must be able to think well on his or her feet and reevaluate your entire value proposition when something—anything—happens to change the criteria that consumers are using to evaluate your brand.

Positioning: Who You Are and What You're All About

Once you've got your strategy in place, your next task is to figure out how to reach your customers. We'll talk more about sourcing and segmenting customers in Chapter 4, but for now, let's just talk generally about how to position your brand.

Like your strategy, positioning doesn't just happen all by itself. But one way or another it does happen—whether you do it or somebody else does it for you. **Like your brand, how you position yourself depends on every aspect of your advertising and marketing mix: your employees, public relations, sponsorships, packaging, and pricing.** It depends on what you do and what you don't, what you say and what you don't, how you say it and how you don't. It depends on what your competitors say about you and about themselves and what you say about them.

The key is to take control of the dialogue early and never let go. Otherwise, your competitors will take over. Think back to Bill Clinton's famous phrase from the 1996 presidential election: "It's the economy, stupid." Every time Clinton said that, he was reminding voters that he was concerned about jobs, unemployment, welfare, taxes, and a whole bunch of other issues that were worrying them. But the best thing about "It's the economy, stupid" was that it positioned Clinton as the only one who cared. Other candidates tried to jump on the bandwagon, but Clinton already owned that space. The public responded to Clinton's opponents by saying, "We already know about the economy. What else do you have?"

In 2000, Ford had some problems with Firestone tires on its SUVs. A number of people were killed because of faulty tires and Ford had to recall millions of them. Congress held hearings to investigate the matter and the industry analysts started writing about how the tire fiasco was opening the door for Ford's competitors to gain market share in the SUV and truck categories. To make matters worse, Firestone sent out a press release blaming everything on Ford, claiming that Ford "had recommended that the tires be underinflated."

Although what happened with Ford was really an exercise in horrible media management (which we'll talk about extensively in Chapter 7), it also serves as a good example of what happens when a company loses control of its positioning. Ford and its flagship Explorer got involuntarily repositioned by Firestone and the media. Eventually, Ford will be able to regain control of the dialogue and may even be able to reframe the issue as a tire problem. But for the time being, they're being defined more by what happened to someone else's product and its impact on safety than by the meaning of the Explorer brand. If Ford is able to reposition the Explorer and align it with their Expedition and Excursion SUVs, they'll have to redefine exactly what the Explorer is. It will have to be the *ultimate* SUV that signifies and represents exactly how people want to travel or that offers other unique benefits, such as a revolutionary way for the family to get in and out of the vehicle easily. It will have to focus on mileage and durability and many other things in order to diminish the importance of tires.

Now, what about Firestone? Did this whole thing affect their business? You bet! Even though they were very successful in sluffing a lot of the blame onto Ford, Firestone almost went out of business because they ended up with a huge number of recalled tires in their warehouses. To get back on their feet, they're going to have to redefine exactly what Firestone is not only in the context of themselves but in the context of the competition.

A similar thing happened to American Express, which let itself get repositioned by Visa. Not so long ago, Amex was *the* international card. But in recent years, Visa has positioned itself as the card that's accepted everywhere, and Amex is the card that a lot of companies and some events don't take.

Visa's approach put Amex on the defensive. Amex introduced a series of new cards: corporate, gold, silver, platinum, and others, and they're making some headway toward eliminating acceptance and availability as factors by which you judge a credit-card issuer. They also signed Jerry Seinfeld, who did a series of very funny and very successful commercials for them. No question, Visa still owns the dialogue on acceptability, but American Express has carved out a new position in the marketplace using color and membership benefits as a package of attributes to differentiate themselves from Visa. Furthermore, they have successfully segmented the market to their advantage.

And to complicate things even more, MasterCard has jumped into the fray and positioned itself as the card that's the everyday answer for all of life's necessities. They didn't compare themselves to the other cards at all. Instead they told us they'd make our lives better. The world is our oyster, they said. There are a lot of things in life that don't have a dollar value, but for everything else, for all the material things, there's Master-Card. Brilliant.

So how long will Visa be able to continue to convince people to use their card based on being accepted in more places than American Express? And how long will MasterCard be able to tell us that we can use their card to buy happiness? My guess is that these messages will lose their relevance pretty quickly. In fact, American Express is back at the top—on the basis of scientific marketing supported by advertising.

As you start thinking about how to position your brand, take a long look at your company's strengths and weaknesses. What do you do best? What do you do worst? Are your strengths helping you achieve what you want or are you ignoring them? **Some of McDonald's great strengths, for instance, are selecting store locations, making burgers, and getting food to customers quickly. And the people who run The Gap are great at store design and layout, sourcing materials, and motivating their employees.**

As important as strengths (I call them *core competencies*) are, they have very little to do with whether a company is as relevant as it could be. **Many companies, for example, confuse core competence with brand essence.** They think they don't need to build a brand because they have locations and they know how to get those locations properly staffed. They spend lots of time improving how they go to market, where they get the materials, how they source all the ingredients, then they forget that the meaning of the brand needs to be refreshed again and again. They also forget that they need to get people in the door to buy their products.

Don't believe me? Like it or not, as successful a company as McDonald's is, a great deal of its corporate growth has come from opening new stores. Same-store sales—a far more accurate way of measuring things—are fairly stagnant. A lot of other companies make the same mistake, opening new stores all over the place and trying to convince themselves that sales are up because their brand is getting more relevant. In reality, all they do is increase distribution and make their product more available. But availability is not the same thing as relevance.

Meanwhile, The Gap spends hundreds of millions of dollars on advertising, which does a great job of getting people into their stores. All these people are obviously willing to buy; otherwise, they wouldn't come in the first place. But once they're there, fewer than 20 percent of them actually make a purchase. The Gap is obviously not giving potential customers a reason to buy. Customers come into the store because of The Gap's selection and location and because of the strength of the brand. But that's obviously not enough.

Part of the architecture of The Gap brand experience is trying on the clothes and getting advice from a salesperson about how they look. If that's not available, either because the dressing rooms are full or because the staff is unfriendly and unhelpful, the total brand experience is not accomplished. So even though The Gap sources great materials, makes great clothes, and finds great locations, consumers won't buy anything and the company won't be able to maximize its assets. They need to expand their proposition so that it transcends product and location. In other words, they have to define their clothes beyond the clothes.

As crazy as it sounds, when you buy a shirt from Polo, you think of the overall imagery of Ralph Lauren. You think of the horses, you think of the Polo logo, and you think of quality. Yeah, you think about the design and how the shirt is going to look on you, but you also think about all of the intrinsic and extrinsic benefits of the brand that will fill you with the feeling that you're doing something good for yourself and that you made the right choice.

Without making some significant changes, the only way The Gap will be able to increase its sales is to spend hundreds of millions of dollars more to bring in more potential customers in the hope that another 20 percent of them will walk out with a package underneath their arm. A very expensive and very iffy proposition.

Differentiation

By definition, a brand is very different from a commodity, which is a product or service that is perceived to be pretty much the same as the other similar products or services in the same category. Typically, the only determinant of a commodity's value is price. Quality is assumed to be identical unless consumers hear otherwise.

Differentiation, on the other hand, is where value is created. It's giving customers a clear message about why they should purchase your product instead of your competitors' product. **The driving philosophy behind differentiation is the belief that customers don't buy sameness (even with commodities consumers will differentiate on the basis of who's cheapest). Differentiation is what separates you from the pack. There are three basic ways you can differentiate your brand:**

1. **More for more.** You're telling your existing and prospective customers that in exchange for a premium, you'll give them more than they can get elsewhere. This is the approach taken by the biggest brands—the Cokes, eBays, and McDonald's of the world. These people say, "Yeah, you'll pay a little bit more, but you're actually going to get more, too—not only product but benefit."

More can sometimes be a tough term to pin down. Depending on the product or service, more can refer to quantity, service, speed, quality, or any other factor that's important to the consumer. But however you define *more*, just offering it isn't enough. You have to get that message across to consumers or you're wasting your time. **A lot of companies make the best-quality products in their category, have the best manufacturing processes, and use the highest-quality ingredients. But they never tell that to the consumers.**

2. **More for less.** Companies in this category say, "Listen, we'll give you more, but you'll pay less than if you go with the national brand." This is exactly what store brands and branded generics (or what we used to call "private label brands") do. They use a lot of the same imagery as the national brand, including knocking off the look, feel, size, shape, and color of the national brand. But their marketing, operating, and distribution costs are lower, which is the positioning they put in front of consumers.

3. **Less for less.** Companies in this category don't actually say much of anything to anyone. But the impression they try to convey is that they offer products or services that are as good as everyone else's, just cheaper. These are the generic products, the ones with "Food" or "Beer" on the label. In a sense, they're competing with the store brands and the national brands on the basis of price alone. Quality isn't even an issue. In fact, consumers actually expect less quality in these products. They don't offer much in the way of nonprice benefits.

Air travel is one of the most generic products out there, and aside from price, airlines have a relatively limited range of options they can use to differentiate themselves. In this kind of environment, Midwest Express has opted for the more-for-more approach: They charge regular airfares and don't offer any discounts. But what really distinguishes them from their competitors is that they offer leather seats, real china, fresh-baked cookies, and free champagne.

In some cases, it's possible to move from one differentiation category to another. Southwest Airlines started as a less-for-less airline. Their original proposition was "We're going to charge you less for taking you to the same places that the big airlines take you, but we're not going to give you any food and we're not going to give you a pre-arranged seat." Over time, though, Southwest has gradually shifted to more for more and succeeded in this move. Today, price is only one of many reasons people fly Southwest. In exchange for giving up plush seats, sandwiches, and a full bar on every flight, customers get an every-hour-on-the-hour schedule into more convenient airports, in the same kind of aircraft as their competitors, served by well-trained people with a great attitude.

As you look at the events of September 11, Southwest was able to weather the downsizing of the airline industry by continuing to fly to the destinations other airlines were cutting from their schedules. In fact, they actually added service to critical airports that had become economically unfeasible for the big airlines. But don't fool yourself—one of the reasons Southwest was able to survive is because they had been so successful in controlling the costs of running a profitable operation and had enough cash reserves to tide them over.

So how important is differentiation? As Roberto Goizueta, my old boss at Coca-Cola, used to say, "Be different or be damned."

The Importance of Being Relevant, or How to Connect to Consumers' Wants and Needs

Being different only works if your customers actually care about the differences. The big difference that Domino's Pizza used to offer, for example, was quick delivery time. If you were rushing around trying to feed the kids and didn't have time to make dinner, you could get a pizza in 30 minutes, which would take care of your immediate needs. Domino's built their business on a worldwide basis on the fact that they could actually deliver a pizza in 30 minutes. In essence, Domino's wasn't selling pizza; they were selling a solution, which was "Here's food that will take care of your time issues."

But when time wasn't as much of an issue, the door was open for Papa John's to come in on a positioning of quality and product. Apparently a lot of people valued quality over speed, and Papa John's took away a lot of Domino's business. Today Domino's is still trying to figure out how to change their positioning so that they can be relevant to more people.

A very similar thing has happened to Levi's. Many years ago, they positioned themselves as a cool brand that fit the lifestyles of cool kids. Unfortunately, they overused the concept and kept on chasing the same group of kids, who over the years got older and fatter. Eventually, Levi's came out with a line of relaxed-fit jeans that were loose in the butt. Although that positioning was relevant to a large group of consumers, it turned off the young kids, who are really the future of the brand.

Sometimes, though, companies create differences for no logical reason. The Gillette blue razor is a great example. Just a few years ago, Gillette introduced the Mach 3, a futuristic razor that delivered a better shave because it had three blades instead of two. Truly brilliant. It was so successful that they expanded the Mach 3 into a whole line of toiletries. Then, out of nowhere, they introduced a "new" Mach 3, whose sole distinguishing factor seems to have been that it was blue. In fact, that's the only thing they could think of to say in their advertising: "It's blue!" Unfortunately for Gillette, no one cared. Sure, blue razors are a novelty, but for most people who shave, color is completely irrelevant. They just want a smooth face, or legs, or underarms without losing too much blood. Not surprisingly, the new product was an enormous flop. Now Gillette has added a lubricated strip that "helps shave smoother"—success!

Or how about Apple's Cube? When Steve Jobs rejoined Apple, he launched the "Different" campaign and came up with a bunch of products that truly were different and had relevance for Apple users to whom being different is important. Giving Macs color and transparency revitalized a brand that people had pretty much given up for dead. Then Steve introduced the Cube. It was innovative and interesting and beautiful, but the colorful, transparent Macs were different enough already and the Cube offered absolutely no additional benefit. Eventually the Cube flopped and Apple had to take it out of the market.

It's important to remember that relevance is a moving target. Just because a message is relevant at a particular time, in particular circumstances, to a particular group of people, doesn't mean it will always be relevant in a similar situation. Unfortunately, too many advertisers haven't learned this lesson. It's pretty unlikely that what got you where you are going will be able to take you where you want to go.

When we introduced Diet Coke in 1982, the positioning was "Just for the Taste of It." **In an environment where taste as a benefit was critical, selling the brand on the basis of better taste (even though it tasted terrible) allowed us to introduce the Diet Coke brand everywhere and quickly grow its market share to over 10 percent, which was remarkable at the time.** But the relevance of the taste message faded and so did the growth rate. In 1992, trying to reinvigorate the brand, Coca-Cola turned to the advertising agency that had handled the original Diet Coke campaign. Their new positioning was "Taste it all."

It was a beautiful campaign. Art directors and marketing execs were jumping up and down, swinging from trapezes, and celebrating. Unfortunately, the "Taste it all" message didn't work. **Telling consumers that they should taste all of what life has to offer was meaningless, irrelevant, and out of place for a brand like Diet Coke.** Sales of the brand slipped even further, to a truly alarming level.

As I explained earlier, Bill Clinton's "It's the economy, stupid" appealed to voters in 1996 because it was an expression that was relevant to them. Clinton was telling consumers (and voters) that the only thing they should worry about—and the only thing the president should be worrying about—was having a better economy in order to have a better life. That was a tremendously relevant message at the time.

But after September 11, even though the economy tanked again, the "it's-the-economy-stupid" message would have been a huge flop. Unemployment rates may be at least as high as they were under Clinton, but today's driving issues are health and safety at home. Sure the economy is important, but overall I think people are more concerned with staying alive than being rich.

Figuring out what's relevant to your target market and redefining your brand accordingly are critical not only for the growth of your brand but for its very survival.

Image and Awareness

Whether you planned it or not, **your company has an image and so does your brand.** Sometimes they're the same and sometimes they're different. Not all that long ago, companies created their corporate or brand image with advertising alone. Today, though, your image is a function of everything in your advertising mix and your marketing mix. In a lot of cases, the ways companies differentiate themselves from their competitors are what drives their image. With Avis (the car-rental company), for example, it's "We try harder." With Visa, it's "Everywhere you want to be." With Southwest Airlines, it's "No peanuts."

Old Spice proved that it's a good deodorant by putting itself into sweaty places like locker rooms. And Heinz defined ketchup quality as thickness, then positioned itself as the only ketchup that had the goods.

The Coca-Cola Company fell into a campaign and position developed by Creative Artists. Actually, I should say, "got pushed," because they certainly didn't get there on purpose. They introduced a tag line of "Always Coca-Cola," which was really pretty clever if you think about it. It had great meaning in the 190 countries where Coke did business by reinforcing the idea that Coke is everywhere and that it's available all the time. It highlighted Coke's 115-plus years of being in business and hinted at the old "Things go better with Coke" line.

So what happened? Sales went up. But after five years, management and bottlers got tired of the commercials—even though the consumers didn't—and decided to make a change. That was a big mistake, because what management wasn't seeing was that "Always Coca-Cola" was creating a position that promoted the meaning of the Coca-Cola brand in more ways than one. They tried to bring in a product benefit instead and launched a new tag line: "Enjoy." Excuse me, but how does "Enjoy" do anything to differentiate one brand from another? Passive at best, stupid at worst. The issue was that some marketing guy (who really wasn't a marketing guy) wanted to have his own campaign! He got it and sales tanked. Brands have campaigns, not people or companies.

Not surprisingly, consumers didn't understand what the "Enjoy" campaign was about, and Coke had the good sense to pull the plug. But then they went to "Life tastes good," which hinted at "Taste it all," which was old to begin with and really didn't connect to anything. "Always" had supported the idea that Coke was a constant presence. The sponsorship of a series of events, from the World Cup to the Olympics, supported the position of "Always," and Coke was able to use a number of promotions to successfully activate and capitalize on these sponsorships. "Life tastes good" never really tied in with the rest of their promotions and advertising, and they were never able to use it effectively.

When you go from "Always" to "Enjoy," you start wondering what you're going to have to do in order to activate all of the things that you have in the marketplace. You end up with a series of conflicting messages that position the brand in a very, very confusing manner: On one hand, you sponsor the Olympics. On the other hand, you talk about life tasting good. On the third hand, you have your graphics saying something else, and on, and on, and on.

Every single thing that happens with your brand and around your brand says something. And the best way to capitalize on this is to make sure that all the messages are linked together and present a consistent image. If you do, guess what? You'll sell a lot of stuff and you'll make a lot of money. If you don't, make sure you have a bankruptcy lawyer's number handy (or a headhunter).

Too many companies make the mistake of thinking that creating an image is some kind of goal unto itself, and once they get their image into the public's mind, they'll automatically see an increase in sales and customer loyalty. Unfortunately, it doesn't work that way. As we discussed at the beginning of this chapter, having a well-known brand and high name recognition might get people in the door, but they don't guarantee that anyone will buy anything.

Ninety percent of companies out there measure loyalty by awareness and likeability. They say, "Gee, look, 100 percent of the people know who I am; 93 percent think I'm their favorite brand; 85 percent say I'm a very likeable brand." And then they can't figure out why they have only a 15 percent market share. Unfortunately, love doesn't pay the rent. It's all too easy to have super-high levels of irrelevant brand awareness or high levels of irrelevant likeability—awareness and likeability that don't motivate people to buy.

Just think of the Taco Bell Chihuahua and the Pets.com sock puppet. Both presented fun, quirky, exceptionally memorable images, and both created the impression that there was something fun and quirky about the products. But when customers went to Taco Bell or logged onto Pets.com, they didn't find what they expected. And neither company could prove that their ads were relevant. In other words, they made promises they couldn't keep. As a result, awareness of the ads continued to go up even as sales went down.

At the end of the day, usage is what creates loyalty. And the only reason to create an image of any kind—just like the only reason to build your brand and the only reason to be in business in the first place—is to make sales so that you can make money. When in doubt, measure brand loyalty and brand awareness on the basis of your sales. It's great to be known and accepted, but it's better to be bought.

Image and positioning go hand in hand, which is why it's essential that you control your image as much as you can possibly can. If you don't, someone else will be glad to use it against you, and once someone else's image of you is out there, it can be hard to shake.

Take Al Gore. He's a brilliant guy with more political experience than almost anyone in Washington. But no one saw that. Instead, the image of him as dry and overly analytical dominated wherever he went. Realizing that he had to shake his stony image, he went on *Late Night with David Letterman*, basically to show that he could make fun of himself. He wore earth-tone suits and even hired Naomi Wolfe to tell him how to appeal to female voters. Still, the wooden image stuck. The 2000 election surveys found that a lot of people thought Gore was smarter than George W. Bush and were convinced that he would do a better job as president, but they decided to vote for Bush anyway because he was more relaxed and generally seemed like a nicer guy. It's kind of scary to think that people will cast their vote based on niceness instead of qualifications, but that's exactly what they do. **If we don't have the right information, we'll make decisions on the basis of information that we have. That's often the same thing that consumers do when they make their purchase decisions.**

Of course, it's possible to shake an image, but it takes some doing. Bill Clinton, for example, is brilliant, but he had the image of a guy who cheated on his wife and then lied about it in front of millions of Americans. I'm not quite sure how he did it, but somehow Clinton managed to divert people's attention back to his other image as a public servant with a remarkable ability to lead the country.

And look at what happened with Tylenol. They offered a pain-relieving solution that was better for the stomach than aspirin. Then they had a tampering scare. **Overnight, people stopped buying Tylenol, and the brand was on the brink of extinction. But the company changed the whole dialogue by going immediately to a tamperproof package. This made consumers feel safe again and breathed new life into the brand.**

Understanding the DNA of your brand is critical because the molecular makeup of your brand will determine how you manipulate its various components. Exxon was able to separate the devastation done by a single ship, the Valdez, from an otherwise-good retail experience. But it didn't happen by accident. It happened because somebody sat down and decided they were going to have a scientific approach to getting this stuff done.

If you connect with people's wants and needs, *not* with their hearts and minds, their wallets will follow. Building loyalty means that they buy a lot of your stuff, not that they love you a lot. Telling people that your laundry detergent will get clothes cleaner than anyone else's is connecting with a want; telling them that your SUV has sliding doors so that their aging grandma will be able to get in and out connects with a need. But telling people that your toothpaste is recommended by four out of five dentists or that you're the number one rated brand of pork sausage is an attempt to connect with the heart and mind. In short, wants and needs generate sales. Hearts and minds generate a lot of "Okay, so now what?" responses.

In a sea of competitive choices and intense price competition, getting your customers to be loyal to your brand is a pretty tough chore. Image won't do it, and neither will differentiation or fancy ads. Launching a multi-million dollar campaign to bring customers in for a one-time sale might help in the short term, but you'll have wasted a huge amount of money if you release those customers back into the market without trying to build a relationship with them. The only thing that makes customers loyal is usage, and the only way to promote usage is to build brand relationships.

Loyal customers are the best possible customers. They're convinced that your brand is the one that can best meet their relevant needs. They often act as a kind of inoculation against the competition, virtually excluding them from the consideration set. Loyal customers buy almost exclusively from you and refer to you as "their supplier," or "their scotch," or "their coffee," or "their car." **To the loyal customer, price is no longer the dominant motivating factor.** In fact, you can have a higher price and still be perceived as delivering superior overall value than anyone else. Loyal customers become missionaries for your product and are one of your most important (not to mention virtually free) marketing channels.

I remember sitting in a meeting in Stockholm not long after I joined Coke the second time, talking with a researcher about the work she'd done analyzing three groups of Coke customers: daily drinkers (people who drank Coke every day), weekly drinkers (people who drank it once or twice a week), and monthly drinkers (people who drank it once or twice a month). Of course, daily drinkers were the smallest group, but they were very, very profitable for us. They also knew us best, connecting with what we stood for and the things that we said. They appreciated that we sponsored their favorite sport, or that we were available in their favorite store, or that we had the colors in our packaging that appealed to them, or that we had messages on television and on our trucks and in point-of-sale that appealed to them, or that we had promotions that actually fit with what they or their children wanted. Those are the true loyal users. Yeah, they like you; they think you're their favorite brand, and they show it by buying a lot of your product.

Be sure not to confuse loyalty with frequency of purchase. Customers are human, and every once in a while—in exchange for points, lower prices, miles, or some other shameless lure—some of them will temporarily shift some of their spending to another supplier in the category. But make sure it's temporary. Truly loyal customers will be back, provided you give them a reason to return. But if they leave you for price and you don't give them a reason to come back, they won't.

So what creates a relationship? It's not discounts, or promotions, or platinum number status, although those things certainly don't hurt. Just like the relationships you have in your personal life, relationships with your customers are based on honesty, intimacy, trust, dialogue, relevance, and a mutual feeling that the other party is providing something unique, something of value.

We'll talk in a lot more detail later in the book about how to solidify your relationship with your customers. But for now, start by thinking of every point of interaction between your brand and your customers as an opportunity to get to know them better and deepen your relationship with them.

Go Back and Do It Again: Change or Die

Okay, so you've developed a killer strategy, positioned and differentiated yourself brilliantly, created a powerful, memorable image, and have become your customers' preferred brand through usage. Great! But none of this is worth anything unless you go right back to step one and do it all over again. **Loyalty is a perishable commodity.**

Take a look at Figure 2.3 and remember this: You want people to think about you, feel something about you, and turn those thoughts and feelings into action—a purchase of your product or service.

No matter how much your customers love you, your competitors are still going to do everything they can to get customers to switch to their brand partially or permanently. **If you don't stay on top of the situation, you'll be right back where you started: building your brand from scratch.** The simple solution is to keep your brand dynamic by constantly refreshing and adding value to it. **Keep moving forward. Make changes before you get forced into them. Obsolete yourself before someone else does it for you.**

It doesn't take much to make customers switch brands. They're always looking for an excuse. Why? **Because too many companies get lazy and customers stop feeling that their wants and needs are being met.**

BRAND POSITIONING BEGINS AND ENDS WITH THE CUSTOMER

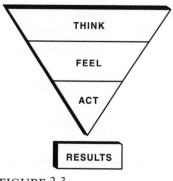

- Brand Positioning must be based on how you want your target to **think, feel,** and **act** regarding your brand.

  – Focus on the most meaningful benefits you deliver.

- Preference is perishable – continually reevaluate and refresh your value proposition and brand.

FIGURE 2.3

Just look at what happened with Charles Schwab and E-trade. They offered a whole different premise than any of the other brokerage houses. The initial foot in the door was based on price. But Schwab and E-trade were also providing every single service that the big brokerage houses did. This eventually turned out to be a very strong proposition and allowed Schwab to get into the market in a serious way, where they then expanded and changed with the times. Merrill Lynch stayed out of the low-cost, online brokerage business. They kept some of their customers but eventually lost enough market share and were forced into it.

Rand McNally has had horrible financial problems in the past few years, mostly because they allowed themselves to be repositioned out of the market by MapQuest. Why go to the store and buy a bunch of maps that you'll spill your coffee on and never be able to fold back up again when you can go online and get an absolutely free map including precise directions from where you are to where you want to go? With its 145-plus-year history, Rand McNally was infinitely better positioned in the map world. If they would have done it right, they probably could have even charged for some of their services. But instead they focused on trying to keep the $3.95 gas-station-map market, which they eventually lost anyway, along with the rest of the company. In 1999, they launched a website that tried to compete with MapQuest, but I think it was too little, too late.

Let me show you how easily this happens by taking you through the steps consumers go through on their way to adopting a brand.

• **Price of entry: Before you can even show up on your potential customers' radar, you've got to get into their consideration set (the group of companies they'll consider buying from).** And the only way to do this is to come up with a price-of-entry proposition, which is a fancy way of saying that you have to meet some basic requirements before anyone will pay attention to you. Sometimes these requirements are tangible; other times they're not. Sometimes the consumer is conscious of using them to make a purchase decision and sometimes not. But the one thing that's *always* true about price of entry is that it's constantly changing and constantly increasing.

For example, when Avis threw its hat into the ring, they did a number of things to differentiate themselves, including having buses pick up their customers at their terminal and take them to their cars. **Customers loved**

the Avis difference and flocked to them. But it didn't take long for every-one else to start offering the same services. After a while, having airport shuttles became essential for every airport car-rental company. Of course, having a shuttle won't get you any business today, but not having one will guarantee that you don't get customers.

The incredible thing about price of entry is that when you use it to dif-ferentiate yourself with physical attributes, in most cases your competitors will follow you and match you. American Airlines started the whole frequent-flyer industry when they created American Advantage. Pretty soon everybody had a similar program. Then they all went to double miles. Nanoseconds later, it was triple miles. Today, if you're an airline and you don't have a frequent-flyer program, you'll have a hell of a time trying to get anyone to fly you regularly. There are dozens more examples. Gillette comes out with a two-blade razor—the first blade pulls the hair out and the second one cuts it off below the surface. Heinz introduces a squeezable ketchup bottle. There are 100,000-mile warranties on cars, fluoride in toothpaste, airline red-carpet clubs, express checkout at hotels, and the list goes on. All these things get you in the door in their respective sectors, but they don't get you the sale.

• **Differentiation: Being different from your competitors is critical. Differences can motivate people and can influence their decisions.** But as important as it is, differentiation by itself doesn't drive sales. Hertz has its Number One club. Pepsi is sweeter than Coke. Tide has more green specks than the other detergent. Starbucks has more stores than anyone, Burger King has the Whopper. So what? Again, if the differences aren't relevant to consumers, they're worthless.

• **Preference:** This is the Golden Fleece. **If you can get your cus-tomers to prefer your product or service on the basis of more than just the product or service itself, you've got it made.** Preference is usually based on intangibles. Sure, some people may prefer one burger to another because of the taste or the size, but usually preference is based on some kind of emotional connection. Earning your customers' preference can propel your brand to leadership in its category faster than any other factor.

Unfortunately, customer preference has a date stamp on it: Today's preference becomes tomorrow's price of entry. When I was at Coke in 1993, I reintroduced a version of the classic contoured bottle design of the

1950s. It was a difference that customers preferred and the results were amazing. Straight-walled bottles of Coke had been selling for 39 cents apiece, but the same-sized contoured bottles went for 89 cents. Customers obviously preferred the unique retro look and were willing to pay a premium to own a piece of iconography.

Never forget, though, that preference is a perishable commodity; you have to earn it every day. Within a month or so, every other soft drink maker out there had introduced a contoured bottle of their own. Our unique advantage—something that had made customers prefer us—had become a necessity, and we had to move on. The contoured bottle had become part of the background, nothing more than another price of entry.

As you go through the process of evaluating your advertising efforts, remember that you constantly have to refresh consumers' minds about the things that make you unique, why they're important, and why consumers should buy your brand over everyone else's. Not following this advice can be expensive. The contour bottle I just talked about is a great example. At one point it was a difference that quickly became a preference. Then it

BRAND POSITIONING & ARCHITECTURE

The brand adoption model leverages the insights about the hypothesis to build a compelling brand positioning.

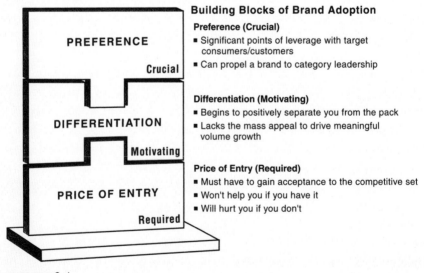

Building Blocks of Brand Adoption

Preference (Crucial)
- Significant points of leverage with target consumers/customers
- Can propel a brand to category leadership

Differentiation (Motivating)
- Begins to positively separate you from the pack
- Lacks the mass appeal to drive meaningful volume growth

Price of Entry (Required)
- Must have to gain acceptance to the competitive set
- Won't help you if you have it
- Will hurt you if you don't

FIGURE 2.4

became the price of entry into the soft drink business. But people forgot why they started using contoured bottles in the first place (because they were cool and retro). As a result, consumers see them as old and dated and no one uses them anymore. Putting something out there without an explanation is a good way to kill a valuable asset.

Admittedly, sometimes this can all be like shooting at a moving target. **The biggest marketing trend today is "me, too!" and technology has advanced to the point where almost any company can come up with a copy-cat product and have it on the shelves in 48 hours. Just look at all the generics and house brands out there.** So remember, even the strongest brands don't stay that way without working at it. **Brands are like muscles: Exercise them, stretch them, and keep them moving and they'll have a longer, healthier life. Let them be couch potatoes and they'll atrophy.**

When it comes to brands, the old adage, "If it ain't broke, don't fix it," doesn't work. If your brand is going to succeed and you're going to stay ahead of the competition, you're going to have to constantly fix things *before* they break and continuously realign your message and your image to your customers' wants and needs.

But does this mean that your brand is always at the mercy of your customers' whims? **What if you want to change direction completely? Whenever I get a client who asks about this, my answer is usually the same: While remaking your brand may offer some attractive advantages, such as bringing in new customers, it also involves alienating your base, the core customers who support your brand right now.** So before you completely overhaul your brand, you'd better have a pretty good reason for it.

A few years ago, I was doing some work for the people who publish the *National Enquirer*. They'd decided that they wanted to start including more entertainment and news coverage. Bad idea, I told them. The *National Enquirer* brand, which is an extremely successful one, is firmly rooted in sensational headlines: two-headed babies, Elvis sightings, alien invasions, and the like. That's why people buy the paper in the first place. **If the *Enquirer* all of a sudden started trying to pass itself off as a *People* magazine–style source of entertainment or a *New York Times*–style source of news, they'd lose their core audience. Plus, it's unlikely that people who currently get their entertainment from *People* or their news from the *Times* would ever switch to the *Enquirer* for either one.**

La-Z-Boy had a similar issue. The company was launching a new ad campaign to introduce some hip-looking chairs that were designed to appeal to today's youth. I don't think it'll ever work. When people hear "La-Z-Boy," they think of Archie Bunker or Frasier Crane's father on *Frasier*—mature guys lounging around watching TV, a remote control in one hand, a beer in the other. That's an image that could only drive young buyers away—unless La-Z-Boy could somehow convince kids that they should buy recliners so that they can be more comfortable when they're playing video games. But in the process of trying to convince the kids, they'd probably lose a lot of their remote-control-toting beer-drinking audience.

This doesn't mean that La-Z-Boy can never do anything other than what they're already doing. Of course they can. But they'd have to truly understand their brand, where it could possibly go, and how they could possibly extend it. It can be done, but it certainly wouldn't be a linear jump.

The same applies to a lot of other businesses as well. Can Johnny Walker sell gin? I don't think so, but they *could* sell single malts and maybe prepared cocktails in cans. Of course, repositioning your brand isn't always just something you might consider. Sometimes it's essential to your brand's success and survival.

Let me give you two cases of companies that dragged themselves back from the brink of extinction by retooling and repositioning themselves in the marketplace: Apple and IBM. Although these two companies seem—and are, in fact—completely different, their stories are somewhat intertwined.

It started a while ago when Apple first went after IBM, which pretty much had the entire PC market locked up, by positioning themselves as the alternative—to Big Blue, to Big Brother, to the lemmings. You may recall that famous "1984" television ad where the girl runs down the aisle at what looks like an IBM convention and she throws the hammer through the giant screen, shattering it into a million pieces, and the convention along with it. To a great extent, IBM's one-size-fits-all approach was a big help to Apple, and it allowed them to carve out a spot for themselves by appealing to people who wanted to be in charge of their computers instead of having their computers be in charge of them.

The big kicker was graphic user interface (GUI). More than anything else, GUI said, "We're here to help you out. No more F7 or control-shift-alt-F3 or any other weird key combinations." All of sudden, it was about icons, which truly revolutionized the industry. Later on, of course, the whole icon idea was copied (or stolen, depending on your perspective) by Microsoft, and icons are now everywhere.

But back then, Apple's icons didn't just reposition Apple; they repositioned IBM. They confirmed in the eyes of the consumer that IBM was rigid and inflexible. With IBM, it was about huge servers. It was about "do things our way, not your way."

Then along comes Lou Gerstner. He figures out pretty quickly that IBM's one-size-fits-all approach doesn't really fit very many people, and he changes the basic philosophy of the company to focus more on customer-based product lines and a customer-based attitude. The numbers speak for themselves. Lou was able to remake IBM back into the symbol of personal computing quality. And that's not all. He no longer sells personal computers through stores but centrally (kind of like Dell). And he backs those computers completely. Unlike Apple, Gerstner isn't constantly touting IBM's innovation, but it's clear that innovation is continuous and that it's driven by consumers' needs. **In short, Lou has changed IBM from a company that services machines to one that services people.**

This, of course, hit Apple right in the profit margin. They were the upstart, but they forgot how to stay on top. Their base was all about innovation, and they defined the landscape in terms of choice and change (sounds like Pepsi, doesn't it?), as opposed to tradition and business as usual.

Apple struggled for a pretty long time and eventually brought back Steve Jobs, the company's original cofounder. They couldn't have come up with a clearer signal that they were getting back to their original mission. As predicted, Jobs went back to Apple's roots, forcing the company to refocus on their target audience—people who are unique, who are looking for an identity, and who are looking for a product that's different, better, and more special than whatever else is in the marketplace. Brightly colored and even transparent computers and the "Think Different" campaign have brought the company back to what it always did best. However, there have been a few mishaps along the way: The Cube, for example, was technologically advanced and beautifully designed but horribly positioned with the consumer, and it was a pretty big flop. We'll see what happens with the I-pod, a product that is the most technologically advanced piece of equipment for downloading music. The downside is that it operates exclusively with Apple computers. And the big question is whether Jobs can generate enough volume—and profits. Or, will he spark a bunch of other companies to create similar machines for PC-based computers?

Overall, though, it seems like Apple is back on track. The latest I-Mac is sleek and futuristic and incredibly easy to use. Plus, now they're opening stores. Yep, stores where they can sell the Apple experience to Apple users—basically mini-clubs where Apple-heads can congregate to buy their machines. Pretty cool, eh? We'll see.

One of the great examples of repositioning happened with Audi. In the early 1980s, Audi was solidly positioned as the Mercedes Benz or the BMW of Middle America. It had a terrific ride, space for everybody, and sleek lines that were reminiscent of a small Mercedes. And then through some fluke they got into the sudden acceleration issue. Supposedly people were sitting at red lights when their cars would suddenly accelerate by themselves. Obviously, Audi really suffered as a result. They tried to reposition the brand in the usual ways, such as changing model numbers (the Audi 2400 became the Audi 2), but it didn't work.

Clearly, cosmetics wouldn't help. They needed a top-to-bottom repositioning focused on redefining what Audi meant. They did it brilliantly with the aluminum car. The A4, A2, and TT were a whole different presentation and manifestation of what Audi was. It gave them a completely new platform in the marketplace and positioned them squarely as the true competitor to the mid-sized BMW series and mid-sized Mercedes series. With that kind of relevance in the marketplace, they were even able to boost their prices.

Somebody asked me the other day whether Britney Spears could be repositioned. My first response was "Why would anyone want to reposition Britney Spears?" But after thinking about it for a few seconds, I realized that Britney, like everyone else, faced a whole new set of challenges after the September 11, 2001, terrorist attacks. Two months after the attacks, she released a new CD that promptly hit number one on the charts. But that's a relative thing: The new CD sold only about half as many copies as the previous one. The Britney message had started to fade. However, Britney responded incredibly well, moving herself more to the center of the music scene. She backed off her aggressive sex-kitten persona and showed some range in a pretty tame movie, *Crossroads*. As a result, Britney's back.

No one repositions herself as well—or as frequently—as Madonna. She started out as a wild and crazy singer who knew how to dance, but remade herself along the way, always slightly ahead of the curve. She was the material girl, she was the slut, she was Evita Peron, and she was even the young mother. When Michael Jackson started prancing around and grabbing his crotch, Madonna started grabbing hers, as if to say, "I can do that stuff, too." **Madonna, unlike almost anyone else in her business, has an uncanny ability to retool the Madonna brand on the fly and stay current without losing her brand's core essence, which, like her, is all about change and outrageousness.**

How and when you reposition your brand is strictly a function of knowing exactly where you want to go at any given time and keeping your eyes focused on that target. That's something politicians do incredibly well. Their goal is to get elected, and they figure out exactly what they need to do to get there. In the process, they change their methods and their tactics and sometimes even their message. Of course, I'm not advocating lying to your customers or making promises you don't intend to keep. What I am saying is that you can't always rely on what worked in the past to get you where you want to go in the future. If you keep your goals in mind, you'll always be able to stand up and say, "Hey, I made a mistake," or "Hmmm, that tactic didn't work. Looks like we need a new one."

CONTINGENCY PLANNING

Of course, something might happen one day that will have a profoundly negative impact on your brand. That's why you should have a contingency plan in place to launch a coordinated salvage effort that will protect what's left of the brand, rebuild where you need to, and relaunch if you have to. This is precisely what Ford had to do in light of the Firestone tire debacle.

Unfortunately, the rules of business (who ever thought them up?) have by and large determined that changing your mind is a sign of weakness, not of strength. What a dumb idea. Every rocket on the space shuttle has double or triple "redundant" systems. And every airplane you fly has two or three computers—just in case. Human beings even have two kidneys for the same reason: It's all about contingency planning.

So what if something does happen to your company or your brand? What are you going to do if your current approaches and strategies stop working? Having a back-up plan is absolutely essential. In fact, in a lot of cases, it's what separates companies that stay in business from those that don't.

Remember a little incident called New Coke? Well, fairly early on, it became obvious that things weren't going to work out. The powers that be at the bottler and within the company's leadership were afraid to introduce Coke Classic—in other words, to admit that New Coke was a mistake.

A small cadre of us prevailed. The choice seemed pretty clear: Admit that we'd made a mistake and take the increased volume or stay the course and lose the volume and maybe even the brand. Gee, which one would you go with?

GIVING YOUR BRAND A KICK IN THE BUTT

What happens when things really slow down for reasons beyond your control? Maybe it's the economy, or maybe it's something else. But the situation is that your category isn't growing, consumers don't seem particularly excited about changing to your brand, and everything—including your bottom line—is flat (or worse).

The soft drink industry was in the doldrums when I first joined Coke in 1979. We were an old, well-known brand with nearly universal name recognition. Business wasn't bad; it just wasn't great. All the big players' market share had remained fairly steady for a few years. This kind of thing isn't uncommon at all. Lego, the building block company, had a similar experience not long ago. The entire toy category was flat and so was Lego's share of it.

In cases like these, a lot of people make the mistake of assuming that just because the market is stagnant, it's okay to let their brand stagnate, too. Not very smart. Slow times are perfect for jumpstarting your brand. Consumers are bored out of their minds, no one's showing them anything new, and the brand that does this will get a huge boost. All it takes is finding creative ways to reactivate consumers.

These times are also perfect for reevaluating your entire approach to your brand and for thinking about some critical things: Are there ways you can let the consumer participate more directly with your brand? And what about your brand image—is it still the best one for your brand and your products? Have your customers' usage patterns changed and have you kept up?

This is the kind of soul-searching we did at Coke, and it's what I helped Lego do years later. **We gave customers in more segments of the market more reasons to buy. As a result, sales took off.**

SOME COMPANIES THAT DIDN'T LEARN THESE LESSONS

The following paragraphs are a who's who of companies that have disappeared completely or are heading that way despite incredible name recognition in their market. Having a big name didn't do them any good. Let me give you a bit of background on them just so that you can see what went wrong and what might have been done to keep them and their brands healthier.

- **AMF Group** used to absolutely define bowling. But then they started getting into boating and other sports and completely lost track of their original focus.
- **Baldwin Pianos** defined the home piano category (although Steinway had a lock on the concert piano market) and had most of the business. But then along came Yamaha and a few other Japanese manufacturers that introduced lower-cost, higher-quality pianos. Baldwin had plenty of chances to extend into related niches (electronic keyboards, for example), but they never did. As a result, the Japanese essentially redefined Baldwin out of the market.
- **Budget Group** had a great value proposition: lower rates for rental cars. But when they started charging as much as everyone else, where was the *budget*? And where was the relevance? Calling a company "budget" and then not offering budget prices completely undercuts the entire message. It would be like Weight Watchers coming up with a line of high-fat foods.
- **Chiquita Brands International** had a huge percentage of the U.S. banana business but tried to coast on their name, never thinking that there was absolutely nothing other than their label to differentiate a Chiquita banana from a Dole or Kroger banana.
- **Converse** used to be *the* athletic shoe but got overshadowed in the 1980s by Nike and Adidas and the other higher-profile makers. In the 1990s, they had a chance to reestablish themselves as a manufacturer of good-quality shoes, which was what they were known for. But they got

caught up trying to "out-Nike" Nike in the high-end market. Unfortunately for them, they didn't have the pockets to finance the battle and they got slapped down hard.

• **Day Timer** for decades was *the* calendar company, practically synonymous with "schedule." Anyone who was anyone carried a Day Timer. But then along came Lotus Notes and Outlook, and, of course, Palm, and suddenly Day Timer and their paper calendars had become the dinosaurs of the industry. There's no reason why they couldn't have continued to dominate the market, but they were just too slow.

• **Fruit of the Loom** was always a maker of cheap, kind-of-generic underwear. They got involved in a big takeover battle just as big name designers such as Calvin Klein were getting into the business and the whole market was getting fragmented. Instead of putting money into telling consumers why they should buy Fruit of the Loom underwear, they dropped every available cent into a leveraged buyout and ended up getting picked up by Warren Buffett. Trying to save the company instead of the business just about killed them.

Interestingly, the issues Fruit of the Loom (FOL) had to face in dealing with their longtime rival, Hanes, were very similar to the ones I had to deal with when I was at Coke and battling Pepsi. Both FOL and Coke were in highly competitive but fairly stagnant markets, faced one primary competitor, and dominated those markets with about a 45 percent share. Both were the best-known brands in their category and had nearly universal awareness.

But all this dominance and awareness weren't doing either company much good. At Coke, we were on the losing end of the comparison to Pepsi. Pepsi stood for choice and change, and consumers were changing their preference. We had to dig deep into Coke's DNA in order to truly understand what consumers expected from the brand and to identify the functional and emotional benefits we needed to deliver. In doing this we made a painfully simple but critical discovery: Coke's DNA was about *tradition* and *stability*, not just thirst-quenching refreshment. We leveraged that discovery into some breakthrough marketing programs that ended up driving the greatest share growth in the company's history.

Fruit of the Loom is in a great position to reinvigorate their brand in much the same way. Although their big-name recognition won't guarantee them anything, they can leverage it to develop a greater mind share among mass merchandisers and shoppers. But to do that they're going to have to dig into their own brand DNA. They'll also have to rethink their relationship with their key retailers and figure out how and where they want to position themselves: Is it going to be fashion or utility (comfort, fit, etc.)? Based on my own experience in a similar situation, I can guarantee that if Fruit of the Loom does the work they need to, they'll be back on their feet in no time.

• **Loews Cineplex Entertainment** invented the concept of smaller screening rooms. It makes sense, I guess, because the more screens you have, the less likely it is that any single flop will result in a loss. But they never developed the brand, and pretty soon Sony and United Artists and everyone else was doing the same thing. So Loews ended up with a lot of real estate that they couldn't make the payments on.

• **Mary Kay Cosmetics** still has a huge amount of icon value—pink Cadillacs, outrageous sales ladies—but they never really figured out whether they were selling unique high-quality products or a unique sales and incentive system. Since they didn't define themselves, their competition did. Personally, I don't think it would take all that much to get this company back on its feet.

• **Revlon** used Cindy Crawford for positioning as a mid- to high-end cosmetics company. But after Cindy left, Revlon dove headfirst into the low-end market and lost their core customers, the ones who'd been buying Revlon because they wanted to look like Cindy.

• **Trump Hotels and Casino Resorts** was a financial model inextricably linked with Donald Trump's ostentatious lifestyle: beautiful women, throwing around money, and so forth. This model ties in well with casinos, but is it translatable to hotels and skyscrapers? Obviously not. **What's the brand essence of a guy who's on top of the world one day and in bankruptcy court the next?**

• **Xerox** has been absolutely hammered by recent events, but they were already under a lot of pressure from analysts and customers long before September 11, 2001. Rating agencies had downgraded them, they had cash flow and liquidity issues, revenues were dropping, and their stock in 2001 was off 85 percent from its 1999 high.

Their employees were hit particularly hard: The company was getting out of certain business segments and sometimes out of entire regions, and they cut their staffing a lot in an attempt to get their costs under control. At the same time, though, the company deserves a lot of credit for some pretty heroic efforts: They reconstructed their business model, outsourced some of their manufacturing operations as well as some noncore competencies, and refocused on a small number of key, profitable growth areas.

But there's still a long way to go. The Xerox brand, for example, is an incredible equity, but is it as relevant as it should be and are they managing it to its greatest advantage? Is "The Document Company" still a meaningful and compelling concept? How well do they know their customers' wants and needs, and does their positioning allow them to adapt when those wants and needs change?

At the end of the day, Xerox needs to fundamentally revitalize their brand among consumers, employees, and shareholders. This means rethinking the attributes the brand stands for and repackaging it in a way that's consistent with the Xerox DNA, and that also takes the brand—and the business—forward. It'll take some work, but if they can make it through their latest accounting scandal, it can be done.

• **The Dot-com** collapse that began in 1999 was no real surprise. Those of us who've spent a lifetime creating and managing brands always knew things would fall apart; it was only a question of when.

It all started with the "ready, fire, aim" attitude that dominated the dot-com boom when it first started: Do anything, even if it's stupid, just as long as you do something fast. The theory was that because business was moving so quickly, you could correct your mistakes overnight and retool before anything drastic happened. **Some people had a vague idea about the importance of creating a brand, but with very few exceptions they had no strategy for how to do it.** Their only goal was an initial public offering.

Consultants and in-house marketing gurus started telling everyone that it would cost $250 million to build a brand, and that figure—ridiculous as it was—became common knowledge. As if that weren't enough damage to do, they managed to convince a lot of people, including venture capitalists, that awareness and eyeballs would guarantee success. (For that reason alone, these people deserve a special place in brand hell.) They pulled out their shotguns and started advertising everywhere whether it was appropriate or not. Customer acquisition costs were staggering, sometimes as high as a few hundred dollars a head. It doesn't take a lot of math to figure out how long it would take to burn through $250 million at that rate. Eventually we had a bunch of companies with huge name recognition but no customers and no profits. Not a good combination.

DOING IT RIGHT

Okay, now that you've seen how easy it is to run a perfectly good brand into the ground, let me leave you with two examples of companies that have managed to avoid the mistakes that so many others around them make. Maybe you're expecting me to spend the next few pages talking about how brilliantly Coke has managed their brand for the last hundred years or so. That may be true, but the reality is that Coke hasn't developed the brand to its maximum potential.

As painful as this is for me, I want to start with Pepsi, a brand that practically came out of nowhere and has built itself into an institution. In their early days, they had some trouble coming up with a strategy and positioning themselves, and they actually went broke three or four times. But they finally pulled it all together, and over the past 50 or 60 years, Pepsi has done an incredible job of managing and developing their brand.

Their strategy? Pretty simple, really. It was all about being different. How many times have you seen political challengers talk about how it's time for a change? That's how Tony Blair got elected in the United Kingdom the first time and how Vicente Fox got elected in Mexico.

Sometimes, of course, proposing change doesn't work. In Canada, the last election was won on the basis of "let's keep the status quo," and in the United States, Bill Clinton got elected for his second term on the same basis.

At the time when tiny David (Pepsi) was contemplating getting into the ring with Coke, the Goliath of the soft drink category, a lot of other companies would have given in to the temptation to copy Coke, to pull a "me, too." But the first thing they did was change their value proposition. At that time, Coca-Cola was selling 8 ounces of Coke for 5 cents. So Pepsi came in and started selling 16 ounces for the same price with the "Twice as much for a nickel" tag line. The message basically was "Pepsi is as good as Coke and we'll give you some incentive to try it." It was an incredibly successful approach—at least until Coke copied it.

But Pepsi had done what they wanted to do, which was to get people to try their product. They then quickly moved on to something even more daring: repositioning themselves from "as good as Coke" to "completely different from Coke." (This was a time when Coke was positioned as the serious family brand that people drank in the living room, and Pepsi was the young upstart, the one the kids were drinking in the kitchen. The twice-as-much-for-a-nickel value proposition had gotten Pepsi out of the kitchen and into the living room, where it could compete with Coke head to head.) They figured that there were two kinds of people: conservatives, whom they were perfectly happy to leave to Coke, and liberals, whom they went after with a vengeance. That's how the "Pepsi Generation" was born. And that fantastic jingle, "You've got a lot to live and Pepsi's got a lot to give," came right out and told consumers that there are Coke people and there are Pepsi people, and it's more fun to be a Pepsi person.

And how about those commercials with the little kid and the puppies? Pepsi took a note from the images Coke had used for years—family and stability and consistency—but put a little bit of a young spin on it. They managed to reposition Coke at the same time as they were positioning themselves: Pepsi is for the Pepsi Generation and Coke is for everyone else, especially older people. They pretty much took the world by storm with that one.

Some people might have stopped there and rested on their laurels but not Pepsi. (On the other hand, that's what Coke had been doing for years, and it took them a long time to start taking Pepsi seriously.) Instead, they upped the ante even further with the "Pepsi Challenge," another elegantly simple campaign. This time the message was "Not only are we different and less expensive, but a lot of people think we taste better, too. We think you'll agree, so check us out for yourself." More than anything else, it was the Challenge that drove Pepsi's sales in existing outlets—and especially in vending machines—through the roof worldwide. Is it any wonder that "Pepsi Challenge" became part of the vernacular? Constantly remaking themselves and keeping their brand alive, Pepsi built on their past successes and launched "The Choice of the New Generation," the now-famous Michael Jackson commercial.

Incredibly, it wasn't until the early nineties that the Coca-Cola Company publicly acknowledged Pepsi's existence and made a serious attempt to separate and differentiate itself. Pepsi was talking about the Pepsi Generation and Coke had been using "It's the Real Thing." The problem was that customers' response was "Okay, so you're the real thing, but would you please pass the Pepsi?"

Sounds silly, but it's absolutely true. It's sort of like the United States saying, "We're the biggest country in the Americas," while Mexico says, "Come to Mexico and you'll have a great time on our beaches." Or Hertz saying, "We're number one," while Avis says, "We try harder." One is a statement of fact; the other is a sales message. And that's exactly the way it was with the Pepsi Generation. Coke was saying, "We've always been here and we always will be," and Pepsi said, "You've got a lot to live; Pepsi's got a lot to give." It was killer stuff and did wonders for the Pepsi brand.

Coke's commercials with Bill Cosby eventually helped us regain some of our footing by saying that the only reason Pepsi had the Challenge was because Coca-Cola must be the best. This approach did a lot to reenergize the Coca-Cola system but didn't have much effect on Pepsi's sales. Pepsi did run into some trouble for a few years when they basically abandoned the essence of their brand. But it didn't take them long to recover and get back on track.

This whole story is a study in stability. As a student of scientific, results-oriented marketing and someone who believes that consistency of strategy and variance in execution is the key to success, I don't think I've ever seen a company that has done as good a job developing and broadening its brand over such a long time. They've done some pretty risky, innovative, and in-your-face things along the way. But with only a few bumps in the road, Pepsi has never abandoned its core essence: choice and change. They've always been the brash up-and-comer, the challenger, the insurgent, never the incumbent. And, amazingly, they've kept it going for over 50 years.

Right after the September 11 attacks, Pepsi started having a little trouble keeping consumers interested in the message. It was obviously a little harder to push change and newness when people seemed to crave stability and consistency instead. That was a great opportunity for Coke—whose brand exudes stability and consistency better than any other—but they didn't move quickly enough. Pepsi retooled in a hurry, creating some new commercials for the 2002 Superbowl (starring the newly repositioned Britney Spears) that were completely true to the DNA of the brand. They were young and different, but at the same time they showed that Pepsi has had a long history of being young and different—an interesting way to combine change and stability.

Yep, Pepsi has had their slumps, but they have bounced back. That's probably why the "Pepsi Generation" will be a part of the colloquial language for generations to come—kind of like "The Real Thing"—and their branding story is a textbook case in how to do things right. They're never afraid to change, and risk taking is an important part of the brand's DNA.

The other company that has done a masterful job of creating and managing a brand is Starbucks, which single-handedly brought the entire coffee category back to life. In 1960, coffee had a 70 percent market penetration. People drank an average of 3.2 cups of coffee per day. By 1988, penetration had dropped to 50 percent and daily consumption was down to 1.67 cups. Everyone was about ready to give the coffee category up for dead. The theory was that newer, younger consumers didn't want hot beverages, didn't like the taste of coffee, and didn't have time for a drink that has to be consumed slowly. Then along came Starbucks, which did four pretty amazing things:

1. They redefined the business. Suddenly going to a coffee place wasn't about ground coffee; it was a social experience.
2. They repositioned the category. No more boring "coffee, please." Now it's gourmet blends, cappuccino, espresso, latte, low-fat muffins, and tables where you can plug in your laptop.
3. They reengaged the consumer. Coffee became a way to excite the senses, discover the world, and indulge yourself.
4. They reignited consumer passion for coffee. "My coffee, my way, damn it!"

As a result, the category was completely revitalized and the downward consumption trend was completely reversed. In 1999, penetration was up to 76 percent and daily coffee consumption was up to 3.5 cups—both higher than in 1960. Even the size of the servings was up: 33 percent of cups are bigger than 8 ounces. In 1988, when the category was left for dead, Starbucks had only 33 stores. Today, they have nearly 5,000. We should all be so lucky.

CHAPTER 3

Fish Where the Fish Are

When I was working for Coke the first time, Pat Garner was the brand manager for Sprite. Pat was a great guy, but he kept telling me that the way to grow the brand from its 15 percent penetration level was to convince everyone out there who wasn't a Sprite drinker to drink Sprite. Sounded logical enough, I guess, but it was completely wrong. The reality is that most of the people who don't drink Sprite just don't like lemon-lime. But that didn't keep Pat and hundreds of thousands of other brand managers all over the world from reciprocal marketing—chasing after the remainder of their market share (which in Sprite's case was 85 percent) instead of focusing on the share they already have.

Sure, if you could only convert all those nonusers out there to your brand you'd be rich, but it'll never work. Politicians always fantasize about getting everyone from the other party to switch to their side, yet they really need to be spending their time making sure their hard-core voters aren't going to jump ship and trying to sway the undecideds. It's the same with products and services: **Fish where the fish are and you'll be a lot more successful than if you fish where they aren't.** It's a three-step process:

1. Find out where the people are who already buy your product and get them to buy more of it.
2. Spend some time giving the undecideds a reason to buy.
3. Forget about everyone else.

If you were more than a few years old in November 1963, you probably still remember where you were and what you were doing when President Kennedy was shot. You also probably remember where you were and what you were doing in 1986 when you heard that the *Challenger* had exploded, or when the World Trade Centers were attacked. But do you remember where you were when the Berlin Wall came down? Probably not. Well, I do. Not because I love politics, but because of what businesspeople started to say the moment the first jackhammer went to work.

"Just think, all those Eastern Europeans—a billion new customers!"

This was a great example of lazy marketing and lazy business. The theory was that if we went into those countries and expanded our footprint, we would grow our business. It was that simple. "Oh, and by the way," they'd whisper, "we won't have to worry anymore about growing the business in all those difficult places we already have our assets in."

Amazing. So they all spent tons of money and not that many years later had to call Mr. Write-off to do something with their bad investments. Hundreds of beautiful plants in Russia and thousands of great-looking trucks in some of the iron-curtain countries were swept under the carpet because the companies that owned them didn't pay enough attention to consumers. And these were the same companies who said, "Think global, act local."

How stupid. That kind of comment (people said the same thing when China opened up) is a perfect illustration of two of marketing's biggest problems: first, the belief that it's all about new customers, and second, the belief that all customers—new and existing—are the same and can be approached the same way. The reality, however, is that you can't just slap a few warm and fuzzy commercials together and hope everything will turn out okay.

After having not sold in India for a long time, Coca-Cola was able to get back in the door. (The first time around the Indian government demanded the formula, and the company, rightly so, refused. So they threw us out.) We bought the Parle Business, a group of franchises that sold a number of popular and successful brands. The big shots in Atlanta decided they needed an Indian to run the show in India, so they found one in the United States and sent him over. Unfortunately, he didn't have a clue about how to manage a series of brands, so he thought he'd try what worked in the United States in India. You won't believe this, but it's absolutely true: This guy actually got a bunch of young Indian kids from all over the country and had them sing a song on a hill (sound familiar?). It meant less than nothing to the local audience and the campaign didn't last a week. What a waste.

It ought to be obvious that different groups of people have different needs and wants and should be approached differently. You're not going to sell a lot of Depends (adult diapers) at an *N-Sync concert. And it ought to be pretty intuitive that you should try to keep your current customers happy before chasing around for new ones. But you'd be surprised at how few companies understand these two points.

The big problem is that most companies don't know who their customers are. If you don't know that, two things will happen: You'll have a tougher time reaching customers who might actually buy your product, and you'll spend a hell of a lot more money than you need to on advertising.

So who *are* your customers? We have to start with who they possibly could be, then slice things thinner and thinner until we get to a reasonable number. A friend of mine came up with an analogy that I think explains this pretty well. Say you decide you want to go fishing. The first thing you have to do is figure out where all the lakes are. Then you have to determine which ones have fish. Then you have to find out what kind of fish are in each of the lakes that have fish. Then you have to decide which lakes have the kind of fish you're looking for. Only then can you actually drop your line in the water.

To put it in slightly simpler terms, as far as your company is concerned, the world is divided into two groups: (1) people who do, could, or might conceivably use a product in your category and (2) people who won't. Get rid of the ones who don't and whoever's left is your potential market. If you're a politician running for statewide office, your potential market is only people who live in your state or who are registered to vote there. If you're a steak distributor, you're not going to sell much to vegetarians.

But even trying to target an ad campaign at everyone in the state or everyone except vegetarians isn't much better than targeting it at everyone everywhere. Your potential market consists of five types of people:

1. **Loyal supporters:** They not only love steak in general, but they love *your* steak best of all. They don't pay attention to competitors' ads, they don't like to try new things, and they're willing to wait in line and pay more for your steak.

2. **Soft supporters:** These people are regular steak eaters and they'd

probably buy yours, but you'll need to give them some concrete reasons why.

3. **Undecided:** This tends to be the biggest group and is by far the most
expensive one to reach. Undecided voters switch from candidate to candidate depending on the last piece of information they hear. Undecided
steak eaters see no real difference between your piece of meat and your
competitors', and they'll buy whichever one they happen to walk by first.
In fact, they might even go with a burger if they feel like it.

4. **Soft opposition:** These people don't like your brand and they won't
buy from you, although if you gave them a really good reason—such as a
huge discount—they might give you a try.

5. **Strong opposition:** You'll never please someone who got food poi-
soning from one of your steaks or someone who bears a personal grudge
against your political party, so don't even bother trying.

Rob Smith, who's a brilliant expert in direct marketing and a good
friend, put it like this:

IT'S THE RELATIONSHIP

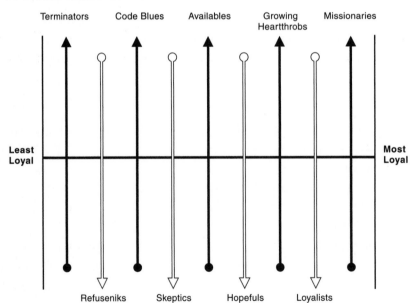

FIGURE 3.1

DETERMINING WHICH MEDIA APPROACH WORKS BEST
FOR WHICH CUSTOMERS

We know that different customers require different media approaches. (After all, you can't use a bass lure to catch trout.) But traditionally advertisers and their agencies took the shotgun approach—hitting as many people as possible regardless of whether they were potential customers. Or, if you want to keep going with this fish thing, we could say that this traditional approach is kind of like dropping dynamite into a lake and blasting as many fish out of the water as possible regardless of whether they're edible.

Of course, the shotgun (or dynamite) approach sounded too crass, so advertising people switched to terms such as *reach* and *frequency*, which are basically the same as dynamite, anyway. Advertising goals were set as reaching x percent of the population y number of times each month (or week or day or whatever)—still pretty indiscriminate.

That approach obviously wasn't going to work for everyone. So the next trend was *continuity*, which was basically a variation on the reach-and-frequency method. Continuity was based on the idea that if you want people to buy something, you have to reach them every day. So the metric became how often you could reach people.

Continuity didn't work, either. Finally, someone spent a little time analyzing customers and their behavior, eventually figuring out that content and placement were really the most important factors of all—that what you say and where you say it are more important than how many people you say it to. For some strange reason, however, the industry decided that television commercials were the only way to go.

Well, conventional wisdom aside, there are—and always have been—plenty of other ways to advertise besides television commercials. Most of them aren't as sexy as getting your face plastered all over millions of TVs, but they're often a lot more effective.

The basic advertising options are broadcast (television and radio), print (newspapers and magazines), outdoor (bus shelters, billboards, etc.), online (banner ads, etc.), and direct mail. Each has distinct advantages and disadvantages. Not all of them are appropriate for every type of company.

Now I know what you're saying: "You used to do advertising for Coca-Cola and you had a gazillion dollars to spend on media. And now you're doing consulting for a bunch of big shots with gazillions more. But what about companies that don't have that kind of money to spend?" The answer is that you do the same thing as the big boys: Understand your target market—who they are, where they are, why they do what they do— and have a firm grasp on what your goal is. Exactly what do you expect consumers to do after seeing your advertising that they aren't doing now? Finally, pick the media outlets that reach the greatest number of consumers in the most cost-effective way. In most cases, you'll want to use an approach that integrates two or more types of advertising. But if you can't afford that, go with the one(s) that is most likely to hit your customers head on. Table 3.1 makes this a little clearer.

CUSTOMERS: WHEN TO GET RID OF 'EM, WHEN TO FIND NEW ONES, AND WHEN TO KEEP THE ONES YOU HAVE

Okay, back to your customers. You've probably sold your product to consumers from at least four of the five categories I talked about earlier (let's forget about the ones who really hate you). But not all customers—and not all sales—are created equal. Here's how things typically break down:

- Eighty percent of your sales come from only 20 to 30 percent of your customers. These customers are referred to as "heavy users" in the fast-food and mass commercial products biz.
- One hundred percent of your profits come from that same top 20 to 30 percent.
- You incur about 80 percent of your sales-related expenses selling to the bottom 20 percent of your customers. Call it reciprocal marketing or call it dumb marketing, but it's the same thing: You're not spending money trying to get people who are already big buyers to buy more. Instead, you're spending a ton of money trying to convert large groups of consumers who have no interest. Why bother?

Recently, a group of banks did a study that backs me up pretty well on these numbers. The banks analyzed their customers and found that they fell into a couple of general groups. One group tended to open up accounts and deposit a bunch of money. They'd use credit cards and ATMs but almost never come into a branch. These were very profitable customers. The other group kept small balances, bounced checks, called the 24-hour service lines a lot, and came into the branches all the time with problems—real or imaginary. These guys cost the bank a ton of money.

When the banks ran the numbers, they realized that the top 30 percent of their customers generated 100 to 150 percent of profits. The rest either didn't provide any profits or were so expensive to take care of that they were actually a drain. In fact, 90 percent of bank costs were generated by 10 percent of customers—the whiny ones with the smallest balances.

This kind of research has spurred banks to make big changes in the way they do business. You've probably seen the results at your own bank: They encourage "good" customers by offering lots of free services in exchange for maintaining high balances and doing things that minimize actual customer contact, such as using ATMs and signing up for direct deposit. At the same time, they almost openly drive away "bad" customers by charging for teller visits, phone calls to the service center, low balances, writing too many checks, and just barely maintaining an account. Driving customers away might seem like a poor business decision, but think about it this way:

- Sixty-five percent of most companies' sales come from existing, satisfied customers. This is the old repeat purchase scenario. Every time you go back to the same restaurant or stay at the same hotel chain or buy gas at the same station, the company's relationship with you grows, which translates into lower marketing costs. And how do they keep growing that relationship with you? By understanding and catering to your needs. It's the hotel that asks you if you want a second wake-up call 10 minutes after the first, the donut shop that gives you 13 donuts for the price of 12, or the software manufacturer that offers discounted upgrades to loyal users. On the opposite end, you've got the magazine that won't give existing subscribers the same reduced rates they offer to new subscribers. Then, after you cancel your subscription, they spend hundreds of dollars trying to get you back.
- It costs six times more to acquire a new customer than it does to retain an existing one.
- A 5 percent increase in retention rate can boost profits 25 to 125 percent.

TABLE 3.1 MEDIA OUTLET ADVANTAGES AND DISADVANTAGES

OUTLET	ADVANTAGES	DISADVANTAGES	ESPECIALLY GOOD FOR	ESPECIALLY BAD FOR
Television	Very visual, attention-getting; glamorous; consumer associations of quality; can combine audio, visual, text, sight, and motion	Hard to target specific demographic groups; lots of clutter; even if you find a particular commercial especially convincing, it's pretty doubtful that you're going to go out and buy anything right then	Products that require a visual demonstration or explanation, such as the GE Arctic Series refrigerators, where there's a new technology that cools different parts of the fridge at different temperatures; good for image building—like Philip Morris and the oil companies telling you what wonderful work they do to help the environment; good for politics—gives candidates a chance to explain positions in some detail and take swipes at opponents	Anything where the goal is to get people to act immediately—except for infomercials

Radio	Easier to target by audience (can pick oldies station or hip hop), less expensive, lends itself to impulse buying because you might actually pull off the road into a store to buy something that's being advertised	No visuals; can't do product demonstrations; audience isn't always paying attention (they're supposed to be driving or talking on their cell phone)	Fast food and others that rely on impulse buys (have an ice-cold Pepsi right now) and daily reminders; good for politics—voting is often an impulse kind of thing; anything where you have to constantly bombard people with the message to buy your product so that they won't forget	Anything where you need a visual demonstration, say a blender or a washing machine
Newspapers	Rated as the most believable media; lots of space to explain your message; can use graphics, can target based on geography	Hard to target based on anything other than geography; very short shelf life (people toss them after one day); lots of clutter; poor image quality	Retail companies that use price as a motivator; good for short-term promotions; good for anything that needs lengthy explanation of benefits (such as medication) and for an immediate call to action	Daily consumption, except to promote a special promotion

(continued)

TABLE 3.1 MEDIA OUTLET ADVANTAGES AND DISADVANTAGES (Continued)

OUTLET	ADVANTAGES	DISADVANTAGES	ESPECIALLY GOOD FOR	ESPECIALLY BAD FOR
Magazines	Can target audience based on demographics or special interests; very long shelf life—people keep them around, will tear out pages and stick them on the refrigerator door	Long lead times	Cosmetics; fashions; computers; cars (some people buy magazines just for the ads); anything where the consumer will spend time looking at pictures; good for brand building	Short-term promotions or anything that is easily dated, such as politicians, groceries, or fast food
Billboards and bus shelters	Can target geographically; can place near point of sale; lots of repeat viewing; good for giving directions to local places	Message has to be short because people are usually moving past it; audience limited to whoever happens to be driving by; lots of clutter	Fast food and impulse buys; local businesses; good for reinforcing television message; clothing; point of sale: dog food, for example—generally a destination product that people buy when they run out, but a billboard might convince them to buy a bigger package	Long-lasting durables like cars; nothing technical or that requires extensive explanation

	Advantages	Disadvantages		
Internet	Precise targeting; easy to tailor your message almost to the individual; if you get permission, there's a good chance it'll actually be read; excellent multimedia possibilities	Can be deleted before it's even read; fancy graphics and audio elements might be missed by people with older systems; perception of spam	Content sites; Elle site good for cosmetics; AOL good for electronics and books	Bulk products or cash-and-carry items; disposable, impulse buys
Direct mail	Very precise targeting possibilities; plenty of room for complex messages; can include special discount coupons; can deliver actual product samples	Often perceived as junk; lots of mailbox clutter	Targeted offers; promotions for local businesses; political messages; solicitations; groceries and other consumables	National companies; air travel; rental cars

Obviously, the way to increase your profits is to figure out which of your customers are in the most profitable group and expand the size of that group, right? If you have to go out and chase down new customers every day, you'll be out of business before you know it. Of course, the trick is to figure out who your best and worst customers are. The solution is simple: Get out there and collect some data.

Go wherever there are likely users of your product or service and talk to these people. Go to the grocery store and stop people who have a package of meat in their cart. If they bought your brand, why? Was it price? Quality? Advertisements? Convenience? What did they prefer about your brand? If they didn't buy your brand, why not? And most important, what would it take to get them to switch to your brand (or at least give it a try)?

For years, Internet companies have done a great job of asking for all sorts of information from the people who buy from them. Grocery stores do something similar: Every time you make a purchase with your credit or ATM card, they know what you bought and how much. If you're not doing business on the Internet, you can do phone surveys or mall intercepts, and analyze some of the internal data you've already collected from your sales-people—you probably have a lot more than you think you do. You may also be able to buy some basic data from companies such as AC Nielsen. However you get it, here's the kind of information you're looking for:

- **Demographic:** Age, income, gender, family size, religion. Most sports equipment buyers, for example, are males 18 to 35. In your business, you might find that the majority of your customers make $25,000 to $50,000 per year and have no children.
- **Geographic:** You'll probably find that most of your customers are grouped in a particular region or state or neighborhood. This kind of information could save you the trouble and expense of selling parkas in Hawaii.
- **Motives:** Why might people be interested in your product or service? People suffering from anxiety are potential customers for tranquilizers; people with bad morning breath are potential customers for mouthwash.
- **Benefits:** People use products and services for a lot of reasons other than what you might think. In some upscale neighborhoods, singles go to certain grocery stores because they're better than bars for picking up potential dates. And teens usually don't go to the mall to buy anything— they go to hang out with their friends.

As valuable as these data will be for helping you retain customers, they have a lot of other benefits as well. You'll find out what your customers like and don't like about your product, what they like or don't like about your advertising, and what you'll need to do to get them to buy from you the next time. These invaluable insights can help you retain existing customers by continually satisfying them, and they can help you tailor your advertising—and your brand itself—to fit each subgroup you want to reach.

Remember this: The whole reason you're gathering data is to establish or deepen your relationship with existing and prospective customers. Consumers don't give a damn how you segment your market or why you think they buy what they buy. All they care about is whether you're meeting their needs. Do so, and they'll give you their business. Don't, and they'll go somewhere else.

Recently, I got hired by a company called Sonosite, which had come up with a great new way to do sonograms. The question was where to focus their advertising efforts: on the obvious—sonograms for expectant mothers—or the less obvious—emergency rooms. To find the answer we had to find out where the money was, which involved identifying the kind of doctor or hospital who would buy this new technology and whose patients would buy the new technology's premise. Bottom line? Highly targeted data yield highly targeted results.

THE IMPORTANCE OF HAVING RESEARCH-BASED DATA

To get where you want to go tomorrow, you need to know where you are today with your consumers. How do they think, feel, and act toward your brand? The only way you're ever going to be able to answer these questions is by doing research. (I can't emphasize enough the importance of doing research *before* you start plunking down your hard-earned dollars buying media.) If you don't know who your consumers are, you won't be able to reach them. It's that simple. Do *not* rely on sales reps at the various media outlets to tell you the truth. Their job is to sell you ad space, and they don't really care whether you move any product. Actually, just doing research isn't enough—it's all about the data that research produces, which means that your research has to be good.

But what is good research? From a scientific perspective, good research is valid and reliable, which means that it accurately measures what it sets out to measure, and the measurement devices will yield a consistent perspective if used over and over. Stated more simply, good research gives you insight that you can translate into actions that will lead to greater purchase frequency, stronger brand equity, and increased volume and profits. On its most basic level, good research excites and stimulates. It tells you things you didn't know and it gives you direction on what to do next.

I recently met with a major toy manufacturer who told me that his company's goal was "to have the most powerful brand in the world." Well, what the hell does that mean? If you take a look at a list (from Interbrand) of the most powerful global brands of 2001, you'll notice that *almost all* of the top 20 (including companies such as Cisco, Sony, American Express, and Citibank) are having some kind of financial troubles. Only two of the companies on the 1993 top-10 list—Coca-Cola and Intel—still made it into the 2001 top 10. And just to pound home my point that awareness and profitability aren't related, only four of the most recognizable brands in a 2000 name-the-first-brand-that-comes-to-mind survey (Coke, Microsoft, IBM, and GE) are on that same year's most profitable ranking. Looks like being one of the most powerful brands may not be all it's cracked up to be. Wouldn't it make more sense to have doubling sales and tripling profits as a goal instead?

Here are some critical things to keep in mind when thinking about doing any kind of market research—whether you do it in-house or you hire an outside vendor to do it for you:

1. **Rather than identify consumers, identify *with* them.** The first rule of marketing is be a people person. No, I don't mean being the life of the party or a good schmoozer. Being a people person means understanding why people do what they do. How? First, understand the world we live in. Current events, social and political trends, movies, books, and headlines all provide context and affect—and reflect on—how consumers think and what they do. You must first understand your consumers as people.

2. **Keep focused on why.** You know your consumers want convenience, variety, and value, and they want to fit in and be successful, right? Of course, you need to know what size, flavor, package type, version, and set of services they like—all the stuff that describes what, when, and where. Isn't that enough? Hardly. But that's what most companies that do

market research come up with, and it's easy to see why: Everyone gets a little lazy and the research becomes descriptive rather than prescriptive. In other words, the focus is on understanding *what* rather than *why*. If you're paying to have research done and you end up with conclusions like those, you're getting ripped off. Chances are you knew all that kind of stuff before you started, anyway, plus that kind of knowledge—even if it is new— won't help you make meaningful connections with people. To be a successful advertiser, you need to know *why*. Where does your brand fit in people's lives? How does it make them feel? What are customers trying to say about themselves when they use your product? How do they want others to see them or think about them?

3. **Design is king.** The goal in designing good research is to come up with something that will give you real insights into consumers' behavior. The big obstacle here, though, is that **consumers generally don't know why they buy what they buy, and if they do, they don't want you to know.** Direct questions alone don't go deep enough to reveal the whys behind the behavior, so you've got to gather information in a roundabout way. To truly understand consumers' behavior, you need to see the relationship between what they think and feel and what they do. If you can, use hypothesis-based research—that is, you should design your research around *what ifs*. What will you do if you learn a certain fact about your consumers and how will it change their relationship with your brand?

4. **Content is queen.** Ask a lot of questions and make sure they're the right ones. Each question should be like a mini-hypothesis. The better your hypothesis, the better the research. One of the best examples of how this can go wrong occurred during the research process that led to the introduction of New Coke. We'd done taste tests and found that consumers seemed to prefer Pepsi's sweeter taste to Coke's more biting taste. So we stopped right there and decided that if we made Coke taste like Pepsi, more people would drink it. You know what happened. We came up with New Coke, and consumers weren't interested at all. The problem was that we'd never bothered to follow up our "Which one do you like best?" question with "If we make Coke taste like this, would you buy it?"

A lot of companies try to do this kind of research by getting focus groups together. Don't bother. People who go to focus groups tend to be professional focus group goers—they've got time to kill, and they like the fact that you feed them and pay them a few bucks for their trouble. Worst of all, though, they generally want to get out of the focus group meeting as quickly as possible, so they'll give you the answer they think you're looking for. Although dealing with smart people is generally preferable to dealing with dummies, when you're doing research, you're looking for respondents, not thinkers. You want honest answers to your questions, not well-thought-out answers that try to explain behavior.

5. **Knowledge only gets you halfway there—maybe even less.** If 0 is the starting point for a research project and 100 is success (i.e., new insights that lead to a positive impact in the marketplace), the best design and content can get you only to 50, no further. Where does the rest come from? From the advertising strategy you develop based on the knowledge your research generates. In sports, war, investing, and pretty much everything else, all the knowledge and insight in the world is worthless unless you can develop a plan to put it into action.

6. **Don't get too bogged down in the numbers.** At the risk of belaboring this point, go beyond the cold hard facts and get to know consumers as people: what their hopes are, their dreams, their values, what's really important to them, how they spend their spare time, what they do for fun. You need to know what's in their heads and what's in their hearts.

7. **Be curious.** When you see someone buy a Snickers bar, ask yourself why she didn't buy a Milky Way. When you see that line of SUVs and minivans waiting to go through Wendy's drive-thru, ask yourself what they're buying, where they're going next, and whether this is a routine or a unique occasion. For every action there is a reason, and you need to know that reason.

8. **Two out of three is all you get: quick turnaround, good quality, inexpensive.** Granted, the Internet has helped make research faster, better, and cheaper, but overall this rule is still true today. If you think you can do all three, you're wrong. And if someone tries to tell you that he or she can do all three for you, keep your hand on your wallet.

I realize that some of this stuff may be a little abstract, so let me give you a few thoughts to tie it all together. I'm not going to cover every single point here, but you'll get the picture.

Take, for example, a huge food retailer with nearly universal name recognition and market penetration. Although that's an enviable spot to be in, it's also a tough one. When you're one of the biggest, all the smaller guys are always trying to eat into your market share, and it's a constant struggle to keep doing the things that made you a success in the first place.

That's what happens with many of the big players, to some extent which is why they need to look for ways to reinvigorate their brands. Reinventing a dominant brand is a pretty complicated task, so you must start with some research on what the brand and company might have to do to get back on track.

In Chapter 2, I say that a brand is essentially a container for a customer's complete experience with the product and company. That's more than theory. For consumers, the fast food brand is more than the iconography and the catchy commercials; it's more than the movie product tie-ins and the community service projects; it's more than the mascots and spokespeople; it's even more than the food itself. The truth is that on some level consumers see, feel, touch, smell, hear, and taste the fast food brand.

One of the main reasons people eat at fast food restaurants is speed—they know that if they're feeling rushed, they can get their food quickly and get back to whatever they were doing before they got hungry. Helping customers get in and out quickly and efficiently is great for the customer, but from most of these companies' point of view, it's hard to build relationships with people who are always rushing off somewhere else. As a result, whatever connections they do have will naturally weaken over time.

To combat this reality, most companies appeal to consumers through one of the following channels: personal happiness, family, and enjoying life. Local banks allow people to "realize their dreams" (personal happiness and enjoying life), movie-rental brands deliver "fun and togetherness" to the home (family and enjoying life), Internet service providers bring the "world to you" (personal happiness). With this in mind, the big question for a fast food retailer is "What value does it deliver?"

Based on accurate research, many companies could tell what consumers were thinking, feeling, and what made them act. But to be on top, a company must come up with advertising that takes advantage of that knowledge and gives consumers what they want.

HOW SEPTEMBER 11 CHANGED THINGS

Frankly, I'm getting a little tired of everyone trying to reference but not draw connections between whatever it is that they're doing and what happened on September 11, 2001. Still, the truth is that along with every-thing else, the advertising world—and what it takes to succeed in that world—has been fundamentally altered.

I'm not talking about advertisers going out of their way—in a com-pletely insincere way—to show their support for New York or the war on terrorism, and I'm not talking about some companies' cynical attempts to capitalize on this disaster to sell products. That sort of pandering and deception have always been around and always will be.

The fundamental change I'm talking about is in the way consumers think about the two very different things that happened on September 11, 2001: the terrorist attacks that started a completely new kind of war, and the noticeable worsening of the recession that was already underway. Each of these events impacted advertising in very different ways.

The attack itself changed consumers' norms, values, and needs. People now feel somewhat less safe than they did before, and they've made their world a little smaller. Country, church, family, social harmony, and secu-rity have become more important while excessive personal gratification, social recognition, and materialism have become less important.

At the same time, the economic recession—which we now seem to be digging our way out of—made many consumers value their jobs a little more and made them more concerned about value, more frugal, and less likely to take risks. The combination of a war and an economic tightening may leave people even more worried about the future than they were before. This brings up an interesting contradiction: Consumers may respond to their safety and security issues by spending more time with their family, but they may feel that they need to work even harder than usual to keep from losing their job.

As a result of these two significant events, people are changing the qual-ities that are important to them and the things they value when consider-ing a brand. In some cases, the driving factor will be price; in other cases, it'll be convenience or something else. Although these might seem like the same qualifications as before, the difference is that now the lines may be drawn in different places. Wal-Mart, for example, has managed to come through these tough times pretty much unscathed. Their sales continue to grow, but they're selling more gardening tools and fewer Game Boys.

Interestingly, this kind of thing happens all the time. Not on the same scale as September 11, of course, but every single day there are things that change the ways people see themselves and the ways they arrange their priorities. If you're going to succeed in business, you're going to have to be prepared to identify these changing currents, and, more important, react to them appropriately.

In unpredictable times, consumers seek out the familiar and safe in their personal lives. And they do the very same thing when they go to the store or consider making purchases: They turn to brands that provide benefits such as guidance, comfort, authenticity, connection, and utility. If you're lucky to have a brand that has forged solid emotional and psychological connections with customers (Coca-Cola, Starbucks, and Disney, for example), this may come as good news. Consumers will be looking for security and value, and they're going to want to spend their money on brands that are category leaders; brands that are respected, innovative, and popular; and, most important, brands that represent stability and that are likely to be there over the long haul.

If your brand isn't (yet) so intimately connected with consumers' hearts and minds, you'll have to overcome some pretty high hurdles if you want to be included in the consideration set of things that they feel are important to them. This gets me back to the point I've made before and that I'll keep making over the course of this book: Making people *aware* of your brand won't work anymore (that's assuming it ever did). In uncertain times, now more than ever, you need to give consumers a clear way of differentiating your brand from your competitors' and a clear reason to purchase it instead of someone else's. And you need to pay attention to *why* people buy what they buy as opposed to what they buy and where.

HIRING ADVERTISING AGENCIES

Here's a message that those of you in advertising should be happy to hear. Chances are you hire someone to do your dry cleaning, change the oil in your car, do your plumbing, rewire your electricity, and more. You might be able to do some of those things yourself, but could you do them well and would it be an effective use of your time and energy? The same goes for CEOs and marketing managers when it comes to managing your advertising efforts. You could probably do it yourself, but really and truly, is advertising what you do best—better than whatever it is that your company does? If so, you're in the wrong business.

To paraphrase Clint Eastwood in one of his *Dirty Harry* movies, you've got to know your limitations. So be honest with yourself. If you're a manager and don't have the resources or the expertise to do the job in house, get some help. Producing, managing, and evaluating advertising can be an expensive, time-consuming process, which is why you need to find the right people who have the skills to get the job done.

In the rest of this chapter I address the person in charge of making advertising decisions. I'm assuming that you've decided to bring in some outside help. Congratulations—that's probably the right thing to do. But this is no time to relax. Making the decision gets you only part of the way there. The real chore is to find the right agency. If you pay attention to the next few pages, you'll be well on your way. And if you're in the ad business, stick around. You really need to hear and understand this information so that you'll be able to live up to your client's expectations.

What Do You Need?

You can't do anything in business without a strategy. You need to be very clear on exactly where your brand is right now, where you want it to be, how you plan to get there, and when you expect all this to happen. And if there's one time when you want to have a firm grip on your strategy, it's when you're about to hire an ad agency. The people you hire will have a tremendous influence on your brand's future. They can make you or break you. The choice is yours.

It's important to have a solid understanding of who your customers are before you bring in an agency. In some cases, the agency will be able to help you out with demographic research, but no one knows your brand like you do (if there's someone who knows it better than you do, you'd better hire him or her fast).

Making Your List and Checking It Twice

Let's start with the big question: What do you want the agency you hire to do for you? Yeah, yeah, I know, you want them to come up with a killer advertising campaign. But what does that really mean to you and to them? What kind of skills and experience do you think the agency should have? What are your minimum requirements and where—if at all—are you willing to make compromises?

The best way to answer these questions is to put together a profile of the ideal agency. This means coming up with a comprehensive list of qualifications and skills that are important to you and ranking them in order. It may sound like a silly grad-school exercise, but it's actually very important. At a minimum, putting this kind of matrix together will help you organize and rank your priorities. It'll also be an excellent tool to use when you're evaluating candidate agencies. (Be reasonable, though. It's pretty unlikely that you're going to find any single agency that satisfies all your requirements.) Most important, it can be used as a screening tool: By sending it to all the prospective candidates, you'll probably eliminate a few who aren't even close to having what you need. The ones who are left will have a very clear idea of your requirements, which will help them better focus their presentations and keep them from wasting everyone's time on a bunch of stuff that you don't care about.

Because each business is different, not everyone will have the same needs, which means I can't give you an iron-clad checklist. But here are a few points I always look for and always advise my clients to look for before signing up with an agency:

• **Business knowledge:** Have they had any experience working with clients in similar categories? If so, they'll probably have a pretty good idea of the media requirements you have. If not, it's not the end of the world, but expect a much steeper learning curve as you break them in.

• **Consumer understanding:** Does the agency have a deep understanding of consumer attitudes and behaviors and can they adapt their work to appeal to different groups?

• **Contacts:** Do they have the right contacts in the business world? Do they know the right people at the right places so that they can make a few calls and get things done, or are they going to have to go through the switchboard like all the other mortals?

• **Stability:** How fiscally stable are they? How long have they been in business? What kind of turnover do they have among their most senior staff? Do they have the horsepower to do the job you need them to do?

• **Clients:** How strong is their client list? Does it include anyone you've heard of? How big a total media buyer are they? How good a job do they do of controlling their media budget? Don't be shy about checking references. And while you're at it, be sure to check their off-limits list, too. You don't want to get involved with an agency that's handling a competitor's account.

• **Breadth and depth:** Have they worked with a variety of media? In other words, some people do great television ads but suck when it comes to billboards or radio. You want an agency that has skills in the areas that are most important to your brand and the ones that will be most important as your brand grows.

• **Creativity:** How strong is the creative team and what kind of a system do they have for generating creative work? You want pros working for you. This isn't the time to let your 22-year-old niece break in her brand-new advertising degree.

• **Planning:** Is strategic planning a central part of the agency's work or is it something of an afterthought? If you have a sense that they're winging it, pass.

• **Production processes:** Does the agency have internal production resources or do they farm everything out? If so, are they watching your wallet as they work?

• **Research:** Do they do research? Do they test sample ads, do store surveys, and so forth? Are they constantly looking for ways to improve their understanding of your customers? If they do this kind of research, do they do it in house or is it done by some third party?

• **Defining success:** How does the agency monitor and evaluate their own work? Is their definition of a successful ad or campaign the same as yours?

• **Promotions and events:** How does the agency view the role of promotions and events as part of an overall brand communication plan? Are they capable of integrating programs into a cohesive plan? Do they have a record of success in this area? Do they have the resources to get the job done?

• **Where do you fit in?** Is the agency going to treat you as the boss or are they going to ignore you and do what they want? Will they share your definition of success? If possible, find an agency where you'll be one of their biggest clients. You'll get a lot more respect and a lot better response time.

• **Do you like them?** You're not looking for friends here. You want people who can do the job you agreed on for the price you agreed on and achieve the results you agreed on. If they're nice people, great. If not, don't invite them to the office holiday party. On the other hand, you're going to be working closely with these people on some very important projects, so if they're impossible to work with, nonresponsive, or just plain jerks, take that into consideration.

• **Compensation:** Are they willing to have at least part of their fee be tied to the performance of the advertising campaign? If not, walk away because they're probably more interested in winning awards than they are in selling your brand. Sound too theoretical? Well, it's not—it's exactly how we hired ad agencies when I was at Coke. The smart ones loved it because it paid well to do well. The dumb ones hated it and started new chapters of the "Get the Ayacola" club.

After you go through this whole process, it's safe to invite a few of the top candidates in to make presentations. When you get to this stage, do everyone a favor and lay out the ground rules up front. Tell the agency how long a presentation you want and what specific things you want to see. And make sure that everyone from your organization who needs to be there is there and that anyone who doesn't need to be there isn't. During the presentation resist the urge to jump in and start debating points. Just listen to the way they put their ideas together, watch to see whether their passion for their work comes through, and see whether they've incorporated your suggestions into what they're proposing. Are you impressed with what they consider the best work they've done for others? And, again, do they understand what success means and how to measure it?

When the presentation is over, let the agency know when they'll hear back from you. Two weeks or so is reasonable. The moment they leave the room, your decision-making committee should evaluate the presentation, with a focus on how well the agency that just left meshes with your fantasy agency. Keep as much clutter as possible out of your decision-making process. A flashy presentation or a big name in the industry isn't enough. Make sure there's some substance behind the form.

After the Interviews

At the end of the process, you'll hopefully have winnowed down your list to one or two agencies you'll use or at least try. Contact the losing candidates first. Thank them for the work they did and offer to give them an explanation of why you decided to go elsewhere. There's no need, of course, to tell who the winning agency is. They'll find out sooner or later.

When you contact the winning agency, congratulate them and let them know which specific factors contributed to your making the decision you did. By the way, don't be afraid to split up the work between several agencies. It's very possible that a single one might not be able to handle everything you need to get done. If you decide to split your account among two or more agencies, get ready for a fight. Over the years, agencies got used to being the ones in charge, and they won't like the idea of sharing control with someone else. But I've found that once I give them a choice—take what I'm offering you or take a walk—they get pretty docile.

Then take care of some of the basics: contract details, nondisclosure agreements, names of team members, and so on. It's critical that everyone agree on who's going to work on your account. Agencies often do a bait-and-switch, sending their heaviest hitters to make presentations, and then, once they get the job, replacing them with more junior people.

Check Them Out Very Carefully: The Three-Step Evaluation Process

You're about to turn over a big chunk of money to someone to invest for you. Yes, *invest*, not just spend. You'd check out a new broker before you turned your portfolio over to him, and you'd check out a surgeon before you let her replace your kidney. Same goes for ad agencies.

Check a few references by talking to the agency's past and current clients, particularly some whose media requirements are similar to yours. Spend some serious time getting to know the key members of the agency team: team leaders, creative directors, and others. Consider giving smaller projects to a few candidates as a way of evaluating them.

Don't make the mistake of thinking that you can pick an ad agency, then head off to the bank to wait for the checks to start rolling in. All the hard work you've put into defining the qualifications you're looking for, listening to presentations, and negotiating contracts will be completely wasted if you don't monitor the relationship between your company and the agency every step of the way. I've streamlined the process into three fairly simple steps:

1. **Think about what you want to achieve.** Really and truly you should have done most of this long before you picked your agency. But at this point you need to make sure the agency knows what your goals are for your brand and what your media and marketing plans are. Get their input on all of this; they may have a different perspective or be able to help clarify things for you. But before you make any big changes in your plans,

make sure you understand why. Make sure everyone's on the same page before you move on.

2. **Define success.** What do you want your advertising campaign to accomplish and how are you going to measure it? Increased sales? Increased customer purchase intent? More people trying the product? More people coming into your store? Reduced new-customer acquisition costs? Improved corporate image? Increased market share? Set up the criteria and agree on every point up front, including the time frame over which you want to see results. If you don't get everything straight early on, you'll probably end up with a bunch of beautiful television commercials that don't help sales instead of a comprehensive campaign that has measurable, positive, bottom-line impact.

3. **Monitor and record the results.** So, how'd you do? Did you achieve your goals? Did the project come in on or under budget? As you're going through this process, keep in mind that as important as financial, measurable results are, they aren't everything. Take advantage of this time to do a little soul searching: Was your plan reasonable? Maybe a little overambitious? Did you do anything to screw it up? Be honest—if one of your execs got caught with a hooker in the back seat of his luxury car and your sales drop, that's nothing to hold against your agency. Finally, how was the agency to work with? All these things need to be taken into account when putting together your next plan.

Know When to Hold 'Em and When to Dump 'Em

In principle, if you did a good job hiring and evaluating your agency, you'll never have to worry about getting rid of them. But sometimes, just like with marriage, things don't work out the way you'd hoped. So stick to your guns: If the criteria you've established aren't being met the way you want them to be, get out of the relationship—for your sake as well as for the agency's.

CHAPTER 4

Celebrity Endorsers, Spokespeople, and Icons: When to Use 'Em, When Not To

Think back to when you were in high school. If you weren't already one of the "cool" people, chances are you wanted to be. And if you couldn't actually *be* one of them, you could at least be *like* them. That meant dressing like them, driving the cars they drove, listening to the music they listened to, seeing the movies they saw. Of course, there was nothing inherently cool about those clothes, cars, music, or movies themselves. What made those otherwise generic assets attractive was the *association* between them and the people you wanted to be like. The "cool" qualities of the cool people—in your mind, anyway—rubbed off on the products and services, and it was as if using them would make you cool, too.

I'm not sure whether it's good news or bad news, but either way the reality is that not much has changed since you got out of high school. People still acquire products and services because they associate them with qualities they find attractive and they wish they had.

From a business point of view, the results of making those links in consumers' minds can be amazing. Just take a look at what using Paul Newman's name and face has done for ordinary, generic products like popcorn and spaghetti sauce. Whether Newman's popcorn and sauces are really any better than Orville Reddenbacher or Ragu doesn't make any difference. The point is that Paul Newman represents certain qualities to a lot of people, and when he lends those qualities to a particular product, people no longer see it as generic. Instead, they see that product as a way of linking themselves to the qualities they associate with Paul Newman. And they're willing to pay for the privilege.

So here's the thing: If your brand doesn't already conjure up the images and associations you want consumers to get when they think it, you'll need to *borrow* those qualities from someone or something that already has them. Otherwise, consumers will never make the connections you want them to and they'll keep looking until they find someone who'll do it for them.

Before you start complaining, I am *not* suggesting that you go out and spend $25 million that you don't have to hire Paul Newman or Tiger Woods or Michael Jordan or even Harry Potter to be a spokesperson for your product. That's not necessary at all. What's important is that the qualities your spokesperson possesses are relevant to your brand. Sure, a big name can help, but not always. The late Dave Thomas, who owned Wendy's, was incredibly successful as his own spokesman for years. And Chevy has managed to sell millions of trucks by associating themselves with a rock! ("Like a Rock" has been one of their themes for a long time.)

WHAT'S IN IT FOR ME?

For some companies, hiring a celebrity spokesperson or endorser can be a great idea and an even better investment—a way to borrow the celebrity's personality and awareness to give relevance to a brand that might not have any. But a big-name spokesperson is no guarantee that customers are going to line up outside your door. In fact, sometimes hiring a celebrity can do a lot of damage to the brand.

Over the years, I've heard all sorts of reasons for hiring celebrity spokespeople. Some have been good (the reasons, I mean) and some have been just plain idiotic. Let me take you through the best and the worst ones I've heard:

• **To take advantage of the celebrity's "equity":** This is really the only reason to hire a celebrity. Sure, having an instantly recognizable big name say great things about your product can help grab the attention of people who might have ignored you otherwise. But what you're really paying for when you hire a celebrity is *associative imagery*, to have the image and values that consumers associate with the celebrity transfer to your brand. That is what's going to get people to buy your products or services.

Remember those Disney World commercials where they asked all sorts of famous people who had just done some amazing thing, "Now what are you going to do?" The answer, of course, was "I'm going to Disney World!" Disney was very successfully linking two ideas: (1) The people you want to be like go to Disney World; (2) if you want to be like them, you'll go to Disney World, too. That approach worked beautifully for Disney, but only because the stars they used in their ads were relevant to the Disney brand and there was a logical association (call it relevance) in consumers' minds with what the company and the celebrities who do the ads stood for. If there's no connection, head the other way, because your spokesperson-driven ad will crash and burn. Having Tiger Woods endorse Nike golf clubs is a perfect fit. But Tiger, famous as he is, is completely irrelevant to the computer or grocery business.

So what are we supposed to think when the New York Stock Exchange goes out and gets Sarah Hughes, the 2002 Olympic skating gold medalist, to ring their opening bell? Huh? What's the connection there? Sure, there are people who want to be like Sarah Hughes, and there are plenty of people who are potential customers of the Exchange. But the two groups have nothing to do with one another. Does anyone at the Exchange really think that a bunch of 11-year-old girls who idolize Sarah Hughes are suddenly going to go out and start trading stocks because they want to be like Sarah? Probably not. I'll talk more about this as we go through this chapter.

• **To break through media clutter, to quickly generate brand awareness and stronger brand recall:** These are perfectly good reasons, in moderation. Having a celebrity spokesperson can be a kind of shorthand, saying a lot about your product in a very short time, and there's no question that having a celebrity endorse your brand can give you a leg up on the competition, highlighting your brand and getting people to pay attention to you. It can bring in new customers and reinforce your brand to existing customers. Done correctly, having a celebrity associated with you can go a long way toward helping you establish a brand, create an identity, or possibly even change your brand's image. Research actually shows that people have better familiarity with and recall of products associated with celebrities. But what's the point? As I say in Chapter 2, the fact that people know who you are is useless unless they're buying what you're selling.

• **To establish instant credibility and/or to reassure consumers:** This is a subset of the two previous reasons. The only way your celebrity will be able to reassure your customers (if they need to be reassured) or get them to believe you when you need them to, is if he or she is seen as a credible, reassuring person. Walter Cronkite, for example, is someone just about everyone in America would believe no matter what he said. Bill Clinton, on the other hand, is someone most people associate with qualities a little short of honesty.

- **To take advantage of the celebrity's media exposure to get even more coverage:** Again, Tiger Woods is a good example of what I'm talking about. Nike pays him to endorse their products and they've been very successful. But Tiger does a lot more for Nike than commercials. He's constantly getting his picture in the paper, appearing on talk shows, and just walking around town. And every time you see him, you see that Nike swoosh on his hat or his shirt, which is additional exposure for Nike. But remember, eyeballs don't always translate into sales.
- **Because your competitors are using them:** Dumb. This sort of thing ends up diminishing the effectiveness of having celebrities in the first place. A celebrity can help you differentiate your brand from your competitors', particularly in categories where there aren't a lot of differences to separate your products from everyone else's. But if everyone has a celebrity, you're back to square one, with no differences.
- **Because your ad agency is trying to impress you or because they've run out of ideas and believe that using celebrities is always a safe bet for advertisers to make:** Dumber. Time for a new agency.
- **Because you want to rub elbows with famous people:** Dumbest. The bottom line is that hiring a big name just for the cachet of having one or because you want a chance to hang out with him on the set of the photo shoot can confuse your customers, undermine your product's meaning, and weaken your brand. There used to be some executives at Coke (who shall remain nameless) who put a lot of pressure on me to hire Tom Watson as a spokesman. Tom was the nicest guy and he truly wanted to help us in any way he could. But Tom Watson and Coke? How was that going to help us reconnect the brand to the youth of the world? I fought hard against Tom but lost. Apparently it was all about Coke execs getting to play golf with Tom, not actually using his associative imagery to help us. Same exact thing happened with Greg Norman: great guy, great golf, no match. And just so you know, I'm not always right about these things. After the 1996 Olympics, I wanted to hire Michael Johnson, the track gold medalist. Here was a guy with a great image who I thought would be able to connect

us to both youth and athletes. But after doing some research it was clear that consumers weren't making the same associations I was. In the end, we didn't use him.

I'm willing to bet right now that whoever made the decision to have Sarah Hughes ring the bell at the New York Stock Exchange has a daughter who's taking skating lessons and really wanted to have her picture taken with an Olympic gold medalist.

Okay, so now you know the reasons why you might want to hire a celebrity spokesperson. But the bigger question remains: Even with all the advantages, can *your company* and *your brand* benefit? The answer, of course, is that it depends on a lot of things, such as the kind of business you're in, your target market, and your overall advertising strategy. There aren't any hard-and-fast rules governing who should and who shouldn't hire celebrities. But let me give you a few rough guidelines that might make your decision-making process a little easier.

Generally speaking, celebrity spokespeople are fine for products that don't involve a lot of risk or technical know-how—food, appliances, cars, clothes, beer, that kind of thing. And if you're selling or manufacturing an essentially generic product, such as coffee or pasta or batteries, a larger-than-life personality may help you connect with customers quickly.

But you'll probably want to hire an expert if you're selling anything that has any kind of physical, technical, health, or financial risk. That's why Peter Lynch, who used to run one of Fidelity's most successful mutual funds, is pitching Fidelity products. And that's why you often hear about how "four out of five dentists recommend . . ." If you're in the market for skis or bungee-jumping equipment, you're going to want to hear from someone who really uses those products. Sometimes there are naturals. Having Lance Armstrong, who is a cancer survivor, pitch a drug that reduces chemotherapy side effects is one hell of an endorsement.

There are exceptions, of course. Charles Schwab had a bunch of commercials in which famous athletes were endorsing Schwab brokerage services. Ordinarily, I don't think most people look to athletes for financial advice. But Schwab was able to use the athletes' celebrity status by having them talk very authoritatively about asset allocation, return on investment, and price-earnings ratios. Great commercials that got the point across very effectively that managing your money isn't very complicated and Schwab can teach just about anyone how to do it.

All those "I'm-not-a-doctor-but-I-play-one-on-TV" commercials for Vicks cough syrup are another exception. Ordinarily, you'd want to have a doctor talk about how great Vicks is, or you'd at least have the usual sick kid or guy-whose-coughing-keeps-his-wife-awake-all-night-long commercials where the cough syrup magically cures everything. But with the "I'm-not-a-doctor" ads, you have a soap opera celebrity with absolutely no medical credibility selling a product he knows nothing about and isn't qualified to discuss. I'm amazed they worked, but I guess it shouldn't be all that surprising, given how many people write letters and send birthday presents to fictional characters.

Whenever you hire an expert, be sure to get the right kind. When Elliptical skis first came out, they got all these hot-shot skiers to throw themselves off cliffs as a way to communicate how cool the skis were. The problem was that Ellipticals weren't made for hot dogs; they had been carefully developed for intermediate skiers, the guys who ski only once in a while but want to do it better. So by having these expert skiers demonstrate the product (although I'm not sure they were actually using Elliptical skis), they ended up missing their target market entirely. All those middle-aged or intermediate skiers thought Ellipticals were high-performance skis and never even considered them.

Sometimes having regular people pitch a product or make a testimonial works better than either a celebrity or an expert. Think about Subway's commercials featuring that guy who lost 200 pounds on a Subway sandwich diet. And all those women who dropped six dress sizes on Weight Watchers or Jenny Craig diets. Having real people say, "Look what I did," can be a lot more effective than having a diet doctor or some athlete with 4 percent body fat tell you how to lose weight.

New Balance athletic shoes also takes the regular-guy route. They leave the big-name athletes to Nike and feature unknowns in their ads. By doing this, New Balance is losing out on the teen market, but they're appealing to the somewhat older buyers who are more interested in wearing a good-quality shoe than in making a fashion statement.

DIFFERENT STARS FOR DIFFERENT CARS

Let's assume for the rest of this chapter that you've decided using a celebrity spokesperson is the way to go. Great. So now what are you going to do? Step number one is to take a few deep breaths and calm down. Don't start making lists, or calling agents, or booking production studio time just yet. I know way, way too many people who've made a decision to hire a star, then went into some kind of celebrity psychosis, constructing elaborate advertising campaigns around the athlete or actor they were going to hire. That's exactly the wrong way to do things.

As with any other component of your advertising strategy, you need to start evaluating your celebrity spokesperson options by reviewing your overall business strategy. Don't be afraid to ask yourself again (or for the first time, if you didn't get around to it before) whether having a celebrity is good for the brand. Unless you're completely clear on what your goals are, you won't be able get down to the task of picking the right person to help you achieve them. It's a time-consuming process but a critical one. And believe me, if you skip it, you'll wish you hadn't sooner than you think.

Before we get into the specifics of how to pick the right celebrity, I want to make a slight detour. Until now I've been using the words *spokesperson* and *endorser* pretty much interchangeably. But although they might seem the same, they really aren't. Most consumers won't notice the differences between the two. But each sends your message in a slightly different way and each can have a very different impact. So knowing when to use one instead of the other is something you need to understand.

Typically, a spokesperson's message is this: "I'm rich and famous (or at least someone you trust) and I'm recommending this product." An endorser, on the other hand, says, "I'm rich and famous and I actually use this product. If you buy it, you can be like me." Endorsers can also send a somewhat different message, which I'm sure you've seen in a lot of commercials where the celebrity doesn't actually say anything about the product at all. The subtle message, which is really more of a third-person narrative, is "There's Bob doing whatever it is that he's famous for. You associate Bob with certain traits and attributes. And, oh, by the way, we're flashing a picture of our product on the screen now. You do the math." Let me give you a few examples.

Spokespeople

• Ed McMahon has been a spokesman for Publisher's Clearinghouse for years. He never says he actually subscribes to any magazines through PC and you probably wouldn't believe him if he did. But he's a trusted, honest figure and you'll probably do what he suggests.

- Bob Dole has been a spokesman for Viagra. He never comes out and says he's taken it to get an erection. Who would? Like Ed McMahon, Bob is a credible guy. He's a decorated combat veteran, someone you can trust. He's also someone who had prostate cancer and was—like a lot of men in the same position—worried that he might suffer sexual dysfunction. The message is that if Bob Dole *were* having any sexual problems, he probably would take Viagra. And if Viagra could help a guy like Bob, just think of what it could do for you. Pfizer recently decided to broaden Viagra's appeal to include younger men, which they did extremely well by sponsoring a racing team and hiring a young driver, Mark Martin, to head the team.

- Bill Cosby was a spokesman for Coke when we were going after the Pepsi Challenge. Bill didn't say anything about either product one way or the other. He was simply chronicling what he was seeing (okay, what we paid him to see), which was that Pepsi wouldn't have come up with the whole challenge thing if they didn't agree that Coke was number one.

- American Express piggybacked on Karl Malden's image as the streetwise cop on *The Streets of San Francisco* to speak as an authority figure. He didn't say he used American Express Travelers Cheques. But he's got that authoritative cop-like manner (even though we all know he's not a cop), and when he gives us a suggestion, we believe him.

- Any product given away on *The Price Is Right* or *Wheel of Fortune* conveys this message: "We wouldn't have these products on the show if they weren't the best." The network isn't saying they use the products and neither are Pat Sajak or Vanna White.

Endorsers

- Cindy Crawford for Revlon puts on her makeup and the message is pretty straightforward: "Use these cosmetics and you can be as beautiful as I am."

- Florence Henderson for Crisco oil looks like someone who might actually spend time in the kitchen. So when Florence says she uses Crisco, we believe her.

- James Whitmore for Miracle-Gro (plant food) has been doing these commercials for decades. Personally, I don't believe for a second that he gardens at all, let alone uses Miracle-Gro, but obviously a lot of people do.

- Endorsers don't always have to be real people. Ericsson and BMW both paid a ton of money for product placement in a recent Bond movie.

There was no overt sales message, but simply seeing James Bond using an Ericsson cell phone to get himself out of trouble and watching him drive his snazzy BMW (at least until it got sawed in half) says volumes about those brands. If they weren't cool and hip and top of the line, 007 wouldn't use them.

MAKING YOUR LIST AND CHECKING IT TWICE

Okay, back to business. Here are the areas you'll want to focus on when you're considering different celebrities:

• **Is there a logical connection between the big shot you're considering and your brand?** When Michael Jackson was putting together his last world tour, he came to Coca-Cola and asked us to sponsor it. Sounded like a great idea—just think of all the exposure we'd get in stadiums and concert halls all over the world. But I turned it down. Michael Jackson was (and may still be) about newness and change, which has nothing to do with the Coke brand. He then went to Pepsi, which was a much better choice, anyway. Michael was a perfect fit with the DNA of Pepsi's Choice of a New Generation, and the whole thing was incredibly successful for everyone.

Soon after that, a lot of Coke's marketing people forgot about how important it is to link the brand and the endorser. Management wanted a personality, so they hired Julio Iglesias—great singer, good-looking guy, charismatic, popular, the whole enchilada. But he simply wasn't right; he just didn't look like the kind of guy who'd actually drink Coke. A single-malt scotch in front of a fireplace, yes, but Coke, no. Well, at the first commercial he refused to touch the bottle, let alone drink from it! The whole thing was a miserable flop, and all Coke could do was try to find a way to get out of the contract and as far away from Julio as possible.

They made a similar mistake when they hired Christina Aguilera. Pepsi was doing incredibly well with Britney Spears, who was perfect for their choice-and-change message, and Coke felt that they needed to strike back. But Christina, who appeals to the same revolution-not-evolution consumers as Britney, didn't make any sense with Coke's brand DNA.

Buick has made the same mistake with Tiger Woods. Tiger is so famous right now that everyone wants to use him. But does anyone really believe that he drives a Buick? Not a chance.

• **Is the celebrity relevant to your target market?** This is especially important if you're selling to more than one type of customer. The celebrity who's perfect in one market may be a total flop in another. With athletes, for example, there's been some interesting research that shows baby boomers and teenagers admire very different types. Boomers like the classy ones, the guys who play clean and follow the rules (Latrell Sprewell wouldn't be a good choice here). And they're much more receptive to messages from athletes or celebrities who've been consistent performers for a long time such as Arnold Palmer. When Arnold says a particular golf club is going to help you swing, you believe him. Teens, on the other hand, appreciate the fast-moving, constantly changing, in-your-face, independent, screw-the-rules kind of people such as Dennis Rodman and Johnny Mosely. But in the post–September 11 world, I wonder whether guys like these will successfully be able to endorse a new way of looking at life. And finally, young kids are far more receptive than any other group of consumers to messages coming from animated characters (more on that later).

Bob Dole's commercials for Pepsi were, I guess, an attempt to attract older people to the brand. The spots were a takeoff of his Viagra commercials, and he introduced the audience to a product that supposedly changed his life and made him feel young again: "my little blue friend, Pepsi." The whole thing was a total flop.

• **Is the celebrity credible?** You'd be amazed how many companies use endorsers who don't make even the slightest bit of sense. Why should I care what Michael Jordan says about phones or hot dogs? And what about Scottie Pippen and Charles Barkley endorsing Gingko Biloba? Okay, they're not as young as they used to be, but are we really supposed to believe that they're having trouble remembering things? Hmmm.

1-800-COLLECT had the same kind of "huh?" credibility problem when it signed up Terry Bradshaw as a spokesperson. Sure, he's a famous athlete and sports announcer, but does a guy who makes a few million bucks a year really need to call anyone collect or even think about saving a buck or two?

On the other hand, Paul Hogan's ads for Outback Steakhouses were a big hit. Thanks to his *Crocodile Dundee* movies, Paul had become the person who Americans equated with Australia, a place where everything is big, wild, and no-frills—just the image Outback wanted to project. And Paul's outback image hit just the right chord with the meat-and-potatoes crowd the restaurant was trying to reach.

- **Can you use the celebrity's "equity" to build your own? (What does this person stand for?)** If the celebrities you're considering don't have the image, values, or other qualities you want consumers to associate with your brand, hiring them will be a waste of money. Take Warren Buffett and NetJets (a kind of corporate-jet time-share). Warren bought the company and wanted to attract wealthy business execs who do a lot of travel and don't want to wait around for commercial flights. By putting himself out there as the spokesman, Warren is lending his wealthy-but-frugal-and-always-makes-good-business-decisions image to the company, which wants people to think that plunking down a few million dollars for a fractional share of a jet is a good investment.

Forbes magazine enhances their brand equity by attracting high-profile columnists who have a lot of brand equity of their own. They've published editorials by Ernesto Zedillo, the former president of Mexico, and they regularly have columns by Caspar Weinberger and other heavy hitters in the political and business worlds. Having these people appear in *Forbes* enhances the magazine's credibility and its cachet.

American Express takes advantage of the star power of just about every big-name celebrity you can think of in their "Membership-Has-Its-Privileges" campaign. The point, which they get across very effectively, is that American Express is a special card for special people. In other words, if you aren't special already, using the American Express card will make you special and will get you special treatment.

California's Milk Advisory Board tried to do something similar with their "Got Milk?" ads—the ones with all sorts of famous people sporting milk moustaches. But most of those endorsers have no connection to milk at all. No wonder the ads are a total flop.

- **Do you like the celebrity's values?** Is he politically outspoken? If so, do you like his politics? Does he belong to any groups or organizations that might hurt you? Remember what happened to Kathie Lee Gifford when it came out that her clothing line was being made by child labor.
- **What's the risk of controversy cropping up?** Like any other part of your advertising mix, you're going to have to stay on top of your celebrities. So do some research. Do any of your prospective spokespeople or endorsers have a drug or alcohol problem? Check the web, PR people, and so on. Do you like their politics? Of course, this is a hard thing to prepare for. Things can change in a hurry and you'll usually be the last one to

know, which means you can be repositioned right into the gutter if you're not careful.

Basketball great Allen Iverson was a very effective spokesman until he got arrested on gun charges. And Ben Affleck was out there endorsing a bunch of products all over the place, then went into an alcohol rehab program and the ads had to be pulled. One minute O.J. Simpson was a hall-of-fame football hero, sports commentator, and celebrity spokesperson for Hertz; the next he was in court accused of killing his ex-wife and her friend.

NASCAR racer Dale Earnhardt endorsed a lot of things and his picture was on all sorts of products. But when he died in a race-car crash, Earnhardt's picture suddenly became a liability. No one, except maybe collectors, would want to buy a candy bar with a picture of a dead guy on it.

• **Is there any danger of overexposure?** Two words: John Madden. Over the years, John has been a celebrity spokesman for a dazzling array of increasingly schlocky products from exercise equipment to face cream. Having him endorse a product does nothing to differentiate the product from the competition. In fact, it may even raise a red flag for some people. You can say just about the same thing for Bruce Jenner. Really and truly, these two guys aren't even endorsers; they're just pitch men, plain and simple.

Michael Jordan is everywhere, but most people can't pull that off, and even he's getting overexposed. I was in an auto parts store not long ago and walked by an end-cap display of Ray-O-Vac batteries. And there's Michael, holding a package of Ray-O-Vacs in his hand and smiling. What's that about? No one seriously thinks Michael uses those batteries (and the display copy doesn't indicate that he does). What are we supposed to think—that if we buy Ray-O-Vac we'll be able to play basketball better? There's no connection at all. In fact, for me, anyway, the net result of seeing Michael's smiling face on that battery display is that I lost some respect for him and I'm probably a little less likely to buy Ray-O-Vac than I was before. If a company goes out and pays a bunch of money to hire a celebrity without any clue as to what they're going to do with him or whether he's relevant to their brand at all, you've got to wonder whether they're putting as little thought into creating a quality product as they are into their advertising.

• **What's the "vampire effect" risk factor?** In the late 1970s and early 1980s, Cinzano (an alcoholic drink that's very popular in Europe) ran a series of ads featuring Leonard Rossiter and Joan Collins. They were all based on the same gag: the bungling fool who somehow always managed to spill his drink down the front of the girl's dress without ever realizing anything had happened. The ads were incredibly popular and very successful for Cinzano. But after a while Rossiter's persona began to overshadow the brand (that's the vampire effect—sucking audience attention away from what they're supposed to be focusing on), and even though the ads remained wildly popular with viewers, they were no longer effective in doing what they were supposed to do: Sell the product. In a way, the same thing happened with Taco Bell's Chihuahua and Pets.com's sock puppet. Both became celebrities and overshadowed their owners.

• **How long will this person's flame burn?** No Excuses Jeans has done a great job of capitalizing on people whose 15 minutes of fame are almost over. You probably still remember Monica Lewinsky, but what about Donna Rice (former presidential wannabe Gary Hart's lover) and Marla Maples (who had just broken up one of Donald Trump's marriages)? This is great for short-term campaigns, but if you're looking to build a long-term association between you and the celebrity, go with someone who's more likely to be around for a while.

• **Honestly, how popular is the candidate?** This is another case of name recognition not being everything it's cracked up to be. Lots of people have heard of Charo and Pauly Shore, but you probably wouldn't want them representing your company. And what on earth was Old Navy thinking when they signed up the Smothers Brothers to pitch winter fleece? First, the Smothers Brothers hadn't done much since the 1970s— before most of Old Navy's target audience was born. Second, does anyone know what the Smothers Brothers stand for or what possible connection they could have to fleece?

One way to get a more-or-less unbiased evaluation of popularity is to take a look at the Q scores for your prospective celebrities. Q scores are basically a popularity quotient—a measure of the popularity and appeal of hundreds of famous people. You can get info at www.qscores.com.

• **How attractive is he or she?** Shallow as it sounds, this can be important. The simple fact is that people generally prefer to look at and buy things from good-looking people. They'll also listen to attractive people longer. This isn't true in every case, of course. Experts and trusted sources don't always have to be beautiful. Think of Wilford Brimley, Florence Henderson, and Ed McMahon. But athletes and entertainers almost always do—unless they've achieved a level of fame that transcends their looks. I'm sure someone finds John Madden sexy, for example, but what's really important is that he looks the part, which is why he's popular. If you're doing ads for Tab or Polo or some other product that's aimed at the beautiful people, you'd better have some beautiful people in your ads. On the other hand, do you really care how good Mr. Whipple or the Maytag repairman look?

• **Does the celebrity actually use the brand?** He doesn't necessarily have to just as long as he doesn't use your competitors'. You've probably heard all sorts of stories about celebrity spokespeople being admonished for using competitors' products. Pepsi actually had to give Britney Spears a list of Pepsi products because she'd been spotted drinking Coke. In a sense, you should consider your spokespeople a separate group of consumers that you have to sell to. If you don't keep reminding them of your brand, they could end up forgetting who's signing their paychecks and start using someone else's products. Revlon certainly wouldn't want to catch Cindy Crawford touching up her makeup with Max Factor.

• **Can you use the celebrity in different media?** Since the most common use of celebrity spokespeople is in television, that's what I've focused on for most of this chapter. But most of what I'm talking about here applies equally well to other media. When that familiar voice comes on your car radio and says, "Hi, this is Larry Bird," he's not just doing it to be sociable. He's doing it so that people will know who they're listening to and make the connection between endorser and product. Call it *associative hearing,* as opposed to the associative imagery that goes along with visual images.

If your strategy dictates doing other-than-television advertising, be sure your star will translate well. Some personalities don't come across nearly as effectively in print as they do on screen. Jerry Seinfeld's sense of humor really comes through in his TV ads for the American Express card. But there's no way a print ad could work nearly as well. As I wrote in *The End of Marketing As We Know It,* even though Mean Joe Green was pretty much a flop in TV ads, he was very effective in meetings with employees and the trades. In the old days back in Mexico, we discovered that there was an American girl on one of our famous hilltop ads. We tracked her down and were able to use her very effectively in a lot of personal appearances.

Sometimes, in the midst of all this planning, you just luck out. We hired a male model named Lucky Vandross—a complete unknown—to do a Diet Coke commercial. Interestingly, Lucky was an instant hit. He managed to associate himself with Coke's imagery and became an overnight celebrity. We were then able to use him to do personal appearances, which made him very helpful to the brand. A similar thing is happening with the young guy who does those "Dude, you're getting a Dell" commercials and with the Levi's guy with the rubber legs.

HEY, WHAT ABOUT WOMEN?

At the risk of offending some female readers, here's the deal: Male spokespeople and endorsers are generally more successful than female ones. I didn't make the rule; that's just the way it is. A lot of this, I think, has to do with the fact that a pretty big percentage of ads involve making fun of someone, and advertisers and ad execs have historically been hesitant to make women the butt of a joke or to make them look bad. Maybe it's because women control about 75 percent of family finances and make about 80 percent of family purchasing decisions (it's true, I'm not making this up), and advertisers are justifiably afraid of alienating their customers. It could also be that men and women both are more comfortable looking to men for advice. Or, it could be that women are just more savvy and careful about what they buy. But what about Oprah and Vanna White? They certainly have a lot of appeal in some quarters.

Also, when it comes to women athletes, there simply isn't enough interest. Male athletes are generally a lot more visible and have longer careers. Plus, they generally appeal to both men and women—both want to be like them. But very few men or boys look at a female athlete as a role model. Maybe girls are just a little more open-minded.

Naturally, there are plenty of exceptions. Candice Bergen and Sela Ward have been very successful for Sprint. Skier Picabo Street has been endorsing ski products and a ton of other things for a long time. Joan Benoit has been very effective for Nike. And then there's Chris Evert endorsing iced tea. Eh? I don't get the connection, but I guess it worked because she has been around forever and seems extremely believable. But overall most things break down along traditional gender lines: Men seem to be more credible for financial and technical brands, while women seem to be more credible when it comes to health, food, nutrition, and department store sales.

OH, JUST MAKE SOMETHING UP: USING ANIMALS, ANIMATION, AND MADE-UP PERSONALITIES

I can't emphasize enough that the most important reason to use a spokesperson is to utilize his or her image and values to bridge the gap between consumers and your brand. In a lot of cases, you can find an athlete, sports star, business exec, or even a regular person to do the job. Sometimes, though, you're better off creating someone from scratch. The trick, of course, is to come up with a character who has or who can at least highlight the personality and attributes you want associated with your brand. Here are a few examples:

• **Mr. Whipple with Charmin:** The guy really looked like a store manager. Wouldn't have been the same with Tom Cruise in the part.

• **Madge the manicurist with Palmolive:** Did she look like a gossiping manicurist? You bet. And that's what gave her credibility.

• **The Maytag repairman:** Okay, I've got to admit that I never thought the Maytag repairman looked the part. Maybe that's why the company has been in trouble for so long.

• **Mikey with Life Cereal:** The impossible-to-please kid. If *he* likes it, it must be good.

• **Ronald McDonald:** The ultimate fantasy in a created character. He allowed people, especially kids, to believe that a character was actually making the Happy Meals.

• **The Marlboro Man:** The perfect embodiment of the independent, macho guy who values his freedom. Years after the last Marlboro Man billboard came down, the Marlboro Man image was so strong that the antitobacco lobby used knockoffs to get some of their antismoking messages across. In one, a tough-looking cowboy stands in front of a gorgeous sunset with a droopy cigarette hanging out of his mouth. The caption reads, "Smoking causes impotence."

Faces from Beyond the Grave

Strange as it seems, spokespeople don't even need to be alive. In the early 1990s, The Gap's "Who Wore Khakis?" campaign featured old images of famous nonconformist types such as Jack Kerouac and James Dean. A perfect fit with the cool, independent, anti-establishment image The Gap likes to present.

Thanks to some pretty incredible digital technology, deceased celebrities can almost be brought back to life to sell products. Nearly 20 years after he died, John Wayne was pitching Coors Beer. Who better than the ultimate macho man? And Fred Astaire dances up and down the walls with a Dirt Devil vacuum to illustrate how light and easy to use it is. Marilyn Monroe is selling Chanel No. 5 and Humphrey Bogart sips Diet Coke with (still-alive) Elton John.

One of the most successful of the dead celebrity commercials digitally reshot the amazing car-chase scene from *Bullitt* with Steve McQueen racing through San Francisco in a Puma (a British sports car). McQueen was perfect: Everyone knew him as a real-life car racer and a tough-guy actor who performed his own stunts. Very credible.

If you're thinking of using a dead celebrity, be prepared. Aside from the possible legal battles, you're undoubtedly going to tick off a lot of die-hard fans who may interpret your use of their idol as shameless exploitation. And I guess they'd be right. On the other hand, you'll never have to worry about your deceased spokesperson saying or doing anything that could embarrass either of you.

Animals

Animals can be great "spokespeople," too, conveying and emphasizing brand attributes. Nipper, the RCA Victor dog, was probably the first of these. Sitting there listening to his master's voice on a record told us that RCA Victor's record players reproduced sound more accurately than anyone else's. Finicky Morris the cat was a great endorser for 9 Lives, which wanted to position itself as the cat food for the truly sophisticated feline. The real-life cougar that used to run through the Mercury Cougar commercials represented speed, sleekness, and beauty—the very attributes Mercury wanted to embody in the car. MGM's roaring lion established right from the beginning of every movie that you were about to watch something created by the king.

The Coke polar bears are some of my favorite spokesanimals. They came out of nowhere and became one of the company's most successful icons. What's interesting about the bears was that they appealed to older people and kids alike with their sense of frankness and naivete. This naturally reinforced people's image of Coke as honest and straightforward. We could have used the bears in every advertising campaign forever but opted not to. As with a lot of animal-driven campaigns, a little goes a long way.

And then, of course, there's the Taco Bell Chihuahua. I've talked about him pretty extensively in this book, but suffice it to say that he was one of the more famous spokesanimals. Let's just forget for a moment that he was remarkably unsuccessful.

Budweiser has a long history of using all sorts of animals in their beer ads, but the lizards may be the best. To a great extent, beer is a regressive product, a way for the drinker to remember the good old days when he was young and had a few brews and went out and did some pretty funny things. Having Louie the lizard do just that gave Bud's core audience a way to reconnect with the brand.

Animated Characters

Using animated characters has all of the upside of using live people but almost completely eliminates the downside: no worry that they'll get tossed in jail for soliciting a prostitute or that they'll get caught using a competitor's product. They'll never have a bad season or get traded to another team, and they never ask for more money.

Animated characters definitely add a much more lighthearted, whimsical feel to ads, whether they're on television or in print, so they're not for every product. Here are a few of the most successful ones:

- **Frito Bandito:** No one in the United States had ever heard of corn chips, and as a marketing gimmick the manufacturer decided to position it as a Mexican snack. (As you probably know, I'm Mexican, and I can assure you that corn chips don't come from there.) To help, they came up with this little guy with the sombrero and serape who was supposed to be some kind of representation of a Mexican, running around like that other famous Mexican, Speedy Gonzales. It was a great way of getting the Frito brand into people's minds.

- **Tony the Tiger:** Getting your box of sugar-coated cornflakes to stand out from all the others isn't an easy job. But Tony and his "G-r-r-r-r-reat!" showed that the product was more than the same old thing—it was fun.
- **Snap, Crackle & Pop:** One of the biggest problems with cereal is that it gets very soggy very quickly. Having the cereal snap, crackle, and pop when milk gets poured on it (as opposed to squish, mush, smash) shows that Rice Krispies won't get soggy like all those others. These guys were great, but you've got to wonder what happened to them and why they lost their edge. Today, the rice-puff (or whatever) market is dominated by private-label brands, and Rice Krispies is back to being an also-ran.
- **Jolly Green Giant:** What could be healthier than a garden full of huge vegetables grown by a green giant? A great differentiator, they eventually lost their edge, too, and virtually gave away market share.
- **Keebler Elves:** Like Snap, Crackle, Pop, and the Jolly Green Giant, the Keebler Elves have been around for a long time. But unlike those others, the company has very successfully refreshed them and used them to communicate that elves actually make the product, it's unique, has a special recipe, and is magical.
- **Pillsbury Doughboy:** Another guy who's been around a long time. Pillsbury made a mistake by dropping him a few years ago but eventually brought him back when they needed to reinvigorate the message that Pillsbury's dough rises faster and better than anyone else's.
- **Chef Boyardee:** Again, character made up for the sole purpose of differentiating one product in a generic category from the others: ordinary pasta with ordinary sauce. It worked for a while, but eventually everyone else in the business copied the idea and the difference became background noise, making the category pretty much generic again.
- **Mr. Clean:** One of my favorites. This bald-headed guy with the earring was a great way to get across the difficult-to-communicate premise that this particular cleaning liquid could do the job of a tough cleaning person. The icon actually helped. Unfortunately, Mr. Clean was as narrow a focus as Wisk's "ring around the collar." They came out with a Mr. Clean line of bar soap, but the whole product line has been drifting aimlessly for a while. Nothing more than lazy marketing.
- **Scrubbing Bubbles:** What can I say? They do the job perfectly. Who knows more about cleaning than the bubbles themselves?
- **Quaker Oats Guy:** I don't think anyone really believes that the guy with the wig is a Quaker (most of us have never seen a real Quaker, any-

way), but that hasn't kept him from becoming a symbol of the product and the symbol of continuity, wholesomeness, and quality. When you pick up a package of Quaker Oats, you know you're getting a top-quality product. And with the recent medical discovery that eating oatmeal may actually help lower your cholesterol, things have really taken off for the brand. Unfortunately, though, they haven't been nearly as successful getting that message across about their other products.

• **Charlie the Tuna:** Yet another example of creating a way to be different in a tough, generic category. Lots of companies have tuna packed in water, with low sodium, high sodium, and every other possibility. But Charlie really communicated that Starkist was different, better, and special. The company probably didn't get as much use of old Charlie as they could have before retiring him.

• **Punchy of Hawaiian Punch:** Like a lot of other products aimed at kids, Hawaiian Punch had the added task of having to convince the gatekeepers—mom and dad—that the product is good. Punchy was a clever way to appeal to both groups.

• **Little Caesar's:** Domino's difference was fast delivery time. And advertising genius Cliff Freeman (the guy behind "Where's the Beef?") came up with the little guy in the toga shouting "Pizza Pizza!" which quickly communicated that the Little Caesar's difference was that you get two pizzas for one low price.

Animated animals are especially effective if you're trying to sell to children. Smokey the Bear was probably the first. He didn't say anything that we didn't know; he just tugged on our heartstrings by expressing the animals' fear of forest fires. And then there was McGruff the anti-crime dog, another campaign pitched largely at kids.

Because animated animals are so attractive to kids, you've got to be careful how you use them. Joe Camel was an incredibly popular icon, but he generated a huge amount of bad press for Camel when it became clear that Joe, who was one of the most identifiable characters among young kids, had probably been responsible for getting millions of them to start smoking.

SINGING A HAPPY TUNE

Now I'm sure most people wouldn't consider music to be a spokesperson (or an endorser, for that matter). But think about it for a minute:

Music is used to sell us all sorts of things. Alfred Hitchcock used that *screech, screech, screech* music in *Psycho* to sell us the idea that we should be scared. And I know I'm not the only one who hears that *bom-bum bom-bum bom-bum* music from *Jaws* every time I go swimming in the ocean.

Music has an amazing capacity to almost instantly evoke emotions, memories, and associations. If you're able to capture the associative imagery and qualities that people associate with a particular song, music can be a powerful tool to convey your brand's attributes. (Even think of Intel's sign-on or sign-off music.)

Ad agencies used to come up with their own jingles that they hoped would stick in people's minds: Just think of "plop, plop, fizz, fizz," "G.E., we bring good things to life," and "Reach out, reach out and touch someone," to name a few. But after a while, companies figured out that they could get even more associative imagery from an established song. Nike may have been one of the first ones to do this when they used the Beatles' "Revolution." (They originally got sued for using the song but later bought the rights.) A lot of Beatles purists hated the idea, but it worked.

Since then, just about every company you can name has used music to promote their brand: Heinz made good use of Carly Simon's "Anticipation" to highlight that their ketchup is thick, but it's worth the wait; Apple used the Rolling Stones' "She's a Rainbow" to tie in with their rainbow logo; AltaVista (the search engine) used Nancy Sinatra's "These Boots Are Made for Walkin' "; Nissan used Lenny Kravitz's "Fly Away" to show how their Xterra SUV gave you the freedom to go places an ordinary SUV couldn't. Even stodgy accountants Coopers Lybrand got into the act, using Bob Dylan's "The Times They Are A-Changin' " to tell us that they're the best place to get your numbers crunched in unstable times. The list goes on and on.

It's especially interesting that the music–product connection sometimes flows in both directions. Some of the songs that advertisers are using are so new that they haven't had time to establish any associative imagery. Take Gatorade's use of Smash Mouth's "All-Star." Sure, Gatorade is using the song to say that top athletes (and future top athletes) drink Gatorade, and using a pop band like Smash Mouth squarely aims these spots at teens and 20-somethings. But you've got to wonder whether Smash Mouth's record label is also trying to sell CDs by linking its songs to Gatorade's image. This two-way street certainly worked for Sting. His "Desert Rose"

CD was going nowhere on the charts or in stores until Jaguar started using it in their commercials. Then it became a hit.

SOME LEGAL STUFF: COVERING YOUR BUTT

I don't want to spend a bunch of time talking about contracts—that's what your lawyers are for. But I do want to point out a few important things:

- **Leave yourself a way out.** If your business suddenly changes, you want to be able to cancel the endorsement contract.
- **Have a clause on conduct.** How your endorsers carry themselves in public can have a big impact on their effectiveness. If you've hired Dennis Rodman, it's because you want him to be outrageous and in your face. If suddenly he stopped dyeing his hair, had his tattoos and piercings removed, and switched from sequins and feather boas to Brooks Brothers suits, you'd want to be able to dump him fast. Ditto for substance abuse or trouble with the law. If a celebrity wants to trash his or her career, fine; just don't let this person take you along. The Florida Department of Citrus ran into a problem like this when it hired Burt Reynolds as a spokesman, which was a strange thing to do, anyway. Burt Reynolds and orange juice? I don't get it. But when Burt's divorce from Loni Anderson got really ugly, the Citrus people had to pull the ads.
- **Get a noncompete clause in there.** Just one photo of your spokesman using a competitive product can undermine your entire campaign. Catherine Zeta-Jones seemed to be the perfect, credible spokeswoman for Sainsbury's, a British grocery store chain. (She's gorgeous, has a big name, and is a mother, too.) But when she got caught shopping in Tesco, Sainsbury's major competitor, it was bye-bye credibility. If something like this happens you want to be able to get out fast and for free.
- **If an endorser's specific job, title, team, or something else is important to your campaign, make the deal subject to cancellation if the endorser loses the reason you're using him or her.**

MONITORING SPOKESPERSON SUCCESS

I've got to get back to a point I've hammered on a lot throughout this book and that I constantly hammer on with my clients: Spending money on anything—in this case, it's a celebrity—is stupid if you're not getting the results you want. This, of course, takes us back to the very beginning: knowing what your strategy is and what you want your new celebrity-driven campaign to accomplish.

It's not all that hard to do. Start by looking at your before-and-after sales figures. If the numbers aren't heading in the right direction, you've got a problem. At the same time, you should be hitting the street (or the mall or wherever your likely customers are) and asking questions. Are people making the connection between your brand and the celebrity? Are they more likely to buy your product since you started using that celebrity than they were before? Do they see your brand as "a brand for me and for people like me"?

As you're putting your results together, be absolutely sure you're measuring actual impact on the brand, *not* just celebrity recall or the fact that the celebrity is associated with your brand. Recall and association are useless unless they translate into sales.

If you aren't getting the results you want, you have two choices: (1) Figure out what went wrong and fix it, or (2) pull the plug and cut your losses. Actually, I guess there's a third option, too: Do nothing. That's the one that the California Milk Advisory Board is going with for their "Got Milk" ads. They spend $240 million a year paying celebrities to have their picture taken with a milk moustache. The ads are kind of cute, but they've been a huge money pit. Sales are up 2 percent, which means that the board is actually worse off running the "Got Milk" ads than not running them. And they won't stop. This kind of reminds me of the old joke about a guy who goes to a store where a tailor is selling nice Italian suits for $25. The guy is amazed that the suits could be so cheap and he asks the tailor how he could possibly make any money at those prices. "Actually," says the tailor, "I'm losing money on every one I sell, but I'm making it up in volume."

Get the point?

CHAPTER 5

Packaging Matters: It's Your Last, Best Shot, So Make It a Good One

Imagine you're about to go out on a blind date. The two of you have exchanged some emails, you've had a few wonderful phone conversations, maybe you've even swapped photos online, and a mutual friend has told you how great your date is. You're getting excited, but before you leave the house for the actual date, you're (hopefully) going to spend some time making yourself look as attractive as possible for this person you've never met. That's pretty much a no-brainer, right? You know that as important as all those premeeting things are, the big decision about whether you're going to get together again, let alone whether you're going to date regularly, is made eye-to-eye. It's exactly the same thing when it comes to packaging your product or service. Stay with me here—I'm going somewhere with this.

Today, most companies spend a ton of money for a gorgeous picture to post online (let's call it your 30-second commercial), they hire my cowriter to craft exquisite emails (call those your print ads), and they get themselves a celebrity spokesperson to give the product some credibility (call that a high recommendation from a mutual friend). Then they show up for their date unwashed and wrinkled. It's all over before it starts.

The connection is pretty obvious: Don't take a shower and don't get a second date. Don't spend enough time making your packaging as attractive to consumers as you possibly can, and they'll walk right by you. In either case, you'll probably never get a second chance.

So here's a question for you: What are you hoping to get in return for all the money you spend on research, branding, ads, hiring celebrity

spokespeople, sponsoring events, and everything else? If you've been paying attention so far, you're probably going to say that the goal of all this
spending is to sell more stuff to more people more often and for more
money. But you'd be wrong, at least partly. What you really want—actually, the very best you can possibly hope for—is for consumers to make you
part of their consideration set (the short list from which they make their
final purchasing decision). If that's all you need to get the sale, wonderful.
But for most people there are still plenty of roadblocks ahead.

Now before you get all upset and accuse me of having misled you,
take a deep breath and relax. No, you haven't wasted your money on ads
and research and branding and whatever. But the truth is that advertising can spark interest, it can get people to think about your product,
and it might even entice them to come into a store or log onto a website. However, no matter how much you spend, it won't make them buy
your product unless you've covered all the bases of communication.
And one of the very biggest is packaging, which is your face in front of
the consumer at the critical time: the moment the final purchase decision is made.

The generally accepted number among research companies is that 75
to 80 percent of a consumer's purchase decision is made at the point of
sale. And it gets worse from there. In grocery stores, for example, shoppers
spend an average of less than 10 seconds in any single product category. No
small wonder that they don't even notice over a third of the products on
the shelf. The same basic numbers apply to just about any retail situation.

Sounds pretty horrifying, but don't just take my word for it. The next
time you go to the grocery store, pay attention as you're walking up and
down the aisles to how much time you spend in a single section. What
makes you stop? As you grab something off the shelf, take a second to
think about why you picked that specific product instead of the one next
to it or on the shelf above or below it. Was it the look or feel of the product? The color? Something you read on the label? The price? The name of
the product itself? Then take another few seconds to notice how many
other options you didn't even see. Pretty surprising, isn't it?

If you're honest with yourself, you'll probably admit that what
prompted you to pick up a particular product was its packaging. And if you
picked up more than one, packaging was still a major contributor in your
final decision. Don't feel bad. Having spent more than 30 years in marketing, I consider myself a pretty sophisticated shopper. But this kind of

"CONFUSING"

FIGURE 5.1

thing happens to me all the time. Just take a look at the photo of the real-live grocery store shelf of hair coloring products. Can you explain to me how anyone who doesn't have three hours to read every package is going to be able to tell one brand from another?

It used to be that packaging existed solely to keep the stuff inside it from getting dirty, broken, or contaminated. But it didn't take long for marketers to figure out that the container a product comes in is a perfect place to do a little last-minute advertising. After all, the last point of defense against your competitors is how your product looks on the shelf. It's especially important in today's environment, where more than 30,000 new products are introduced each year, including multiple versions of the same product—deodorant that comes in 15 different scents, toothpaste that whitens, controls tartar, or contains baking soda, and so on.

Contemporary packaging attracts attention, soothes, agitates, urges, and, most important, communicates volumes about the product it contains and about your brand. Just think of Tiffany's little blue box. That box—that package—sends a message that's nearly as powerful as the stuff inside it. It lets Tiffany's get away with selling jewelry that is essentially generic for a lot more than anyone else. And think about the original 1964 Mustang. A perfectly ordinary car inside a very hot package that people were willing to pay a premium for.

Even though just about everyone agrees that packaging is important, most companies make two big mistakes:

1. They think about packaging only when they're launching a product, then they forget about it sometimes for years or forever.
2. They define packaging too narrowly. In a world where everything communicates, packaging is more than the can, tube, box, bag that a product comes in. It's also how (and how many) multiple products are sold, the size and color of the trucks that deliver the products, store interiors, the buildings themselves, and a lot more that you may never think about. I'll give you some specific examples of what I'm talking about as we go through this chapter.

So what makes good packaging? Simply put, if the packaging makes you buy the product, it's good. If not, it's bad. On the most fundamental level, good packaging has three major ingredients:

1. Good looks (aesthetically appealing)
2. A message that's consistent with and reinforces your other advertising
3. An ability to cut through clutter

That's pretty much it. Let's take a look at these components in a little more detail.

DON'T JUDGE A BOOK BY ITS COVER? OH, PLEASE . . .

"Don't judge a book by its cover" is a great expression, telling us that looks aren't everything and we have to judge things on their true attributes instead of their superficial value. Well, that's all wonderful. But on this planet you could have the most amazing product in the world, made of the best ingredients, and offer it for the lowest price yet still not sell a single item.

Studies find that only 7 percent of communication is verbal—that is, the words we say. The other 93 percent is nonverbal—that is, how we say what we say, tone of voice, speed, hand gestures, facial expressions, posture, and so forth. Similarly, people get a lot more information about a product by looking at the pictures on the package than from reading the text.

Bottom line? If your product doesn't communicate your brand's message visually, you're pretty much out of luck. Consumers are basically shallow people who judge books—and just about everything else—on how they look, and if they don't notice your product, they'll never pick it up. So either your package shouts, "Buy me!" and breaks through the clutter in some serious way, or it stays on the shelf while someone else's product gets bought.

How your product looks is especially important if it's available online. In a lot of cases, a prospective customer's first—and only—interaction with your product is a picture. She won't even be able to pick it up and hold it. So, again, you either communicate your message visually or not at all.

Now, as important as looks are, they aren't everything. Words can certainly play an important role. Phrases like "new and improved," or "30 percent more free" or "new easy-to-open package" are all good. They help explain your brand and tell the consumer why he should buy it instead of the other options. As you know very well at this point, if you don't give consumers a reason to buy, they won't.

Whatever you do, keep your text short and to the point. Research has shown that having a lot of messages on a package actually decreases the chance that people will read any of them. And be sure to spend some extra time reading your own packaging to make sure you're saying what you really mean. Here are a few actual examples of packaging text that could have used another round of editing:

- The package of snack foods that proclaims, "You could be a winner. No purchase necessary. Details inside." And how are you going to get those details if you don't buy the package?
- The frozen dinner manufacturer that puts "Serving suggestion: Defrost" on the package. Are there really that many people who eat frozen dinners cold?
- And what about the box of tiramisu dessert that says on the bottom of the box, "Do not turn upside down."

- The laundry detergent box that says, "Remove clothing before distributing in washing machine." Gee, thanks. I might have tried to climb into the washing machine if I hadn't read that.
- And the package of bread pudding that warns people, "product will be hot after heating." Now there's a surprise.

Your packaging has to function well, too. This isn't a book on package design or engineering, so I'm not going to tell you how to create ergonomic packages. But the importance of functionality shouldn't be underestimated. Does your package make the product itself easier to use (think squeeze bottles for ketchup, detergent bottles with built-in measuring cups, individual portions, etc.)? Or does your package act as a deterrent (think of those plastic packages you have to have a chain saw to get into, CDs that require a college degree to figure out how to open them, or those extra safety seals that come with some bottled products that take 10 minutes to get off)?

Consumers aren't the most forgiving lot. Give them a clunky, inconvenient package or nonsensical messages and they may never come back.

COLOR

Color is a very powerful communicator. It can inspire us or repel us, make us happy or sad. Like tastes or smells, colors carry all sorts of emotional weight. Certain colors mean certain things. Sepia instantly communicates "old-fashioned" without the need for any further explanation. A certain shade of yellow practically says "school bus," and if you saw another kind of vehicle painted that color, you'd probably think for a second that it was actually a bus. The red, white, and blue pattern on our flag says "America" so strongly that you might not be able to identify a flag on which the colors were reorganized or changed. And no matter how old you are, you know that tie-dye says "1960s."

Colors play an equally powerful role in marketing and advertising. A one-second flash of a particular shade of red and gold from three blocks away tells you there's a McDonald's nearby. A one-second flash of slightly different shades of red and gold says Shell Oil instead.

Color also communicates a huge amount about products. The messages evolve over time and get ingrained in the culture, just like school-bus yellow. Burgundy and gold packaging, for example, conjure up images of quality. Peppermint is almost always red and white; spearmint is green and white. White is the color of choice for low- and non-fat dairy products. Cinnamon-flavored candies are red. Antibacterial soaps are often gold. Using a color is a great way to shortcut communication with consumers. It instantly conveys certain benefits, telling people where your product is positioned and what niche it serves in their life. All that without you having to say anything.

Interestingly, very few companies actually understand the meaning of the color they chose or fell into. When I was at Coke, we found red to be a powerful color for us. It all started when we went to China, where red meant a lot of things: power and strength but also superstition and fear. Wow. We wondered whether we could capitalize on red in other countries, so we hired an advertising agency/consulting firm, Weiden and Kennedy, to explore it on a worldwide basis. We found amazing things: In Spain, red is passion and a sign of aggression. In India and Pakistan, it's the color of cricket, and by extension, the color of competition and pride. (Interestingly, it didn't have any particular significance in the United States even though it's all over the flag.) We used this knowledge of red to link with consumers where it made sense, but we deemphasized it where it didn't make sense.

Be sure to do your homework before using any color on your products, especially if you're doing business overseas. In the United States, white communicates light, coolness, purity. But in China it means death—not the image you generally want to convey in a package of breath mints.

I haven't got the foggiest idea why certain colors get associated with certain categories. But I do know that there are very few exceptions and that going along with the established program is usually a good idea. I know that I've spent a lot of time talking about how important it is to differentiate your brand, to make your product noticeable on the shelf. No question that's essential. But unless you have a really, really good excuse, think long and hard before you try to buck a color trend.

If you're in the beer business, why waste valuable space on your package telling a consumer that the can he's holding is filled with lite beer when simply making the can silver would get the same point across a lot quicker? Making your antibacterial soap pink (or, in the case of your razor, blue), or introducing a line of lite beer in orange cans just for the sake of being different or being noticed, won't get you anywhere. In fact, you'll have to spend a ton of time and money explaining to the customer why you made a change that doesn't serve any particular purpose. Consumers already know that differences are differences. What they need to know before they buy is how the differences are relevant to them.

Colors can change their meaning from time to time. Green, for example, used to be completely off-limits on food packaging. Then Healthy Choice took a risk and put green on their packages. Now green has become a shortcut, instantly conveying health and nutrition in the frozen foods category. Black used to be taboo, too, but then along came Minute Maid, which used it to signify premium quality.

Remember that both Healthy Choice and Minute Maid were exceptions. Healthy Choice was introducing a completely new category, and by going with a new color, they communicated boldness and newness. Minute Maid, on the other hand, was entering the existing chilled juice category, but it was a category in which Tropicana had 100 percent of the market. If Minute Maid had any hope at all of getting noticed, they were going to have to come up with something radically different.

HEY, ME, TOO! WHEN TO BE A LEADER AND WHEN TO BE A FOLLOWER

Okay, so if you can't express your brand's individuality through color, how about differentiating yourself with an eye-grabbing design? Well, maybe. If you're in the music business or you're hoping to sell a lot of products to young people (or maybe their parents), unique and innovative packaging is essential. Whether you're a rock star or a video game, you've got to be cool before you can be relevant. Nowhere is the contrast between follower and leader more obvious than in your local supermarket. Any kind of food product aimed at adults comes in pretty straightforward packages that communicate the traits that are important to adults—usually health and value. But anything aimed at kids—Go-gurt (Yoplait's yogurt in a tube), chocolate milk, green ketchup, breakfast cereals, for example—screams (or tries to, anyway) "I'm cool" all over the package.

A bunch of magazines have experimented—some successfully, some not—with snazzy covers and formats in an attempt to communicate "different." And airlines such as Europe's Easy Jet have even painted their toll-free numbers on their planes. This kind of thing can work, but only if it stems from a legitimate strategy to differentiate.

Most of the time, when it comes to the overall package—the physical shape and layout—you're better off *not* differentiating yourself too much. In fact, often the perfect way to neutralize your competitors' packaging is to match it.

My trusty co-author told me once about an experience he had buying Tide liquid laundry detergent at Costco. He grabbed a couple of large bottles off the shelf, but it wasn't until he got home that he discovered that instead of Tide, he'd actually bought Costco's store brand. Sounds like a dumb mistake, but there are probably tens of thousands of people around the country who make the same mistake every day—not only with Costco detergent but with hundreds of other products as well. It's a mistake that many manufacturers count on.

I'm sure that when Costco decided to start selling a house brand of detergent, they didn't want to spend a bunch of money designing new, distinctive, or innovative packaging. So they deliberately piggybacked on Tide, hoping to leverage Tide's brand equity to sell Costco's products. Walgreen's does the same thing with their Wal-tussin line of cough syrups, which look suspiciously like Robitussin. Go to the store and take a look at these products next to each other.

The retailer stocks their store brand right next to the big brand—same-size package, similar graphics, same colors, same font. If you're in a hurry, you might accidentally pick up the wrong brand. Even if you're not, the message you're getting from the generic or store brand's packaging is that the *only* difference between the products is price.

WHAT ARE YOU TRYING TO SAY, ANYWAY?

Most people define packaging too narrowly as simply the thing that's wrapped around their product. But it's a lot more. Here are a few examples of nontraditional packaging and the powerful messages it sends:

• Southwest Airlines' long lines, no-reserved-seating policies, and nothing-but-peanuts meal service are packaging. A lot of times, Southwest's prices aren't any better than anyone else's, but they sure *seem* cheaper. Their uniforms—shorts and polo shirts—are packaging, too, positioning Southwest very differently from the airlines whose employees wear more professional-looking clothes.

• Banks and brokerage houses use huge buildings with massive columns and 30-foot ceilings as packaging. Those solid structures send the message that the company itself is solid, it will be there forever, and it's a safe place to put your money. (Online financial institutions have to deal with the same issues: Various attempts to create an online bank have failed. Even at Charles Schwab, one of the most successful online brokerage houses, most new customers still open their accounts at a branch. People just don't feel comfortable sending money to a place they can't see.) The packaging is so successful that most people aren't bothered by the fact that those gargantuan buildings don't use space very efficiently and cost a ton of money, which increases operating costs and reduces your yield.

• FedEx's trucks are packaging. Their clean, uncluttered paint jobs make them easy to spot. And the fact that there are so many of them all over the place subtly communicates that FedEx will get your package anywhere you want whenever you want. Because trucks are generally pretty big, they offer a particularly important packaging opportunity. When I was at Coke, we once calculated how much money we could bring in by selling ad space on the back of all our delivery trucks worldwide. It was millions a year. Of course, we weren't going to sell space on our trucks to anyone else and neither are you. But the point is that too many companies overlook a tremendously valuable asset that's sitting right under their butts.

• Costco's open warehouse design and the constant beeping of forklifts are packaging. Costco isn't always the cheapest place to buy stuff, but there's something about being in a warehouse and having to buy a case of something that makes you feel that you're getting a deal.

• Long presidential motorcades of bulletproof limos and the tough-looking Secret Service guys with sunglasses and those curly things sticking out of their ears are packaging. They say that our president is a real big shot who is worth protecting. Celebrities do the very same thing, using the packaging of the limo and the bodyguard to communicate that they're special.

- The huge bags that Harrod's gives away during its annual sale are packaging. One look at that bag and you think you're going to get an incredible deal. The fact that Harrod's sale prices are still higher than most other stores' regular prices doesn't come into the discussion.

- Webvan's trucks were packaging. Webvan offered fresh groceries delivered right to your door. To reinforce that idea, the trucks had to look fresh and fast like a traveling grocery store. Ultimately, of course, the company folded. I think part of the problem was that people would be stuck in traffic next to a Webvan truck and start imagining that everything inside was slowly rotting. Not the kind of message the company wanted to project.

- When Vicente Fox, the president of Mexico, campaigned wearing cowboy boots, open shirts, and riding a horse, he was wearing his package. The message was "I'm not your typical stuffed-shirt politician. I'm something new. I'm one of the people." Very successful.

- In a somewhat more traditional way, the boxes that Gateway ships their computers in are packaging. Those splotchy cow prints evoke a more relaxed, leisurely country image where costs are lower and where salespeople have the time to custom design a computer system for every customer.

- Sometimes even a name can be packaging. Southwest Airlines' stock ticker, for example, is LUV. While most CEOs try to get a ticker that is similar to the name of the company, Herb Kelleher realized that LUV tells investors a tremendous amount about Southwest's culture, attitudes, and commitment to satisfying its customers. Lexus is a great name too—sounds kind of like "luxury" and kind of like "sex"—not a bad combination. Aleve, the pain reliever, combines "alleviate" and "relieve," and Paxil, the antidepressant, draws on the Latin *pax* for peace. Great names. On the other hand, what kind of image does Zocor bring up? Sounds like some kind of Japanese monster who might gang up with Mothra to try to defeat Godzilla. You'd never know it's a drug for lowering cholesterol.

Sometimes the wrong name can be dangerous. Doctors and pharmacists have been known to get mixed up between Celebrex (an antiarthritis drug), Cerebyx (an antiseizure drug), and Celext (an antidepressant). And what about Zyban, a drug that helps people quit smoking, and Zyban (yep, same exact spelling), an agricultural fungicide? It's entirely possible that a patient with a prescription for the antismoking Zyban could see a can of the other Zyban on a shelf in a gardening store and think that it's the same stuff. Don't laugh—this kind of thing happens all the time.

HOW'S THAT? THE IMPORTANCE OF CONSISTENT MESSAGES

I'm assuming that you have a pretty good handle on what your brand's value proposition is and what message you want to get across to consumers. And, of course, you remember that *everything* you do communicates. But simply communicating isn't enough. **If you're going to get the biggest bang for your communication buck, everything—your ads, your sponsorships, your branding efforts, and, naturally, your packaging— has to communicate a *consistent* message that ties in with everything else in your advertising mix.** Inconsistent messages can undermine your advertising efforts faster than anything else.

What is a consumer supposed to think when you package your line of low-fat potato chips in 5-pound bags? On one hand, you're saying these chips will help you lose weight. On the other hand, you're saying here's 5 pounds of them, which completely defeats the purpose of the product.

When we reintroduced the contour bottle at Coca-Cola, we were able to sell it at a premium. The bottle communicated cool, unique, and different, which were things Coke drinkers were willing to pay a little more for. But then someone had the bright idea of putting the contour bottles in six-packs. The problem was that this sent a completely contradictory message to our customers. Those little plastic things that hold six-packs together are packaging that says *value*. That's not a bad thing, but selling the contour bottle individually said something else altogether: *premium*. I vetoed the six-pack. (After I left Coke, they did it, anyway, and contour bottle sales dropped considerably.)

The makers of Strata golf balls had a similar problem. The rest of their advertising supports the idea that Strata balls are superior quality, which they are. But then they introduced a 15-ball pack. The problem is that every other golf ball manufacturer sells 12-packs. A 15-pack gives the impression that there's something inferior about the balls; otherwise, why would they sell them in bigger lots? Instead of helping, Strata's 15-pack managed to take a pretty healthy divot out of their sales.

KNOWING WHEN IT'S TIME TO MAKE SOME CHANGES . . .

As you know, one of my big themes is that you've got to keep adjusting your message to those ever-changing consumer needs. The same goes for packaging. As with the rest of the piece of your overall advertising mix, it's essential that you regularly monitor how things are going.

Your biggest clue is your sales. If they're not going up, you have a problem. Whether it's packaging related will take some time to figure out. Start by asking yourself these questions:

- Is my message still relevant to consumers?
- Am I communicating with the right people?
- Is my packaging making use of the most effective shapes, colors, and symbols?
- Am I taking advantage of the natural colors of the category?
- If I'm doing something to be different, am I getting an incremental benefit from the difference?

If the answer to any of these questions is no, it's time to make a change. But make sure that the answer didn't come from in house. You are *not* your own target group. Get your answers from your customers, not from focus groups, which are largely a waste of time because you end up with a bunch of professional focus group goers who may or may not be actual consumers of your product. You don't need theoretical answers; you need solid data.

Finding solid data isn't any harder than going to the places where your products are sold. Grab a bunch of actual customers and ask them whether your packaging is making them buy your product. If so, why? If not, why not? Then show them a few variations of your package and ask them which one they would be more likely to buy and why.

Make sure you use actual products and actual packaging. Don't show people pictures and ask which one they like best. People have to see a package in front of them and hold it in their hands to properly judge it. And don't ask people to help you design your product or ask them for abstract help. ("If we added a stripe here, what would you think?")

This is going to cost you some money. There's no target amount or percentage of sales. It doesn't have to be a lot, though—just enough to get *quality information*. Doing anything with your packaging without a damned good reason is a terrible mistake. It's like driving your car blind-folded and hoping you get where you're trying to go alive.

Let's go back to the previous questions for a minute. If you didn't get a no answer, there are still plenty of other situations that are major red flags that something's got to change. Here are a few:

- Your product has lost its individuality and has become more of a com-modity.
- Customer expectations have changed.
- You want to communicate to consumers that something big has changed with your brand or product or service.
- You want to move into new markets or expand your target market.
- You've made a significant improvement to your product or service.

. . . AND WHEN IT'S NOT

Okay, okay, so you've got the point that change is a good thing—essential, in fact. But there are lots of times when change isn't such a hot idea. The first, of course, is if your research and results indicate that your packaging is having the desired effect. But remember, don't let a few packaging industry awards go to your head. It's not a beauty contest. Success is mea-sured in dollars and sales.

Change simply for the sake of change is a rotten idea. Smuckers (the jelly people) paid a big price for that. They had a great advertising campaign that brought people to the jelly aisle of their grocery stores, their packaging tied in perfectly with the ads, and made the sale. But someone in the organization decided that Smuckers needed to liven up their old-fashioned label. The result was some kind of modern-looking bull's-eye thing that had nothing to do with Smuckers's message. They promptly lost 15 percent of their market.

Years ago, to celebrate their 100th anniversary, Coca-Cola decided to refresh the packaging on all the primary brands. I fought the idea as hard as I could, but eventually Don Keogh, who was the president, and Ike Her-bert, the executive vice president of marketing, told me to shut up and sit quietly in the back of the room.

They brought in this consulting company, Landor, which did a real bang-up job: They convinced the company that we should have a single look for all of our cola brands, with only minor variations for the "flavors"—diet, cherry, caffeine-free, and so forth. Unfortunately, they lost track of packaging's primary function: to differentiate the product from everything else around it on the shelf and to provide one last chance to tell the story of the brand before the consumer makes his or her final buying decision. Make everything look the same and the consumer will pay you less.

The company went along with Landor's dumb tactical plan and essentially eliminated all of Coke's differentiation on the shelf. The new look basically said, "Yo, kids, Cherry Coke is the same as Coke. It's old and stodgy and not any fun, just like your parents." All of our brands suffered, and it took us a long time to undo this major blunder.

The moral of the story is that if you're fortunate enough to have a packaging icon, think long and hard before you make significant changes. What do you think would happen if Quaker Oats put Tiger Woods on their box instead of that Quaker guy who's been there for 100 years? What if Disney decided that Mickey Mouse sounded too anti-Irish and changed his name to Fred? What if Campbell's Soup suddenly went to a label with vertical stripes instead of their trademark red-and-white horizontal bands? What if Chanel or Chivas Regal decided they could save a few bucks by putting their products into ordinary bottles? And what if Tiffany's changed the color of their box, Coca-Cola decided to go with a different script, or MGM replaced their lion with a chinchilla? Hopefully, you get the point. The answer is that people would be confused. Their entire image of the company would be changed, and it would take a lot of expensive explaining to convince them that the change was truly necessary.

There are some exceptions, but they tend to be incremental rather than earth-shattering. Car manufacturers change their body styles every few years, but overall there's usually plenty of similarity from year to year. Universal Pictures got rid of their plump lady with the torch and replaced her with someone much thinner. But it was still a lady with a torch, not a mouse riding a bicycle.

The important thing to keep in mind when contemplating changing or updating an icon is that the essence of the product—the specific value it communicates—has to remain the same. Remodeling the Apollo Theater in New York to upgrade the number of exits and install more comfortable seating could be a great idea, but the Apollo meaning must remain. It still has to be a place where young performers get a chance to fail or fly. Not maintaining your icon's meaning can turn it into nothing more than wallpaper.

Ford made a colossal mistake when it took its classic sporty Thunderbird and changed it into a family car, almost killing the T-bird brand altogether. But when they brought back a retro-looking T-bird coupe in 2001, the waiting lists were miles long. Pillsbury made a similar blunder when they had their doughboy do a rap commercial. What's next? A tattooed doughboy? A doughhboy with a belly-button ring? It just didn't work.

Not everyone is lucky enough to have an icon. But even if you don't, there are plenty of times when making changes isn't necessarily a good thing. If you're operating a fleet of limos in a competitive market, for example, painting polka dots on yours will certainly help them get noticed, but it probably won't get many people to ride in them. When it comes to limos, black (and sometimes white) represents wealth and respect. Polka-dot limos represent fun and Elton John.

Similarly, a school district would be crazy to paint their school buses black. Even with the words *school bus* written on the side, black just wouldn't convey "school bus." As a result, the message would get muddled. People would get confused and probably wouldn't be as likely to drive as carefully around them or slow down before passing.

The most valuable advice I can give you is to do a lot of research before you make any major changes. But even doing research isn't a guarantee that your changes will be for the better. A few years ago, Wendy's did some research and found that people didn't like waiting in line for their burgers. So they tried to reduce the time between when customers placed their orders and when they got them. Sounds like a responsible thing to do, right? Unfortunately, it backfired.

In the fast-food industry, the time it takes customers to get their orders delivered is actually part of the packaging (just think of the big Jack-in-the-Box head who takes your order at the drive-thru). As it turns out, although Wendy's customers didn't like waiting in line in the restaurant, getting their order almost immediately after placing it gave them the impression that it wasn't as fresh and had been sitting around baking under a hot lamp for a while.

Freshness was an issue for Bumble Bee Tuna, too. They did a bunch of research and found that tuna eaters have two major complaints: The cans are a pain to open, and having to drain the water is a mess. So Bumble Bee came up with a great idea: tuna in an easy-to-open pouch with no drain-ing required. They launched a big advertising campaign, but no one was buying. Why? A few reasons. First, the pouch cost a lot more than a regu-lar can of tuna. More important, though, was that when people looked at the pouch, they imagined that the tuna inside wasn't fresh and that it would be too dry. (How we got to a point where a can is a symbol of fresh-ness I'll never know.) They thought the pouch was a very interesting idea, but when it came right down to it, draining the can is part of the experi-ence and the ritual of eating tuna. It's part of the DNA of a can of tuna, and it's something that buyers accept as part of the deal when they buy it.

AND SOME COMPANIES THAT DO IT RIGHT

Packaging done right is a beautiful thing. Let me give you a few examples of some companies that have raised the bar for everyone else:

- **Absolut vodka:** Their packaging single-handedly changed the pub-lic's perception of an entire category. Before Absolut came along, the vodka biz had always been driven by price—the cheaper the better, in most people's minds. Smirnoff was the entire category. Anyone else who came into the market had to come in cheaper than Smirnoff. Even though Smirnoff sounded Russian, it was actually an American vodka distilled in Stamford, Connecticut. When the *real* Russian vodkas (Stolichnaya and others) came into the market, they had a lot of snob appeal—after all, they were imported—and they positioned themselves as the drink for sophisticated, cool people.

Then Absolut showed up, and instead of telling us how their vodka was different from the others, they focused entirely on their bottle. By showing the bottle in every conceivable situation, they've managed to convey ubiquity and tremendous popularity. It was and still is absolutely brilliant.

The whole Absolut phenomenon fundamentally changed the way the entire wine and spirits category advertises, putting the focus on packaging instead of contents. So now each new entry into the category has to use a distinct bottle to communicate "premium." A great example is Pisa, a slightly better-than-average hazelnut-flavored liqueur whose main distinc-tion is that it comes in a bottle that tilts a little to one side, just like the famous tower. Big deal.

When packaging didn't work, some of these companies went back to using product attributes as a way to differentiate themselves, but too often they settled on the most superficial things. Blue Goose, for example, didn't have much going for it except that it was imported from France. And Chopin was from Poland. Actually, Chopin's real claim to fame was that it was really made from potatoes, which came as a surprise to me, since I thought all vodkas were.

Interestingly, throughout this entire repositioning revolution, Smirnoff stayed pretty much on the sidelines. All they did was put a silver label on their original bottle. The idea was that silver was going to communicate "premium," which it usually does. But putting silver on a bottle that people associated with a product that was decidedly un-premium made absolutely no sense.

- **Altoids:** Who would have thought that anyone in his right mind would be running around making a big deal of an aluminum box of impossibly strong mints? For years, Certs pretty much defined the mint category by focusing on a product attribute that made them different from everyone else: retsin (whatever that is). Retsin, we were supposed to believe, would make it possible for us to kiss longer and more often with no worries about bad breath. Then Altoids turned the whole thing upside down. Actually, they started differentiating themselves by focusing on the strength of the mints. The idea was that Altoids weren't for everyone. Only the truly sophisticated could handle them. But there was no way they could convince anyone that a sophisticated product could come in a foil-and-paper wrapping. So they came up with an idea that completely transcended the product: the box. It's a strong statement and it's being copied by a lot of other players in the category.

Some companies have such great packaging that they've actually been able to reduce the amount of other advertising they do. Think about these:

- **Tiffany's:** The word itself conjures up images of quality (or at least of Audrey Hepburn and George Peppard, if you're old enough). And a great deal of that image comes from their little blue box, which communicates more than what's actually inside the box. Tiffany's customers become an unpaid advertising force, walking around flashing their blue bags and blue boxes. They may be empty, for all I know, but they still communicate quality and have for a long time. The company got into some trouble not long ago, but it wasn't because of their image. Instead, they'd overextended themselves and lost track of what they were all about: generic jewelry at a premium price wrapped up in a perception of luxury.

• **Big Bertha:** No, it's not a cannon or a train—it's a golf club made by Callaway Golf. (In this case, the product and the package are the same thing.) Ely Callaway's philosophy was that Callaway was in the business of making golf a more enjoyable game for the players. Nothing more. One of the things that makes golf fun is getting your score down, and one of the best ways to do that (besides playing a lot) is to buy a club with a big, heavy head that helps you hit the ball farther. So Ely came up with Big Bertha, which does exactly that. And who needs to spend money on advertising when the name of the product alone communicates big and fat. One look at the head of the thing says you can't miss. And when your golf buddy suddenly starts smacking the ball 10 yards farther than he did before, you can't live for a moment longer without one.

Callaway built on the success of the Big Bertha woods by introducing the Bigger Big Bertha and Biggest Big Bertha, then put the Big Bertha name on a set of irons as well. Naturally, everyone else started doing the same thing, but Callaway was there first and has managed to stay a few steps ahead of the pack.

• **Cup-a-Soup:** This one is really the ultimate definition of successful packaging. The name pretty much says it all, and the package drives the point home: It's a single serving of soup in a cup. It doesn't take long to communicate the message. You walk down the grocery aisle and it only takes a second to know what you're getting. That's it. The concept was such a great one that it's been copied by all of the Japanese noodle companies and just about everyone else (you can even get a kosher version!). Interestingly, the Cup-a-Soup concept is such a powerful way of communicating "single serve" that now manufacturers are piggybacking on the idea by putting all sorts of other things in similar packaging.

• **Whatchamacallit:** I can just imagine the meeting where they named this candy bar. "Gee, Bob, what do you call a candy bar that has all sorts of different stuff in it?" "Kind of reminds me of a, you know, a whatchamacallit . . ." "Hey, why don't we call it that?" The name in itself communicates everything about the product without having to say anything more.

• **White Castle** and **Krystal**: Both of these companies sell tiny little hamburgers. Supposedly, you can eat a bunch of them—which may or may not be a good idea. Both also make their burgers square, which sends two messages: First, you're getting more meat (a square seems bigger than a circle); and second, because they're easily stackable, they fit neatly into a box and it seems like you're getting more of them.

• **Smart Car:** An idea that could work only in Europe. Here's a tiny, ugly car that has almost no aesthetic appeal and violates every premise of what a car is supposed to be. But Smart Car wanted to communicate that the vehicle is not only small enough to park anywhere but it's fun. So their dealers sometimes have displays of eight or ten of them stacked right on top of each other.

Obviously, this isn't a comprehensive list of companies that have done a great job with their packaging. But the point is that it is possible. It takes understanding what you want to do with your brand, coming up with a consistent strategy, and sticking with it. If you do these things, you can't help but get the maximum advertising benefit from every package you sell. Guaranteed.

CHAPTER 6

To Sponsor or Not to Sponsor: That Is the Question

In the Introduction I explain that I wrote this book because I wanted to take a long, hard look at the one aspect of marketing where the most money is spent and wasted: advertising. In this chapter I focus on the aspect of advertising that's the most misunderstood and potentially the most financially risky: sponsorship.

It doesn't matter whether you're running the marketing department at General Motors or a local dry cleaner. No matter how big your company is, you probably spend some time every day listening to impassioned pitches from every Tom, Dick, and Sally about why you should sponsor their event. It's just a question of scale: If you're at GM, they'll be asking you to sponsor Major League Baseball. If you're the dry cleaner, it's a little league team. In 2001 alone, thousands of corporations worldwide gave in, spending about $25 billion—up from less than $6 billion in 1987—for the rights to put their names on just about everything in sight, from local AIDS walks to Formula 1 auto races, from video games to sports stadiums, and from art exhibits to rock concerts. That makes sponsorship the fastest-growing form of advertising, according to IEG, an events-tracking consulting company. But $25 billion in rights fees is only the tip of the iceberg: Companies typically spend three times more than that to create, advertise, promote, and implement their sponsorship programs.

Here's the question you knew I was going to ask: Is the incredible growth in rights fees being matched by a similar growth in sponsors' business results? Not even close. If it was, I wouldn't have had to write this chapter.

SO WHAT'S OUR GRIPE WITH SPONSORSHIPS?

Our biggest complaint is that the vast majority of sponsors have no clue what they're doing. At the very root of the problem is a series of mistakes most sponsors make even before they start cutting checks:

- **They don't know *why* they're sponsoring.** Too many do it because they always have or because their competitors are. I've seen far too many white elephants—sponsorships that were purchased in the heat of the moment only to find later that they offered little more than the opportunity to wallpaper sports stadiums with irrelevant company logos.
- **They don't know what they hope to accomplish.** As obvious as it sounds, sponsorships are *not* about getting free tickets to events and schmoozing with your buddies. And they're not all about capturing eyeballs, either. Evaluating opportunities involves more than estimating whether the event is going to attract enough viewers, attendees, or participants from your target audience. Far more important, it involves determining whether sponsoring a particular event will generate increased sales and equity for your brand.
- **They don't understand the balance of power between themselves and the property sellers.** Too many sponsors go along with property sellers' demands and whims even if they're directly contrary to the sponsors' needs. As a result, they don't know how to protect themselves from being railroaded.
- **They don't focus on getting a return on their investment.** The goal of sponsorships—like that of any other advertising element—should be to sell more stuff to more people more often for more money. I hope that's starting to sound familiar.

If you're considering sponsoring something, you're going to have to rethink your strategy from the ground up. Sponsorship, the way it's done today, is dead, and we know what killed it. So read this chapter carefully. By the time you're done, you'll know how to properly evaluate a sponsorship opportunity and assess the strategic objectives and potential benefits.

All you have to do is follow the six imperatives in this chapter. They will help you make sure any sponsorship you get involved in will enable you to generate a proper return on the investment, just as all the rest of your advertising efforts should do. At the risk of sounding a little arrogant, you can't get this information anywhere else. The rules we're talking about here aren't academic and they aren't based on theories or statistical modeling. Instead, they're based on something better: experience.

Coca-Cola is probably the most extensive, experienced user of commercial sponsorships in the world. During my tenure there as chief of marketing, we paid to sponsor the Olympic Games, 3 soccer World Cups, 10 Super Bowls, the Oscars, dozens of other major events, and hundreds of smaller ones. There's no question that some of the sponsorships we ran were remarkably successful. But there were plenty of times when we didn't even come close to success.

After the 1996 Olympics in Atlanta, I had a nagging concern that we hadn't gotten a very good return on the hundreds of millions we'd invested worldwide in leveraging this sponsorship. So I created a new group in our global marketing department to evaluate the situation and to lay out a strategic approach that would make sure we got a strong return on every future sponsorship.

One of the key people I hired to lead this effort was Chris Malone. Chris had worked at the NBA and the NHL Players' Association before coming to Coke, and he knew how to play the sponsorship game from the seller's side of the table. The project he and his team did completely reshaped the way we thought about the Olympics and sponsorships in general. Chris developed a lot of the sponsorship principles that I now advocate everywhere I go, and I'm grateful for his many contributions to this chapter. (The "we" in this chapter refers to Chris and me.)

Since leaving Coke, I've worked with dozens of other companies, many of which have also spent millions on sponsorships. I've served on the board of directors of The Gap and 15 other companies, from dot-coms to Honey Baked Hams, and I even did marketing consulting for a presidential campaign. I know what works and what doesn't.

Frankly, I wish I would have known what I know now when I first started running marketing at Coca-Cola. Instead, each lesson was a painful exercise in trial and error.

WHAT'S IT ALL ABOUT? A BRIEF HISTORY OF SPONSORSHIP

When I was at Coke, I had a strong suspicion that a company that runs seminars on how to find sponsors had published a manual promising the first surefire step to success would be "Buy three airline tickets: one to Atlanta (Coke), one to Purchase, New York (Pepsi), and one to Portland, Oregon (Nike)." It was as though they thought of us as the Bank of Coca-Cola. The assumption that Coke and other large companies will sponsor sports events is so strong that when professional sports teams put together their profit-and-loss projections for a new stadium, they often have a "Coca-Cola Sponsorship" revenue line item in there from the start, as if it's a given. Now that's chutzpah!

In a lot of ways, though, it's not all that hard to see where that impression came from. For a while, we had a running joke at Coke that said, "If it stands still, paint it red. If it moves, sponsor it!" Out of an annual worldwide marketing budget of $5 billion, we spent nearly a third of it each year sponsoring everything from the Olympics to the Venice Flower Show.

Again, it's a question of scale: No matter how big your company is, a lot of people simply *assume* that you're going to send some sponsorship dollars their way. It's an assumption that's really a naive throwback to the days when wealthy individuals "sponsored" artists and musicians who couldn't otherwise support themselves.

These rich people weren't looking for a return on their investment. They were really kind of like groupies. All they wanted was a chance to hang out with Michelangelo or Beethoven and maybe show up in the background of a painting. It was clearly a kind of philanthropy. For Michelangelo and Beethoven, on the other hand, the wealthy sponsor was a necessary evil.

Amazingly, not much has changed over the past few hundred years. As recently as 1974, for example, the Royal Philharmonic Orchestra stated, "Sponsorship is the donation or loan of resources by private individuals or organizations engaged in the provision of goods and services designed to improve the quality of life." You'll notice that according to the Royal Philharmonic, it's very much a one-way street: Sponsors write the checks; the orchestra cashes them. Everyone's happy.

Fortunately, businesses have finally started to wake up to the idea that they've been taken advantage of. And things have started to change—very, very slowly. In 1991, for example, the *International Journal of Advertising* wrote, "Sponsorship is an investment, in cash or in kind, in an activity, in return for access to the exploitable commercial potential associated with that activity." That's a big step forward, but even in this model all the seller is obligated to do is provide *access* (not profits or success) in return for the sponsor's investment. A nice gesture, but nowhere near enough to meet the needs of today's marketers.

The solution?

IMPERATIVE 1: DUMP THE TERM *SPONSORSHIP*

The only way to correct this fundamental misunderstanding of what sponsorships are all about is to completely drop the whole sponsorship mentality. The words themselves, *sponsorship* and *sponsor,* refer to an outdated marketing concept. They suggest a completely one-sided relationship based on philanthropy.

Remember, the goal of advertising—including sponsorship—is to boost your bottom line. And unless you're running a nonprofit, the whole reason you're in business is to do exactly that. You should consider every expense an investment, including the fees you're being asked to shell out to sponsor an event. And an investment that doesn't show a return should be cut off.

This isn't to say that there isn't a place for corporate philanthropy or that you shouldn't give back to your community. Of course you should. Being a good corporate citizen is extremely important. But don't confuse sponsorships with charity, and make sure you keep charitable sponsorship expenses out of your advertising budget unless you seriously expect to see a return.

Really and truly, there is no upside to calling yourself a sponsor. And there may even be a downside. Most football fans assume that all those Gatorade coolers on the sidelines don't really have any Gatorade in them, just water, and that the reason they're there at all is that Gatorade paid big bucks for the privilege. And people know that FedEx pays even more to put their name on the stadium where the Washington Redskins play.

Overall, calling yourself a sponsor tells people that there's a financial transaction involved. They may question your integrity from that point on. For teens, it's even worse: Saying you're a sponsor is the kiss of death. It tells them that you're a corporate entity and that all you're concerned about is money. It makes your message completely irrelevant. So remove the word *sponsorship* from your vocabulary, and, more important, remove the sponsorship philosophy from your advertising and marketing spending.

Of course, no matter what I say here, people are still going to use the word *sponsor,* and you'll still be asked to sponsor events and causes. Realistically, though, I want you to think about things in a different way: in terms of what you really intend to do. So instead of *sponsorship,* let's say *marketing property utilization:*

- **Marketing:** The role this activity will play for the business
- **Property:** The entity must have proprietary value to extract
- **Utilization:** The purpose of our involvement with it

At Coca-Cola, we came up with new terms to distinguish between three types of sponsorships:

1. **Marketing assets:** properties with proprietary value that can be leveraged in marketing programs to generate sales volume and build brand equity. Examples include the Olympics, the Super Bowl, and even Christmas.

2. **Availability account:** sports stadiums, theme parks, and resorts where a significant volume of beverages are sold and consumed, but which lack the proprietary value and meaning of a marketing asset. Owners of these attractions often charge steep sponsorship fees for the right to sell a particular beverage there. The value of this type of arrangement is exactly equal to the profit that can be generated from product sales, not a penny more. Knowing this has helped Coke avoid paying more for sponsorships than they could possibly recoup.

3. **Constituent expense:** sponsorship events such as a Wal-Mart charity golf tournament or a $100-a-plate retirement dinner for the local heath inspector. These are important causes for key constituents that Coca-Cola does business with, and Coca-Cola supports them to help maintain a good relationship. Coke is very careful, however, not to confuse them with marketing assets, and Coke never throws additional money at them in the hope of generating a return on their investment. The bottom line is that this kind of sponsorship is essentially a charitable donation and should be treated that way.

Making terminology changes like these—even if it's just in your own mind—will help you keep focused on the idea that properties (sponsorships) are nothing more than advertising tools whose goal should be to help you sell more stuff.

Why Would You Want to Sponsor Anything, Anyway?

The first step is to take a good look at why you're thinking of marketing property utilization in the first place. Are you looking for a way to get free tickets to events and rub elbows with famous people, or are you trying to find a way to connect with your consumers and build your business?

Chances are that you'll say you want to build the business. In fact, according to a report by IEG, the top reasons companies decide to sponsor are to increase customer loyalty, increase awareness, and change or reinforce their image. The problem is that for most people there's a big gap between what they think would be a good idea and what they actually end up doing.

If you're going to be successful in today's business climate, though, you're going to have to bring the two options a lot closer together. And it starts by going back to the "why-am-I-doing-this" issue. If you can't answer that question, you'll end up with a white elephant on your hands—a sponsorship that turns out to be completely irrelevant or inappropriate for your target consumers.

White elephants are a double problem: They divert valuable advertising dollars from something worthwhile to something that's a waste of time. They also act like a black hole, sucking good money after bad as you flounder around trying to figure out a way to make the sponsorship work.

If you're unlucky enough to find yourself with a white elephant on your hands, the only thing you can do is what you would do with any other bad investment: Get out as fast as you can, cut your losses, and put the freed-up marketing resources to use on something productive. Of course, a far better approach would be to prevent white elephants from being born in the first place, which is what effective property screening and selection is all about. Property screening starts with a review of your current business and brand-building objectives. Answer these questions:

1. **What specific business results are you trying to achieve?** Property utilization is just one of many marketing tools available for helping you achieve your business objectives. It's not a destination unto itself. Therefore, you have to be clear about what you want to sell, where you want to sell it, what business results you want to generate, and over what time period. If the answers to these basic questions aren't perfectly clear in your mind, you're not ready to begin evaluating properties. Remember, property utilization is simply a means to an end, and you've got to start with the end in mind or you'll never get anywhere.

2. **Who are you trying to sell to and what do you want to say to them about your product or service?** Properties are a communication vehicle, and like any other form of marketing communication, you've got to be clear about who you're trying to reach and why. You also need to know the specific features or benefits you want to emphasize and communicate to your target audience. Are you trying to convey a new benefit that your competitors don't have or just reinforce an existing one that really drives the customer purchase decision? Once you can answer these questions specifically, you'll be ready to begin evaluating the properties that can help you achieve these objectives.

3. **Does the property in question possess the associative equity you need to achieve your business objectives?** In other words, does it reach your target audience and is it strongly associated with any of the features or benefits that you're seeking to communicate to your target audience? Just as with celebrity spokespeople, effective property utilization is all about tapping into the equity possessed by a property and transferring some of it to your brand. If the property doesn't have attributes that you want to be associated with your brand, there's no sense in linking your product or service with it, and you'd be wasting your money buying it. It's that simple.

4. **How much will this property cost and how much business will you need to generate in order to achieve the revenue and profit objectives you identified earlier?** No matter how much associative equity a property possesses, if you can't realistically achieve your financial objectives by utilizing it, you'll do yourself more harm than good trying to find a way to make the numbers work.

5. **What are the opportunity costs?** Would the dollars you're thinking of allocating for property utilization net you a bigger return somewhere else? Is property utilization the most effective and cost-efficient way of achieving your business objectives? Some companies completely opt out of sponsoring. Nike, for example, figured out that they get a lot more out of having individual athletes wear the swoosh than they do from putting their name on tennis matches or stadiums. A number of high-tech companies, including Intel and Logitech, have started investing in video game tournaments. They've found that the tournaments are a great way to get their message to their target group of Gen-X-ers without having to shell out millions on slick television and magazine ads.

Once you get a handle on these questions, you'll be in a better position to judge which properties, if any, have the associative equity you need and how you can use them to achieve your objectives.

The Biggest Question of All

Perhaps more important than any of these questions is whether you can be sure your use of the property will be relevant and persuasive to your consumers. This is *not* about whether the property has significant viewership, attendance, or participation among your target audience. It *is* about whether the property you're considering will generate increased sales and equity for your brand.

How does the property you're considering fit with your brand? When I first joined Coke, we were sponsoring the Davis Cup. It had absolutely nothing to do with Coke and the sponsorship was a waste of money. Why did we bother? Because someone in control of a promotions budget was a tennis fan. A stupid reason that cost the company hundreds of thousands of dollars.

A few years ago, I was driving along an empty stretch of road in California and I saw a sign for the Red Barn Animal Auction, sponsored by Pepsi. Hello? What possible benefit could Pepsi get from sponsoring an animal auction? Were they trying to ingratiate themselves with the community? Probably not. Someone—probably someone whose kids love cows—just decided that having a big sign on the side of the road would be nice.

Should Coke have sponsored Michael Jackson on his world tour? Not a chance. Coke's image and brand are based on stability, continuity, and consistency. Michael Jackson was all about change, choice, and youth, which are Pepsi things all the way. If Coke would have put their name on the Jackson tour, the consumers would only have gotten confused. Personally, I would have loved to sponsor the Beach Boys tour, but it wouldn't have done much for the brand.

Should Keebler (the cookie and biscuit people) sponsor the X Games that feature extreme sports? Absolutely not. A conservative cookie can't possibly earn any associative equity from a property that appeals to young people who skateboard and pierce their tongues. On the other hand, the X Games are a perfect fit for Mountain Dew, which has a cool, young, extreme image.

There are plenty of examples of perfect fits between property and buyer. One of the best is Timex's utilization of the Iron Man Triathlon property. Chances are that when you think of Timex, you think of their old tag line, "It takes a licking and keeps on ticking," and some of the great commercials (like trains running over watches) that Timex has run for decades to communicate the quality and durability of its watches.

But as successful as those ads were, it wasn't until the mid-1980s that Timex launched a highly effective property utilization strategy and the idea really became solidified in the minds of consumers around the world (after all, who really believes that a watch can get run over by a train and still work?). The property was the Iron Man Triathlon, where hundreds of relatively unknown athletes with superhuman strength and endurance chose to wear the Timex Iron Man watch during the tortuous and grueling competition.

Having strong, tough, durable athletes choose the Timex Iron Man showed consumers more about the watch's strength, toughness, and durability than anything the company could ever say. The triathlon was the perfect setting for Timex to associate their brand with those qualities and demonstrate the key benefits their watches could deliver.

Consumers made the connection, too: The Timex Iron Man was the best-selling watch *worldwide* for *10 straight years* after its introduction (1986–1996) and is still a top seller today! Not until 1997 did another watch, the Expedition (also from Timex), surpass the Iron Man. Now that's what we mean by effective property utilization!

In our experience, there's only one way to tell whether the property fits with your brand (as well as to answer the other questions in this section), and that's to follow Imperative 2.

IMPERATIVE 2: CONDUCT PROPERTY RESEARCH
BEFORE THE PURCHASE

It always stuns me to see how little time and money most prospective property buyers spend investigating what they're getting themselves into. They usually buy first and ask questions later.

I meet people all the time who say they want to spend $50 million over 10 years to sponsor a stadium. I ask them what kind of research they've done to make sure they're going to effectively reach their target customers.

The response is almost always the same: "Oh, we don't have any money to do that." Believe it or not, this attitude is much more the rule than the exception. Overall, more than 75 percent of corporate sponsors spend less than $5,000 per deal doing research before a sponsored event. A third actually spend nothing.

This isn't brain surgery. If you were considering building a new facility, buying a large piece of capital equipment, or making any other major business investment, you'd do some pretty careful due diligence to make sure you were going to get a positive return, wouldn't you? You'd even do some pretty serious research before investing your IRA money.

The same should go for property utilization. If you don't allocate some of your budget to analyze what you expect to net from your investment, you're asking for trouble. This means going out into the real world and figuring out how your consumers and customers would react if you sponsored the event you're considering. Would it make them more likely to buy your products or services? Would it make them think any differently about your brand? Does the property have enough associative equity to reinforce your brand positioning? When you've got all that figured out, there's one more critical question: Is spending your money on this particular property more effective and cost-efficient than your other advertising alternatives?

Honestly, this isn't all that hard. When we were considering having one of our brands sponsor professional volleyball, we spent a lot of money interviewing fans to find out what feelings and images that sport evoked. The goal, of course, was to determine whether the images people had of volleyball were images we wanted people to associate with our brand, too. It turned out that volleyball had a very limited appeal in most of our markets. And even in areas where volleyball was especially popular, the league we were thinking of getting involved with didn't have any strong equities in the eyes of our target audience. What we found instead was that it was the *sport* of volleyball more broadly, as opposed to the league, that had the equities we were after. As a result, we were able to leverage volleyball as a property in the markets where it was relevant by putting up nets on beaches and organizing local competitions, which we were able to do without paying a nickel in sponsorship rights fees. Thanks to a small investment in research, we achieved our business objectives and saved millions of dollars in the process.

I understand that most people aren't going to be able to spend a ton of money on pre-event research. But there are options for every budget.

Before the event, for example, you might give away some tickets to the event, run a trial promotion, or place some ads that link your product or service with the property. Then do some consumer surveys to measure their response (you can do them by phone, in person, or online depending on how much you want to spend). Ask whether your association with the promotion made consumers more or less interested in buying your product. As a rule, if you're considering investing a substantial amount of money in a particular event, you should be willing to spend up to 5 percent of that investment in advance to make sure you're getting the value you're looking for.

In the end, if the prospective property isn't the most effective and cost-efficient way to achieve your business objectives, then it shouldn't be used at all. Properties are just one of the advertising tools in your arsenal. Use them only when they are the best way to accomplish your objective.

What's in It for Me?

Okay, so you've done all your research and picked out a property that meshes well with your brand and your business. The next step is to make sure you buy only the rights you need to achieve your objectives. There are nearly a dozen different ways you can use a property to communicate something about your brand to your current and prospective customers in a way that that will deepen the relationship with them and market your products or services. To streamline things a little, I've divided them into three broad categories:

1. Brand marketing
2. Customer development
3. Corporate development

Brand marketing activities include:

• **Product exposure:** If you were Revlon or Max Factor, would you want to provide all the makeup for the Miss America contest? Hell yes! It would tell everyone in the world that beautiful women wear your company's makeup.

- **Media vehicle:** If a particular event precisely captures the target audience you're trying to reach, it may make sense to become the exclusive advertiser for your product or service category within that event. Examples would be Super Bowl advertisers that purchase category exclusivity during the game broadcast and local advertisers that purchase exclusive rights to air their advertising in the town's baseball stadium.
- **Consumer and trade promotion:** One of the most common forms of property utilization is giving away or selling property-related merchandise or prizes along with your product or service. Fast-food chains like McDonald's and Burger King rely heavily on property-related promotions that link them to everything from movie releases to sporting events.
- **Product sampling:** Again, if a particular event attracts precisely the target audience you're after, you could get a lot of mileage out of distributing samples there. This approach is especially good when you're introducing a new product to a very specific target audience.
- **Brand communication:** Properties can act as powerful metaphors for something you want to convey about your product or service in your advertising or promotions. Remember Timex and their Iron Man watch. Another example is Coca-Cola's longstanding use of Santa Claus in their holiday advertising and packaging.
- **Brand publicity:** Getting involved with a newsworthy property or event can also generate valuable publicity and imagery for a brand. IBM has used their Deep Blue competition with chess grand master Gary Kasparov to generate positive publicity for their brand.

Customer development roles include:

- **Acquiring new customers:** You may be able to use the broad appeal of certain properties to gain access to potential customers who might otherwise be difficult to reach. For example, Verizon might be able to meet with and register new business cell phone accounts by inviting corporate purchasing managers to a prominent golf tournament.
- **Developing tailored customer programs:** In industries where competition between distribution channels is intense, manufacturers sometimes use properties to create unique and customized promotions for different distributors. This is what happened when Wal-Mart told Procter & Gamble that they didn't want to support the same national promotion

on Tide that had already been offered to Target and every other major chain. Naturally, they wanted something unique that other retailers wouldn't be able to offer. In this case, Tide was able to leverage their involvement with NASCAR and driver Ricky Craven to create customized promotions for each retail chain. This gave Tide a nationwide promotion but still allowed each individual retailer to offer something unique and different.

• **Providing customer hospitality:** Although this form of property utilization is a little overused, if you manage it properly, it can still be effective. Basically, it involves using the property event as an opportunity to entertain and hopefully bond with key customers in ways that you might not be able to do in a strictly business setting.

Corporate development roles include:

• **Corporate image building:** Some companies get involved with high-profile events as a way to improve their corporate image. For example, tobacco companies like Philip Morris have tried to improve their battered image by becoming much more public in their support of charities such as Meals on Wheels and the National AIDS Fund.

• **Employee incentives:** For some companies, property-related incentives can be a great way to motivate employees. John Hancock, for example, sponsors the Olympics mainly so that it can offer free trips to top-performing agents.

If you step back and look at all the different roles that property utilizations take on, it's clear that they often focus on different parts of the value chain. So as you consider property utilization for your business, you need to take a close look at your own value chain and decide how properties can add the most value to what you are trying to accomplish. Once you've done this, you'll be in a much better position to judge which rights, if any, you really need to purchase to accomplish your objectives.

Don't expect your friendly neighborhood property sellers to help you out here. They have a vested interest in selling you the biggest bundle of rights they can, sort of like the prix fixe menu at a fancy French restaurant. If you're thirsty and all you want is a Coke (what did you expect me to suggest?), you'd be an idiot to buy a 12-course dinner just to get the drink. In the same way, don't go out and buy a bunch of property rights that you don't need or can't use just because some property seller is hocking a "package." Just buy, à la carte, only those items that add value to your business and your brand.

For example, John Hancock pays about $50 million every four years to be a worldwide Olympic sponsor, which entitles them to exclusive advertising and promotion rights in the insurance category worldwide. However, since they're primarily using the sponsorship to give away trips to the Games to their employees and run a few ads in North America during each Olympic broadcast, they're paying for a ton of rights that they're not using. They could probably achieve their goals for a lot less money by just buying tickets to the Olympics and giving them to their top salespeople. Okay, John Hancock's senior executives wouldn't get to hobnob with the Olympic Committee types at the Games, but hopefully that's not why they're sponsoring in the first place.

IMPERATIVE 3: USE THE PROPERTY TO DRIVE YOUR BUSINESS

If you're going to survive in today's business environment, you have to make sure that every dollar you spend on advertising drives the business model and creates economic value. Like every other component that makes up your overall advertising mix, property utilization must deliver tangible, measurable results. David Letterman summed this up perfectly in February 1994 while humorously referring to Coca-Cola's sponsorship of the Olympics: "I don't really care who wins. I don't really care who loses. I'd just like to see Coca-Cola make a little money out of this thing."

David was obviously poking fun at Coca-Cola for their overtly commercial involvement with the Olympics. But apparently, not enough CEOs watch *Late Night,* because the fact is that most sponsors use their business to drive the property, not the other way around.

How does this happen? Often, it's because "sponsors" get caught up in the glamour and emotion associated with a particular property and lose sight of what they're trying to sell. In a way, that's understandable, although certainly not acceptable.

The fact is that property utilization is one of the most complex forms of marketing communication. Fundamentally, it involves introducing a third party into the dialogue you have with your customer about your brand. For example, when Mountain Dew leverages the ESPN X Games, they're probably hoping to illustrate to their teen male consumers that the Mountain Dew brand is cool, edgy, and young. Along the way, Mountain Dew may run advertising and special offers that promote the brand's involvement with the X Games. But often, in their quest to run the coolest X Games advertising and promotions around, they forget to stay focused on conveying a message that sells more Mountain Dew. Instead they provide great promotion and publicity for the X Games and nothing for their own business. Happens all the time, and property sellers, of course, are delighted to play along.

So how do you evaluate the effectiveness (or lack thereof) of property utilization? The short answer is, quantitatively—the same way you measure the effectiveness of any other business investment. And believe it or not, it really is that simple.

What amazes me, though, is how few people do it. Zyman Marketing Group's proprietary research indicates that only about 10 to 15 percent of sponsors actually measure their return on their property utilization investment at all, and most of those who do some calculations spend only 1 percent or less of their sponsorship budget monitoring their return during and after the events. Even more amazing are the excuses I've heard for why people don't calculate their return:

- "We don't know how."
- "It can't be done."
- "With so many other factors—media ads, promotions, and so on—going on at the same time, it's too hard to separate out sponsorship-related cause and effect."
- "We don't because we're afraid of what we might find."
- "We evaluate based on our gut, not some scientific formula."

When I start asking questions, it quickly becomes obvious just how little thought these otherwise intelligent CEOs and advertising managers put into property utilization. "Before you started the sponsorship, did you define success? Did you plan out how you were going to measure it? Did you set up a mechanism for measuring results? Did you code your expenses so that you could separate out the property utilization costs from the rest of your spending? Did you make sales projections? Did you estimate what you needed to sell so that you could net a profit after you pay off your investment in the property?" No questions I ask ever generate more blank looks than those.

Measuring the effectiveness of utilizing a specific property isn't any harder than measuring the effectiveness of anything else. Make projections, course-adjust along the way, establish baselines, and measure results against them. Of course, you'll need to make some assumptions about how to allocate certain costs and revenues. But guess what? That's exactly what your finance and accounting people do every day to measure the performance of every other aspect of your business.

Property utilization isn't any different. Some of the metrics will vary, of course, depending on how you're defining success, but the mechanics are basically the same: Does *success* mean increasing sales, loyalty, awareness, or purchase intent? If so, compare pre- and postutilization sales figures, or compare results in one region where you're leveraging a property with another region where you aren't.

And don't even think about renewing a property rights agreement without first having measured the effectiveness of the previous one. Did you spend too much? Divide all your property utilization expenses by the incremental change in your sales and compare that number with your usual cost-of-sales figures. Despite how straightforward this is, most of the small number of companies that do measure concurrent and postsponsorship results do it in ridiculous ways. The two biggies are:

1. **Rating success by attendance figures:** This is complete lunacy. As we've talked about here and in Chapter 2, awareness is meaningless unless it translates into sales. If your company manufactures tofu products, sponsoring NASCAR won't make any of their millions of steak-and-potato spectators any more likely to buy your vegetarian hamburgers.

2. **Measuring cost-effectiveness as a factor of advertising media impressions:** The rationale—as voiced by the property seller—goes like this: "You paid $500,000 for the sponsorship and over the course of the season your logo and banners got 17 hours, 27 minutes, and 28 seconds of exposure. If you were to have bought all that media, you would have paid more than $2 million." All I can say is "What a load of crap." Flashing your logo on a television screen or having a sign up on the 50-yard line is fairly useless unless you're telling the viewer why it should make a difference. So chances are that spending $2 million on 17 hours, 27 minutes, and 28 seconds of well-designed, targeted, masterfully placed media buys

will help your bottom line a lot more than $500,000 worth of logo flashing and poster viewing. Plus, with a sponsorship, you're probably locked in for a while, which means that an unsuccessful match will cost you a lot more than a one-shot media blitz.

Pay No Attention to That Man Behind the Curtain: Exposing Myths About Sponsorship

The sponsorship world is filled with myths, half-truths, and faulty assumptions that supposedly dictate how properties should be acquired. Over the years I've learned to ignore them, which has probably saved my employers and my clients millions of dollars. I can't promise you that kind of savings, but I can promise that not falling prey to the following myths will help you enormously.

Myth 1: Sponsor awareness is an important measure of effectiveness.

Reality: Sponsor awareness is virtually meaningless to consumers.

As we've discussed throughout this book, eyeballs don't equate to sales, and using a property simply to make people more aware of your company is a waste of time and money.

Take Monster.com. When they first started out, they sponsored everything in sight and their name was everywhere. And what about Beyond.com? Their naked guy commercials were among the most memorable and popular of the late 1990s. Too bad no one was buying anything. Consumers really don't care that company X sponsors event Y. They've become savvy about sponsorship and recognize that it's a transaction that doesn't involve them.

The exception to this rule, of course, is if no one has heard of your company at all. Naturally, building awareness is important. If consumers don't know you're out there, they can't even consider you as an option. But once you've achieved wider awareness, then what? There's a difference between noise and meaning. If you don't give people a clear reason to buy, they won't.

That last thought—that you've got to give people a reason to buy—is really what it's all about. Research consistently shows that consumers will support sponsors who support things that are important to the consumers.

That's why companies sponsor individual NASCAR racing teams instead of sponsoring the races themselves. Their perception is that sponsors' financial support makes it possible for the drivers to have the cars and pit crews they need to win.

Coke had sponsored the Olympics for decades. We put the Olympic rings on our packages, aired slick commercials of athletes doing their stuff, and ended them with a tag line saying that Coke was an official sponsor of the Games. Sometime before the 1996 Games in Atlanta, we spent a lot of time talking to people and asking them what it meant to them that Coke had been a sponsor of the Games for decades. Their response? It meant that Coke had a lot of money. Not exactly the takeaway we were hoping for.

Myth 2: Consumers notice and derive meaning from stadium naming rights and sponsor event signage.

> *Reality: Stadium names and signage are essentially wallpaper to consumers. They barely notice them at all.*

Just think of all the hotel rooms you've stayed in and all the conference halls you've sat in. How often did you notice the wallpaper? You know it was there, but did you actually pay any attention to it? The very same thing goes for stadium names and signage. It's a very weak and restricted media vehicle. It's a blank space in the vicinity of a crowd that's interested in looking at something else. You know there are signs everywhere, but aren't you watching the game?

The size and format of the space generally restrict the creative message to little more than a brand logo. (In some cases, this can be an advantage: The Gap, for example, capitalizes on this by putting huge billboards in the gaps in left-center and right-center fields. Having the gap brought to you by The Gap makes sense.) But would you buy outdoor billboards along a highway, then put nothing on them but your logo? Of course not. Consumers would ignore them. So why should we be surprised when they ignore stadium billboards filled with logos that are already household names.

Why would United Airlines, FedEx, Heinz, Pepsi, and others pay to have their names on a stadium? They're already big names, everyone knows who they are, and the customers make no connection between the names over the main entrance and the game.

And can someone explain to me the connection between Pacific Bell and a baseball stadium? Everyone in the western United States who has a phone knows exactly who Pac Bell is. So why pay a ton of money to build a stadium? Are they trying to build goodwill so that when the local phone service is finally deregulated people will stick with them? Hard to say. But it would have been a lot more successful to tell the people of San Francisco that they built a new stadium because the city needed one and Pac Bell loves baseball.

Sometimes renaming a stadium can alienate consumers. Every sports fan in the country had heard of Candlestick Park, where the San Francisco 49ers play, but no one had heard of 3-Com when they bought the rights to rename the stadium. They got a huge amount of negative press, but at the end of the day a lot more people knew about 3-Com than before. Still, the connection between 3-Com and football is unclear, and I doubt that anyone has bought a Palm Pilot (before 3-Com spun them off) because of the name of the stadium.

Now don't get me wrong: We're not saying that buying stadium ads or renaming a stadium are always bad ideas. But we've yet to see any that make much business sense. If companies put the tens of millions of dollars they're spending on stadium naming rights toward strategically sound advertising and sales efforts, they'd accomplish a lot more in the way of quantifiable business results.

Myth 3: It's important to prevent your competitors from ambushing your sponsorship programs by restricting their access to similar or related properties.

Reality: Ambush marketing is even less relevant to consumers than sponsor awareness.

Basically, *ambush marketing* occurs when a company that isn't a sponsor of a particular event gives the impression that it is in order to capitalize on the goodwill earned by the actual sponsor. Nike does this a lot. They won't sponsor an event or even the broadcast of that event, but they'll take out billboards and paint murals near the stadium. If Visa were to sponsor the Super Bowl, American Express might try to ride Visa's wave by running sweepstakes and giving away prizes at the game. In all cases, the goal of the ambush marketer is to confuse consumers about who exactly is the sponsor.

But remember Myth 1? The point is that consumers don't care who sponsors what. So if being a sponsor is irrelevant, it follows that impersonating a sponsor would be even more irrelevant. Consumers are impacted by advertising messages and images that convey a benefit to them in a meaningful way. Forget about the sponsorship. If a particular property has some associative equities that your brand can benefit from, then those equities should form the foundation of your message to consumers.

So let your competitors run around implying that they're sponsors of anything they like. They'll do themselves more harm than good by looking and acting like a "sponsor."

Still, if you've paid a bunch of money to utilize a property, you're going to want to maximize your value and get the biggest return you can. So naturally you'll want to keep people from piggybacking on your property and potentially stealing value from you. Coke once had a situation at the Olympics where even though we were the official sponsor, Pepsi set up booths in the street, gave away product, and proclaimed that they "salute America's athletes."

Frankly, Pepsi has no credibility whatsoever in trying to associate themselves with the Olympics. Their brand positioning is completely incompatible with what the Olympics stand for to consumers. Their ambush attempts were certainly an annoyance, but I don't think they had any significant impact on consumers.

Nevertheless, it's up to the property seller to make sure this kind of thing doesn't happen and to shut it down quickly if it does, if for no other reason than to protect their own ability to continue offering exclusivity to their official sponsors. If they've sold you category exclusivity and they fail to adequately prevent or shut down ambushes from your competitors, it's time to have a little chat with them about getting some of your rights fee back.

Myth 4: Sponsors must give consumers an interactive experience to create a lasting impact.

Reality: Interactive experience events and attractions tend to benefit the property, not the sponsor.

You may have noticed that nearly every major sporting championship now has its own interactive theme-park-style attraction to go along with it.

The Super Bowl has the NFL Experience theme park, Major League Baseball puts on its Fan Fest event during each All-Star Weekend, and so on. The property owners hit the road trying to round up sponsors to fund these high-cost undertakings. "Giving people a chance to hold a football or shoot a basketball or smack a puck with a hockey stick is valuable," they say. And they're right. Property sellers are perfectly delighted to emphasize that connection even more by making sure they tell everyone, "Look at all the fun we're giving you." This happens a lot at theme parks as well, where sponsors line up to put their names on every roller coaster and movie-based attraction. But the truth is that consumers associate all those fun experiences with property, not the sponsoring brands. The time they spend at the NFL's football theme park, for example, simply reinforces fans' connection to the NFL and does nothing for the sponsor.

Myth 5: Property sellers must be handled gently to ensure their favorable treatment of your interests.

Reality: Fawning "sponsors" are the least respected and receive the poorest service from property sellers.

In any other business, sellers generally try to keep buyers happy. If they don't, the buyers take their business elsewhere. But in sponsorships, everything seems to work backward. Too many buyers lose track of who's paying whom, and they end up in a situation where even though they're the ones shelling out millions of dollars, they still treat sellers like royalty, tiptoeing around, trying to keep them happy. Something is very wrong with this picture, but no seller in his or her right mind would ever complain about it.

Having sellers in the driver's seat increases the leverage they have over the buyer and creates a one-sided business relationship that undermines the buyer's interest after the deal is finalized. The solution is Imperative 4.

IMPERATIVE 4: REMEMBER THAT PROPERTY SELLERS ARE SUPPLIERS, NOT CUSTOMERS

Property sellers should be falling all over *you* trying to keep *you* happy. Frankly, I've never been able to understand why more people don't get this. It's not like you're going to get a better deal if the supplier likes you.

In fact, falling all over yourself trying to please them just sends the message that you're an easy mark.

You need to restore the buyer–seller relationship to its proper balance by putting a heavy emphasis on the kind of cost reduction, competitive bidding, customer service, and value improvement that you would use with any other supplier. Establishing the ground rules up front for the kind of relationship you want to have with property sellers will help ensure that you get all the support and services you bargained for later on.

The Heart of the Beast: Why Property Sellers Are Not Your Friends

Over the past 30 years, I've met and done business with enough property sellers to know exactly what to expect from them along the way. One of the most important things I can tell you about dealing with sponsors is to be damned careful: Nowhere does the phrase *caveat emptor*, buyer beware, apply more accurately.

Property sellers love to smile sincerely and say, "Our property is a great fit with your brand positioning." But what they're really thinking is "I smell deep pockets." Or, as Chris Malone found while selling sponsorships for the NBA and the NHL, "Traditionally, the goal of sponsorship selling has been to find the biggest fool in the market."

Another thing to prepare yourself for when dealing with property sellers is frustration. In any other business, sellers generally try to accommodate their customers and provide them with some kind of service. But not these sellers. These guys feel that they have a license to jerk their customers around any way they want.

Here's a typical example: When you agree to pay a fee for a property, what you're getting is the right to associate your brand with the property's trademarks and likenesses. However—and this is a big however—in order to protect their trademarks and likenesses, the seller generally retains the right to approve anything and everything you do relative to the property: advertising, promotions, banners, print ads, whatever. If they don't like something, no matter how inconsequential, they'll make you change it.

Now I certainly appreciate the need to review and approve the use of a trademark or image before it goes into production—we do it all the time for our clients. But having to wait weeks at a time for every last package design and line of copy to be approved can grind the entire program to a halt.

A number of times, sellers took so long to get back to me that I had to move forward without waiting for their answer. It was either that or miss a critical media placement date and blow the whole campaign. The sellers' response? Screams of bloody murder that I'd violated the terms of the agreement by sending out something that wasn't approved. They just didn't seem to grasp the idea that we were trying to manage a business and that the trains had to run on time. Speed and efficiency meant nothing to them, and neither did deadlines, production schedules, rewrite turn-around, or anything else.

I'm completely convinced that the only reason sellers drag things out is because they can. So if this happens to you, push back. Be assertive. If you submit something for the sellers' approval, give them 48 hours to review it and get back to you or you'll consider it approved. You absolutely must regain control and make sure everyone involved knows who's the customer and who's the supplier.

Thinking buyers are stupid and trying to jerk them around are only two examples of beliefs and practices that are rampant among property sellers. Here are a few more:

• **All business relationships must be governed by a lengthy and onerous legal contract.** These one-sided contracts get the business relationship started on the wrong foot and set a tone of inflexibility. But think of it from the property seller's point of view: If you could get someone to pay a flat fee up front without having to guarantee any kind of return or performance, you'd want the longest, hardest-to-get-out-of contract you could come up with. After all, you don't want to have to find a new fool after a year. David Stern, commissioner of the NBA, and I created a much different kind of relationship when we put together a 100-year deal between Coca-Cola and the NBA on nothing more than a handshake. I kid you not. To this day, there is still no formal contract and no annual rights fee payments.

• **The role of broadcasters, sponsors, licensees, and municipalities is to finance, market, and grow my property.** We've talked about this a lot throughout this chapter. As a rule, property sellers do not have your best interests at heart. Fortunately, buyers are getting a little savvier these days and they're less likely to get hoodwinked by sellers into pouring money into a completely inappropriate property because they didn't do enough research before signing that huge contract.

- **The success or failure of my sponsors is not my responsibility.** Too many property sellers believe that once the sponsorship agreement is signed, their job is done and the rest is up to the sponsor. They take no risk or accountability for the success of their business partners. This almost gives them an incentive to deliver lousy service and support. You, the buyer, need to make them accountable for your success, and the first step is to follow Imperative 5.

IMPERATIVE 5: TIE PROPERTY SELLER COMPENSATION TO YOUR BUSINESS RESULTS

If you're going to have any chance of putting together a successful property utilization program, you absolutely must require property sellers to share the risks as well as the rewards of the business relationship. One way is to structure your property utilization deals so that the fee you pay is determined by how much incremental business the property generates, or on whatever other success criteria you decide. That'll certainly get their attention and give them a vested interest in your success.

That kind of deal has great upside potential for both buyers and sellers. Buyers may end up paying a little more in the long run, but they won't be in it on their own: The seller will be helping to maximize the buyer's return, which will probably more than offset the increase in fees. Sellers, on the other hand, can bring in more money. The kicker here, though, is that for this system to work, the seller has to be held at least partially accountable for the success or failure of the event.

Although this kind of thing is still rare, it is happening. One bank that sponsored a NASCAR event was able to negotiate a deal in which they paid NASCAR a set amount for every new account that the bank opened.

A lot of sellers will refuse if you ask them to take a financial stake in an event. But as buyers get more aggressive, sellers won't have much of a choice. Eventually, they'll have to agree to these deals to get the business. The ones that don't take responsibility and don't actively help buyers achieve their goals won't be able to find buyers anymore. And without sponsorship fees coming in, the property itself may be seriously hurt. To paraphrase Darwin, it's adapt or die.

The Olympics may be one of the first major casualties. Two longtime sponsors, IBM and UPS, recently announced that they're no longer sponsoring the Games.

We Have Met the Enemy and It Was Us

Despite everything I've said about property sellers, the truth is that they aren't the only ones responsible for the miserable state of affairs in the sponsorship industry. Buyers have really aggravated the situation by rarely missing an opportunity to shoot themselves in the foot. They've bought into the idea that sponsorship is some kind of secret in which the traditional standards, procedures, and rules of return on investment don't apply. They've blindly followed conventional sponsorship wisdom, and they've set themselves up as easy marks by relying too heavily on property sellers to tell them how to run their businesses. Not surprisingly, the playing field is steeply tilted in favor of property sellers.

One of the most dangerous traps that buyers fall into is being lured into supporting events and activities that are far removed from their core business. This brings up Imperative 6.

IMPERATIVE 6: STICK TO YOUR KNITTING

Property utilization must share the same strategic and financial strategies that guide the rest of your business. Accordingly, every activity in your property utilization programs must stick close to the core business you are in. Often, sellers' enthusiasm for a particular property leads buyers to invest in vastly unrelated activities.

Coke learned this lesson the hard way. In 1996, we spent $32 million to build the Coca-Cola Olympic City, a 13-acre interactive theme park in downtown Atlanta, for the 1996 Olympic Games. The theme of the park was "Be an Olympic Athlete." Visitors had a chance to run 100-meter races, try a high jump, and more. Over the course of the four months leading up to and during the Games, 500,000 people paid $7.50 to get in and even more once they were inside.

We did exit interviews asking people about their experience at the park and overall they loved it. But when we asked whether they were any more likely to drink more Coke, the answer was no. Sure they had fun, but in their minds we were just the sponsor of an Olympic theme park.

All told, we brought in $13 million in revenues, leaving us with a $19 million net cost. If they lived to be 120, those 500,000 park visitors could never drink enough Coke for the company to recoup that $19 million.

The problem was that we strayed from our core business. We got into the theme-park business for four months and ultimately lost sight of the need for every advertising activity—including sponsorships—to directly drive our brand objectives and results. Neither Coke nor I will ever do that again.

TRADITIONAL SPONSORSHIP IS IRRELEVANT, SO DON'T BE CAUGHT DEAD USING IT

Despite *sponsorship's* questionable track record, I am convinced that *property utilization* can be a powerful driver of business results. When it comes to talking about themselves, people aren't always the most reliable sources of unbiased, objective information. As a result, we tend to pay more attention to what they do than what they say. The same goes for brands and companies. Property utilization provides wonderful opportunities for a brand's actions to speak louder (and more credibly) than anything it can say about itself in advertising. Let me give you an example.

WORLDWIDE SPRITE CASE VOLUME GROWTH

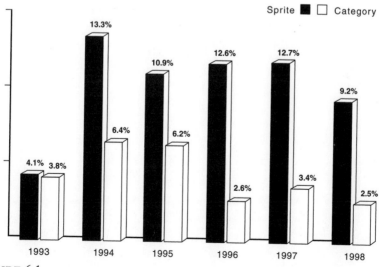

FIGURE 6.1

Since 1994, Sprite has utilized the NBA property as the centerpiece of its fully integrated marketing strategy. They've woven the property into advertising, consumer promotions, packaging, publicity, and special events. The results have been startling: Since the deal began, Sprite sales have grown at a pace that has far exceeded that of the soft drink category as a whole for five straight years.

So how much is Sprite paying for this gold mine? Nothing. The deal is based entirely on collaborative marketing efforts. In exchange for not paying rights fees, Sprite is helping the NBA get additional awareness. It has ads with NBA players and sponsors broadcasts of NBA games. What Sprite gets in return (besides a huge financial savings) is a chance to borrow associative equity from the NBA, a chance to use the NBA image to tell consumers something about the Sprite brand. Our repositioning strategy has shifted Sprite from being seen as the best lemon-lime soft drink on the market to the preferred soft drink for young, independent-thinking, urban teens who want to make choices for themselves, just as NBA players do. Our strategy hit the mark.

CHAPTER 7

Free Media—Your Best Friend or Your Worst Enemy

In today's business environment, where *everything* communicates, everything you do (or don't do) is a branding event. Despite the old adage that any publicity is good publicity, the truth is that getting your company's name in the newspaper or on the nightly news may not be all it's cracked up to be. Free media is rarely free; it might not cost you any cash, but if you don't manage it properly, the consequences can be incredibly expensive.

You don't have to take my word for it. Just ask all those dot-coms that used "free" media to get themselves on the map and raise money, then stood by helplessly as that same media uncovered the weaknesses of their business models. The sock puppet got tons of free media and tons of attention relating to the fact that Pets.com wasn't selling enough to pay for the ads. Or how about all the media that Microsoft got thanks to the Justice Department? Or the coverage Coke got with its contamination scare in Europe? All free, no cost, no good.

So how do you manage free media? Hopefully this won't come as a surprise: You start with a long-term plan with lots of contingency plans built in. But before I get too far into planning, I need to take a second to clear up three terms that you'll hear a lot about and that seem to confuse a lot of people: *advertising, publicity,* and *public relations.* All three communicate, but no matter what you think and no matter what anyone tells you, they are *not* interchangeable. Not everyone will agree with my definitions of these terms. I have two things to say about that: (1) My definitions are the correct ones, and (2) you didn't buy this book to hear me spit out what everyone else is saying, did you?

Okay, back to business. To some extent the difference between advertising, publicity, and public relations comes down to a question of control:

- **Advertising is something you have almost total control over.** With most of the other forms of advertising I've discussed—print and electronic ads, packaging, sponsorships, using celebrity spokespeople, and so on—you control both the content and the context, or at least you should. *You* decide what shows up with your name on it and how it's used, *you* approve the ads, *you* design the packaging, *you* slap your name on the stadium, and *you* hire the spokesperson. In short, advertising is purely offensive (as opposed to defensive).

- **Publicity is about managing—or at least trying to manage—your company's image, with the ultimate goal being to build goodwill.** As with advertising, it's all offense in the sense that publicity efforts are initiated by you. But you don't have quite as much control. Madonna's record label can send her out on the road to promote her latest CD. They can get her on *Entertainment Tonight* and every other appropriate show, but they can't control the context. I saw her on *Late Night* a few years ago and she made a complete fool of herself trying to match wits with David Letterman—always a dangerous thing to do. That couldn't have helped sales. You can give out samples of your new shrimp dip at Costco, but what if someone gets salmonella?

Publicity activities might include making a speech to the Rotary Club, writing letters to the editor, sponsoring your local little league team, donating an original van Gogh to the Girl Scouts, or, if you're a dentist, publishing one of those newsletters that tells your patients how to reduce cavities.

- **Public relations can be either offensive or defensive.** On the offensive side, it's similar to publicity in that you initiate the contact: You can send out press releases to publicize some special event, to suggest that the media write about your new CEO, or to publicize your latest quarterly earnings report. Public relations can also be initiated from the outside, say the *Wall Street Journal* does a profile of your company or interviews you for an article, or *PC Week* does a review of your latest chip. In these cases, though, how the story gets covered, how the reporter spins your quote, and whether the review is favorable are completely out of your control. That's where PR's defensive side comes in. Basically, whenever you're put in a position of having to *respond,* it's PR. In fact, one of PR's most important functions is crisis management, which I'll talk about in a minute.

The line between publicity and PR can sometimes get a little blurry, and what starts off as publicity can unexpectedly change to PR. When we introduced New Coke, we had a huge publicity campaign, including special events, promotional tie-ins, even a news conference at Rockefeller Center with the Rockettes on stage with us. But a few days later, when it became obvious that New Coke was a flop, we were suddenly on the defensive, trying to figure out the best way to respond to a highly negative public relations situation. And remember what happened to Pee Wee Herman? One day he's publicizing a new children's television show; the next day he's caught masturbating in the back of a Florida porn theater—a real public relations disaster.

One of the biggest distinctions of all between advertising, publicity, and public relations is the way consumers react to them. People are generally pretty cynical and they often attribute the worst to everyone. They know that companies pay for advertising and they know that companies sponsor events for no other reason than to get their name in the paper. That, of course, makes people a little suspicious of both. But when a piece of information is put out there by a supposedly neutral third party, people are a lot more likely to believe it: What the media says about you often has a much more significant impact on your business than almost anything else.

That's exactly why it's so important to keep control of the dialog, to be on the offensive instead of the defensive, to manage the media so that it doesn't manage you. And the way you're going to do all that is by having a media plan.

THE MEDIA PLAN

In its simplest form, your media plan should contain the answers to the same questions as your overall advertising plan: What do you want to say and to whom? What do you want people to believe about you? Your annual reports, for example, are produced for investors or prospective investors, while your company newsletter is aimed at your own employees. (I'm including annual reports and newsletters here because they're both important ways of communicating important messages about your company and of managing its image. I'll talk more about communicating with employees in the next chapter.) Meanwhile, sponsoring the Olympics and buying bus shelter ads are advertising activities that are hopefully aimed at anyone who does or who might buy your product or service. If that's not your goal, you haven't been paying attention to anything I've said so far, so go back to Chapter 1 and start this book again.

Keep in mind that the media is an unintended audience to whatever you do. So always make sure that they have the exact information you want them to have. Know what you want them to say, how you're going to communicate it to them, and how you're going to manage the communication to minimize the risk. Otherwise, the media is in control of the dialog and you are at their mercy. Here is what's involved in putting together an effective media plan:

1. **Remember that everything communicates.** This is the most critical step. Never forget it and never let anyone in your organization—from the guy who sweeps the floors all the way up to the chairperson of the board—forget it, either. If everyone keeps this idea in the back of their minds, you're less likely to have anything happen that will reflect poorly on the company.

2. **Put one person in charge of all media-related activities.** If you don't control exactly what you want communicated, your inaction or mistakes will do it for you. So appoint one person to come up with the strategy, issue press releases, outline the relationship your company will have with the media, and ensure that the company gives the media a consistent message about your brand.

You'll also need a media spokesperson—could be the same person, could be someone else. The qualifications are a little different, though. Your media spokesperson absolutely must be someone who is articulate, makes a good first impression, looks good on camera, and thinks fast on his or her feet. This person also has to be very conversant with any issues that could possibly affect your company, good with sound bites (sometimes you have to make your entire case in only 10 seconds), and able to gently take control of interviews and redirect reporters back to the points *you* want to make. I'm not talking about lying, just turning the conversation so that your position is the one that dominates, not the media's.

Everyone else in the company must be trained to refer the media to your spokesperson. In a crisis, reporters will talk to anyone they can reach—secretaries, lathe operators, even temp workers—and all of a sudden these people become the face and the voice of your company. Do you really want to trust your brand's image and future to someone who's been working for you for two weeks?

3. **Target your messages.** John Wiley, the company that published this book, also publishes books on psychology, architecture, cooking, biology, geography, and a bunch of other subjects. And they have a pretty big department that's staffed by wonderful people whose entire job it is to generate publicity for their various titles. They've got huge databases of newspaper and magazine editors, TV and radio producers, product reviewers, feature writers, professors, speakers' bureaus, and every other publicity-related resource you could come up with.

The possibilities are endless—but they shouldn't be. Although the mechanics of how Wiley publicized this book aren't all that different from the way they'd publicize a cookbook, what *is* different is the people and media outlets they approach. This may seem obvious, but it's horrifying how many companies send out hundreds of press releases and make thousands of follow-up phone calls to completely inappropriate places, trying to get their name or their brand or their product or their service mentioned anywhere anytime. What a massive waste of time and money.

Avoiding this kind of dumb mistake is incredibly simple. All it takes is targeting your publicity efforts—having a firm grip on what you want to say and to whom. Since this is a business book, getting me quoted in *Gourmet* magazine would be fairly worthless and so would a three-page profile in *People* or *Home and Garden* (even though it would make my wife happy, but that's a whole different thing). At the same time, not all business books should be publicized the same way. Since the audience for this book is middle and upper management and entrepreneurs, it makes sense to target media outlets that reach those groups. An interview on CNBC or CNN, an excerpt in *Adweek*, a profile in *Forbes*, and doing keynote speeches at all the advertising clubs in the country is just what we're looking for. A review in *At-Home Business* magazine or having me talk to 60 advertising majors at Harvard won't be particularly helpful.

Targeting the media is especially important if you've got a publicity or public relations firm working for you. These firms usually set their fee schedule so that you pay them for every single piece of publicity they score, using some kind of elaborate matrix that reflects how much time or space was devoted to you and the size of the audience. To them, a paragraph in

Bassmaster or *American Rifleman*, which have huge circulations, could be worth more than a page in *Ad Age*, which reaches far fewer people.

4. **Generate publicity.** Take advantage of every natural opportunity to get publicity for your brand. If there's something you want people to know about but you don't have a natural opportunity, make one up. The trick, of course, is to spin it to make it interesting. In the mid- and late 1990s, the dot-coms did this brilliantly. The whole culture of the Internet was new and the media loved to report new twists or anything that seemed like a new twist. Companies took advantage of the nearly unlimited opportunities for publicity, sending out press releases to publicize everything, whether it was truly important or not.

When some company installed a bright red slide that employees could use to go between floors, the media called it an example of building an employee-friendly workplace. Leasing entire floors of abandoned warehouses was billed as a sign of a company's explosive growth. Extravagant parties, BMWs, and stock options were proof of success. And announcing that Jack Welch or some other well-known business personality had joined the board of directors showed stability and good management.

The combination of a news-hungry media and an attention-starved sector spawned an entirely new business category: high-tech PR—firms that did nothing but come up with press releases to publicize their clients' every sneeze to try to keep them in front of the cameras. That whole approach was remarkably successful and it enabled dozens of companies that didn't have a lot of money to spend on advertising to still get a huge amount of free publicity for their brand. (The goal of all the publicity was to generate buzz that would pique the public's interest and get them to drive up the stock price. It never seemed to occur to anyone to use all that media coverage to generate sales.) Unfortunately, companies that live by free media can also die by free media. When the novelty of companies that hadn't made a penny of profits but were worth more than GM finally wore off, the same media that had essentially created many of the dot-coms was delighted to destroy them.

Fortunately, you don't have to be a dot-com to generate publicity and buzz. When Ford announces that dealers are already sold out of the new retro T-Bird, they're really trying to let the public know that the car is a success. And when Richard Branson sends out a press release claiming that he's going to drive a tank through Manhattan to introduce Virgin Cola, he's showing us that he's a guy who doesn't play by the same rules as Coke and Pepsi and that he's going to fight them head on.

I don't mean to give you the impression that you have to be a big company or have a lot of money to blow on stunts in order to get publicity. Sure, it's easier for big companies. Every time Bill Gates scratches his nose, the media is all over it. But the truly essential ingredient to successfully generating publicity is to do something unique that emphasizes your brand's core attributes. If you own a small pizza place, you could announce that you're going to try to set the world's record for the biggest pizza in the world. Invite the high school football team to roll out the dough and have the kids in a nearby kindergarten smear sauce on it. You'll get plenty of coverage.

Recently, a nonprofit group called Community Creative for Non-Violence was trying to focus the country's attention on the amount of food Americans waste. They put out a press release announcing that they were going to prepare a lunch in Washington, D.C., made out of food that they'd collected from dumpsters. Yuck. Hunger and wasted food might not be a particularly glamorous media topic, but it's a good political one, and the group actually managed to get a few Congressmen to climb into dumpsters and pull out food. Since members of Congress rarely do anything out of sight of a camera or reporter, the dumpster lunch got plenty of ink.

Remember, though, that when it comes to publicity, *where* is far more important than *how much*. Giving a radio station a bunch of CDs to give away won't get you on the nightly news, but it sure will get your product and your message into the hands of the right people. I once did some consulting for an entrepreneur who had come up with a revolutionary way of helping independent veterinarians get services, do better work, and become more profitable. He planned to do all this by getting people to his website, vets.com. There were two major vet conventions that were attended by exactly the right people, but my client didn't have enough money to sponsor booths or even to take out ads in the event programs. So I suggested that he rent vans to take the vets from their hotels to the convention center. On each van we had signs saying, "Taking you to the future." We didn't get a single word in any news outlet, but we got a huge amount of really great publicity among the veterinarians.

Be sure you spend a lot of time planning out your media event before you launch it because these things have a nasty way of backfiring. Remember Michael Dukakis's disastrous tank ride? And in the fall of 2001, a park ranger shot a shark that had just bitten the arm off a little boy. For some reason, PETA (People for the Ethical Treatment of Animals) thought they could capitalize on the coverage about the boy to get out their "people mistreat animals" message. So they put up a billboard that said, "Would you give your right arm to know why sharks attack? Could it be revenge?" Hmmm. And Donald Trump, who doesn't much like competition, financed what seemed like a grass-roots group, which placed ads warning that the Mohawk Indians—who happened to be trying to build a casino that would have competed with Trump's—would bring crime and drugs to the community. The ads pictured lines of cocaine and drug needles and asked, "Are these the new neighbors we want?"

Think about how many companies tried to hitch a ride on the goodwill that flooded the country after September 11 by donating food to help the workers and families of the victims. The ones with a decent plan did it right. The ones without a plan got slammed in the media or ignored. One of those who got slammed was David Bouley, a well-known New York chef whose restaurants had to close when the World Trade Center collapsed. Bouley was paid nearly $6 million to produce more than a million and a half meals over 50 days right after the tragedy. The problem was that some of the food he used was donated by the Red Cross and a lot of the work was done by volunteers, including some of his employees who'd lost their jobs when the restaurant shut down. There may not be anything wrong with what Bouley did, but the issue was that he didn't tell the whole truth from the beginning. And sooner or later, the whole truth always comes out. So Bouley ended up getting a pile of bad press in the *New York Times* and other places, and he's probably had to hire a PR firm to do damage control.

Sometimes it's possible to turn a PR blunder into a success. Dallas Mavericks owner, Mark Cuban, criticized the NBA's head of officiating, saying, "I wouldn't hire him to manage a Dairy Queen." The first thing that happened was that the NBA fined Cuban $500,000 for shooting his mouth off. Then he became a bit of a laughingstock when Dairy Queen issued a press release saying that managing a DQ isn't all that easy and inviting him to try it for a day. Cuban very cleverly turned things around by actually taking up DQ on their offer. As a side note, ESPN.com estimated that Cuban's remarks and the flurry of publicity that followed were worth over $1 million in advertising to Dairy Queen.

5. **Have a crisis plan in place.** Unexpected and even horrible things can happen to any company, and assuming you don't bring them on yourself, you can't always stop them. But you can control how you react to them. If you don't, a single poorly managed public relations crisis can

destroy your brand or even your company overnight. Here's what you need to do when things go wrong:

- **Have your response come from the top.** When things really go bad— say your product causes a death or a serious illness—people want to hear from the head of the company, not some fresh-faced press secretary.
- **Tell the truth, tell it all, and tell it fast.** In other words, take control of the dialog. When some nut put poison into bottles of Tylenol and killed a few people, the CEO responded immediately, admitted the problem, and laid out the company's plan for dealing with it: new tamperproof containers. Tylenol turned what could have been a company-destroying crisis into a public relations victory. Unfortunately, not everyone does quite as good a job. In 1999, 200 people in Belgium and France, including a bunch of school kids, got sick after drinking Coca-Cola. Doug Ivester, the CEO, waited 10 days, if you can imagine that, before flying to Brussels to apologize. He was forced out of the company very soon afterward.

  There's an old saying that "it doesn't matter what you say as long as you say it first." Although that's not exactly true—you always want to tell the truth—there's a point here: Respond fast. When it comes to corporate crises, no news is definitely bad news. It just makes you look guiltier. People remember the front-page story, not the follow-ups on page 29C. Take Martha Stewart, who tried to ignore her recent insider-trading scandal. She and her company are being pounded by public opinion. Her stock price is the proof.
- **Do something to make things better.** Apologize, offer compensation, act contrite, and above all show empathy. A few years ago, an 81-year-old woman walked in front of a truck and got killed. The trucker's insurance company, in its infinite wisdom, sued the poor woman's estate for negligence. When the media found out about the story, they had an absolute field day skewering the insurance company.
- **Have a theme and stick to the script.** You or your spokesperson should always know exactly what points you want to get across. It's your job to keep the interview focused on those points as much as you can. As Bill Cosby told me once, "Always rehearse your improvisations." In crisis situations the media may try to put words in your mouth and you'll have to bring the discussion back to where you want it to be. At our famous New Coke press conference, some reporter asked Roberto

Goizuetta what would happen if the product didn't work. And Roberto, who really should have been prepared for that question, said, "You don't understand. It *will* work." Naturally, the media made it their life's work to prove him wrong.

- **Know when to shut up.** Do not make up answers on the fly. If you don't know something, say so and tell whoever asked you the question exactly when you'll have the answer. Very few people can think fast enough on their feet to come up with an intelligent answer to a completely unexpected question, and it's easy to get stumped and end up looking like an idiot. And while I almost never recommend answering "no comment," there are times to hide. During the O.J. Simpson trial, for example, the PR people for Bruno Magli (shoes) and Isotoner (gloves) were very, very quiet, just as they should have been.

- **Keep your PR people in the loop.** I've seen cases where a company got into some trouble, and instead of getting their PR people on the case, they sent out their lawyers. At the end of the day, the strategy has to come from the businesspeople, but the PR folks have to execute that strategy, which means they need to know what's going on. It's not that lawyers shouldn't be involved—they should when it's appropriate. But being on solid legal ground won't help you when you're being sucked down into the swamp of bad press. At the same time, don't let your PR people run wild all by themselves. They're sometimes like ad agency people: They'll try to convince you that what they do is art and that you should keep your nose out and let the artists handle things. Granted, there may be some art involved in managing publicity and public relations, but PR is far too important to be left to only PR folks.

- **Keep your checkbook ready.** No matter how perfectly you've handled the situation, there may be times when you still won't be able to overcome a PR problem in the free media. In these cases you may have to resort to some paid ads to counter your bad press. During the junk-bond scare of the early 1990s, Drexell Burnham Lambert, which had written a lot of those bonds, was getting hammered in the media. If all the information you'd had was the media coverage (which was the case for most people), you'd have thought that the company was run by a bunch of shysters selling worthless bonds to unsuspecting old ladies. The truth was that junk-bond redemption was over 80 percent, but once the media smelled a scandal, they couldn't be bothered with a little thing like the truth. So Drexell struck back by buying full-page ads in the *New York Times* explaining what junk bonds really were: high-risk, high-reward bonds that served an important function in the financial world. These ads were directed more at educating the media than the consumers, and they were remarkably successful, changing the dialog overnight. Of course, Drexel fell apart a little later on, but for completely different reasons.

6. **Forget about viral marketing.** One of the most important things the Internet has done is take down huge communications barriers. In a lot of ways, it's become a free system that allows people everywhere to communicate about almost everything in real time. That means that news—good or bad—travels fast and snowballs even faster. Somewhere along the line, some people got the wacky idea that they could control this information flow and use it to their own advantage. They were wrong. Viral marketing happens by itself and there's very little you can do to stop it once it gets going. All your advertising efforts may give you a little impact, but the fact is that nothing you do can guarantee that people will stand around the water cooler talking about your ads or that they'll tell everyone where they got that great pair of shoes or which search engine they used to find that killer piece of research. On the other hand, to the extent that it exists, viral marketing is much more effective at spreading bad news than good. Do something wonderful and people may or may not tell their friends. Screw up and they'll tell everyone they know as fast as they can.

7. **Measure your results.** As I have mentioned, free media isn't truly free. Although media coverage itself won't cost you anything out of pocket, managing your publicity and public relations effectively will. At the very least, you'll have to hire people, either in house or at an agency, to stay on top of things. Even if it's not a full-time job, you can still put a dollar figure on the opportunity cost. And, as with anything you spend a nickel on, you absolutely must generate a return or you're wasting your money.

That may seem almost impossible, but it really isn't. If you're a non-profit and you're able to get some public service announcements for your event aired on TV or radio, the station will always give you a precise figure of what your PSA is worth. And a lot of PR agencies are starting to come up with estimated values for each media placement they make.

But watch out. Booking your CEO on a completely inappropriate television show may not be worth anything, even if it reaches 4 million viewers. People who sell sponsorships will always try to convince you that you should pay to have your company's name on a billboard behind home plate because your logo will be on screen an average of 12.5 minutes over the course of a game, and buying 12.5 minutes of advertising at the 60-second spot rate during the same game would cost you a lot more. Ridiculous. In most cases, you'd probably be better off spending your money on targeted, well-thought-out advertising than on a series of meaningless flashes.

As I keep saying, awareness by itself does nothing. You want to know whether your ads, or, in this case, your publicity efforts, are making more people want to buy your product more often and for more money. PR agencies and talent agents are notorious for inflating the value of association. Getting quoted in an article on fitness tips for busy executives—even if it is in *Forbes*—won't sell a lot of books or bring in any new consulting clients. A picture of your state-of-the-art carving knife in Emeril Lagasse's kitchen is obviously a good thing, even if Emeril doesn't say anything about it. But an article that mentions Jack the Ripper had a fondness for carving knives isn't nearly as helpful.

I recently bumped into a guy I'd worked with when I was at Coke who was the agent for singer George Michael. He told me that George had agreed to be in a Coke commercial—provided he didn't have to touch the product, drink it, or even say anything about it (sounded like Julio Iglesias all over again to me).

Granted, some associations can be positive. Having Kobe Bryant doing slam dunks in a sports drink commercial, even if he doesn't come near the product, makes sense; the audience makes the connection themselves. But what does George Michael have to do with Coca-Cola? Nothing that I can think of. However, somehow this agent had managed to convince someone at Coke that simply having George there was enough. Anyway, the point here is that even getting quoted in the right place might be useless if the context is wrong.

Okay, so now that I've told you how *not* to measure the return on free media, let me tell you in three words how to do it right: *Measure your sales*. Did you sell more product or get more orders after that company profile came out? If you did a radio interview, compare before and after sales figures for that market with another market where the interview didn't air.

If you're not in the kind of business where sales happen instantly, you can measure purchase intent. With very few exceptions, the best way to do this is to hit the street and ask people. If you were quoted in an article in the *New York Times*, poll some *Times* readers and ask them whether they read the article. If so, were they now more likely to buy your product than they were before?

HIRING A PUBLICIST OR PR AGENCY

As easy as I've tried to make all this sound, the truth is that publicity and public relations shouldn't be left to amateurs, and that probably includes you. For most businesspeople, just running their company or department is enough. Having to also worry about managing your company's image is over the top. So if you're not 100 percent up to the job, hire someone who is.

The process for hiring publicists or PR agencies is basically the same as for hiring ad agencies. It starts with being clear on what you want the agency to do. Once you've got that down, check their references, take a look at their client list, read some of their press releases, and get a list of media placements they've done. In addition, pay special attention to these things:

- **No contacts, no hire.** It's that simple. No agency can guarantee you any specific results. If they claim they can, they're lying, so get away as fast as you can. Still, you need to have people in your corner who have access to reporters and producers in both the good times and the bad. That way, if you do need some press in a hurry, you'll have a better-than-average chance of getting it. You're hiring someone to manage one of the most important aspects of your business, so be damned sure they can do the job right. At the same time, keep your expectations reasonable. Even the most connected publicist can't get you on the *Today* show if you don't have anything worthwhile to say.
- **Hire an independent thinker.** Your publicists shouldn't just rely on you to tell them when to contact the media. Part of their job is to stay up on breaking news and to get your views out there on any topics that might affect your business, even tangentially. If you're running a chain of flower shops, your publicist should be pounding the pavement trying to get you

interviewed for any number of things: a strike by gravediggers, the death of a prominent figure, a new dye made from the leaves of a rare plant, unexpectedly high temperatures in Holland. The idea is to keep you in the public eye and to maximize positive associative imagery as much as possible.

• **Agree on compensation.** None of this pay-for-placement stuff. Instead, pay on results, however you define them. This will come as a shock to most PR agencies and publicists, but if you insist on it, you're guaranteeing yourself far better performance.

CHAPTER 8

Making Your Employees Part of Your Message and Your Product

I've talked about how important it is to identify your customers and to understand their wants and needs. Hopefully you've got a pretty good handle on that. But one thing I haven't discussed in depth is how contradictory consumers can be. For example, I said that in the aftermath of September 11, consumers are slowing down and considering their options a little more carefully before making purchasing decisions. They now place more value on stable, reputable, familiar, proven brands.

The most important thing to remember about the effects of September 11 is that it's not a passing thing. This event has changed the fundamentals of how we market and merchandise. But the number of companies that completely ignore this amazes me, and I'm predicting that those companies are going to get themselves into trouble really soon.

Consumers are getting more and more cynical—and less loyal—by the day. Advances in manufacturing and communications technology have nearly eliminated any substantive physical differences between competing products. As a result, consumers are frustrated: They want everything cheap, they want it yesterday, and, in a lot of ways, they really don't care who gives it to them.

Why is this happening? Lack of relevance and the absence of any other worthwhile benefits. And where those things are missing, price quickly becomes a substitute (whether that's a good or bad thing depends).

It's pretty hard to retain customers in an environment where they don't perceive any difference between your product and anyone else's. But hard or not, that's exactly what you have to do. The big question, though, is how. And the big answer goes all the way back to the basics: **You do it by differentiating yourself, by giving consumers something they can't get anywhere else. In this case, that means satisfying their** *emotional* **wants and needs, their desire to be feel unique, special, and valued.**

WELCOME TO THE WONDERFUL WORLD OF CUSTOMER SERVICE

Actually, this whole customer service thing isn't particularly new or innovative. It's always been natural to want to spend your money on people you know and who work hard to satisfy your needs. But the idea that *customer service is advertising* is new and innovative. It means that although you may still have a customer service department, the people who run it will have to work closely with your brand managers, marketing managers, and everyone else who's involved in defining and selling your brand. They'll all have to agree completely on the role customer service will play in executing your advertising strategy.

The butcher your grandmother went to 50 years ago always remembered her name and would save her a special cut if he knew she was coming in. He'd ask about her husband and the kids and give her a bone to take home to the dog. Sure, the butcher down the street had the same meat at the same price, but he didn't appeal to your grandmother's emotions or make her feel unique or important.

American companies in every line of business have been going on nonstop about customers for years: "Customers are our most important asset," "Customer service is critical," "Our customer service is better than anyone else's," blah, blah, blah. The truth is that most of this is just talk. Of course, there are a few companies that have finally realized the key to business success isn't increasing awareness or opening more stores; it's keeping their customers happy. But those are much more the exception than the rule. Don't believe me? Well, here's what Harvard Business School professor Rosabeth Moss Kanter said: "Despite the recent media coronation of King Customer, many customers will remain commoners. Most businesses today say that they serve customers. In reality, they serve themselves."

I've talked to all kinds of managers at many companies who think that all there is to customer service is keeping customers satisfied—in other words, the customers aren't complaining. That's true in part, but only in part. Of course, you want your customers to be satisfied, but in the same way that high levels of awareness don't necessarily lead to high sales, the fact that a customer is satisfied is no guarantee of anything. If you're hungry, you might go out to eat at a restaurant. Okay, now you're satisfied. But does that mean you'll be a regular customer at that restaurant? Hardly. This time it was pizza; next time it might be Thai food.

Customer satisfaction is really about defining expectations and delivering on them. British Airways, for example, defines their product as comfortable seats, whereas Southwest defines theirs as fun and inexpensive. Jet Blue defines theirs as low-cost but comfortable, offering brand-new airplanes, leather seats, and on-board DirecTV. All three deliver very well, but if someone else came along and was able to fulfill those same expectations, customers would have no problem taking a walk.

By contrast, United defines their product as "the friendly skies," but they don't ever say what "friendly skies" means, and they end up leaving it up to the consumers' imagination, which is something you *never* want to do. **Customers are dangerous, and if you let them decide how they want to be satisfied, *you're* going to have a terrible time living up to their dreams. It's better if you can control both the promise and the delivery.**

Or what about the difference between Burger King's "Have it your way" and all the other stuff they've done and said over the years. "Have it your way" was great. All they were really promising was "hold the pickle, hold the lettuce," which was pretty simple to deliver on, so why did they get rid of it? It was certainly a lot better then Herb the Nerd and all the other dumb shenanigans they've tried. But most likely the people running the business were more interested in advertising slogans and novelty and less interested in sales. Or am I missing something here?

Satisfied customers can—and do—defect all the time, especially from brands where the "cost" of switching is minimal (food, beer, tobacco, shoes, soft drinks, anything online). If you don't like what you have, get rid of it and get some of what the other guys are selling. (Consumers tend to be a little less fickle with more durable items—houses, cars, major appliances—where it costs more to switch.) If there's no differentiation and no downside, why *wouldn't* someone switch? After all, new brands usually come in with a splash, or, if nothing else, with an introductory low price. Ah, the tactics of lazy marketers and predators.

Remember that consumers aren't all that bright: If you don't tell them exactly what to do and what to believe, and you don't keep giving them reasons to buy your brand, they'll take their business to someone else who does. Overall, it comes down to what I like to call DAD: *define and deliver.* Like the old Southern preacher said, "Tell 'em what you're going to tell 'em, tell 'em, and then tell 'em what you told 'em." And I'd add, "Tell 'em over and over and over and over."

WHAT MAKES PEOPLE SATISFIED?

A customer's level of satisfaction is based on three things:

1. **Product or service performance:** Does whatever it is that you're selling do the job it's supposed to? How does the product's performance compare to customers' expectations?
2. **The kind of experience the customer has with your brand:** Is it fun? Is it pleasant? Is it what she expected?
3. **The kind of interaction you have with the customer:** How did the customer feel during your brief relationship? How do you resolve problems when they occur?

Yeah, yeah, I know. You already knew all that, right? But before you get all upset about how much money you just gave this clown Zyman for a book full of stuff everyone already knows, answer me this: If everyone already knows it, how come they aren't doing it? Enough said? Read on . . .

Of these three points, numbers 2 and 3 are by far the most important. That's not to say that you can forget about number 1—it's always nice when things work the way they're supposed to. But in most cases the product itself is almost an afterthought. **It's the *experience* of the product that really counts.**

If you have cable television, your experience with the brand probably started with a commercial you saw on TV or maybe a direct-mail ad that showed up in your mailbox. From that moment on, every single thing that happened colored your experience—and satisfaction—with the brand. When you called to place your order, how many layers of voicemail did you have to wade through before getting a live body and how long did it take? Did you like the music they played while you waited? Was the customer service rep nice? Polite? Chatty? Rude? Sullen? Did she answer your questions knowledgeably or act as if she wanted to go on to the next call? Did she schedule your installation appointment at a time that was convenient for you or did you have to take a day off from work to wait for an installer? And when the installer showed up, was he on time? Was he presentable-looking? Did he block your driveway so that you couldn't get out? Did he tell you what he was going to do and how long it was going to take? And so on.

You go through the same kind of mental evaluation whenever you do almost anything. When you check into a hotel, you either consciously or subconsciously check out the lobby, elevators, ashtrays, bar, employees, towels, gym, proximity to transportation and the airport, and more.

Sometimes the decisions you make may seem a little irrational. Your decision to boycott a gas station, for example, might have less to do with how well the brand of gas performs and more to do with the fact that the last time you filled up at that particular station the bathrooms were filthy.

But whether consumers make rational or irrational decisions is really none of your business. You simply have to accept that it's the way decisions get made. You also have to accept that consumers are sometimes going to hold you responsible for things you have no control over. A good friend of mine who's on the board of directors of Delta airlines says that the customer's transaction with Delta starts at the moment he or she pulls into the parking lot. Frankly, I think that the transaction starts long before that—back when the customer saw a full-page ad in the newspaper and picked up the phone to make a reservation. But the point is a good one: If there's traffic on the road on the way to the airport, or if there's a sudden ice storm that delays the flight, or if the short-term parking lot is full and the customer has to walk half a mile from the other lot, those things will be included in the Delta experience.

One essential part of a customer's experience of a product is how the company handles the inevitable problems. Say you buy an expensive coffeemaker at Starbucks. You get it home, plug it in, and it starts spewing coffee onto your $300 cashmere sweater. Naturally, you're going to be pretty pissed. So you storm back to the store in your stained sweater, ready to choke someone. At this point, a couple things could happen: The clerk could ask you a bunch of questions obviously formulated to demonstrate that you're a mechanical idiot, the problem was your own fault, and you shouldn't wear cashmere while making coffee, anyway. Or, the clerk could apologize profusely, immediately replace the product with an upgraded model, give you a coupon for 5 pounds of your favorite blend, and insist on sending your sweater out to be dry cleaned. That would take the wind out of your sails, wouldn't it? It would also probably make you a Starbucks customer for life. Best of all (from Starbucks' point of view), you'd probably tell everyone you know how wonderfully they treated you. The fact that the product was a dud won't even come into it. I absolutely guarantee you that word-of-mouth recommendations travel faster and are far more valuable than having some babe with a nice tan and big teeth on TV tell you how great Starbucks is.

For the most part, consumers understand that things sometimes go wrong and they're usually pretty forgiving, provided they get treated properly. Imagine that your Hertz rental car breaks down in the middle of the desert. If you call their toll-free number from your cell phone and they leave you on hold until your battery runs out, they'll never get another nickel of your business. But if they send a car—even if it's a beat-up van— to pick you up and take you to your appointment, you'll probably forget the whole thing. You will remember how important, valued, and special they made you feel.

Bottom line? Happy customers come back and bring their friends. Unhappy customers don't come back and discourage everyone they know from doing so, too. Whether a customer becomes an evangelist (spreading the good word to everyone) or someone who never misses an opportunity to say something nasty about your brand depends on how you treat him or her.

Let me get back to defining customer service. Remember I said earlier that customer satisfaction was about defining expectations and delivering on them? Well, customer *service* goes beyond that. It's about *overdelivering* on expectations; it's about creating an emotional bond between your customers and your brand. Looking at it another way, customer service is kind of like a magnet: Do it right and it will draw customers to your brand and keep them there. But do it wrong and it will repel customers away. **In short, customer service is the thing that turns customer satisfaction into purchase intent (or, better yet, actual purchases).**

As obvious as this sounds, the reason you aren't selling more is because consumers aren't buying more. And the reason they aren't buying more is because you haven't given them a reason to. If that goes on too long, you're out of business.

I can't give you a checklist here of exactly what makes for good customer service. In some ways it's like how the U.S. Supreme Court tried to define "obscenity" in the 1960s: I'm not quite sure what it is, but I know it when I see it. Sure, you want to treat people nicely, smile when you serve them, get their orders out on time, and all that good stuff. And you want to know when to stick to your policies and when to bend them. But it's a lot more than that.

Sometimes it's easier just to say what customer service isn't. It's not waiting in line at the grocery store for half an hour when there are plenty of clerks around not doing anything. It's not when the clerk sees you coming and closes the cash register. I guess they call that one "closed for your convenience." It's not getting ignored when you need help. It's not getting spoken to rudely or having some automaton of a person insist on following a company policy that seems to have no function except to inconvenience you as much as possible.

Not long ago, I got to the airport and through security with enough time to spare to catch an earlier flight. I wasn't checking any luggage, so I went to the airline's customer service counter to ask them to change my ticket. The response? "Your reservation doesn't show your middle name, so you'll have to wait for your original flight." Gee, my reservation doesn't show my cholesterol level, either. What difference does that make? All in all, a great incentive not to fly that airline next time.

Maybe the best definition of all is that customer service is advertising, pure and simple. It communicates—just like everything else you do—huge amounts of information about your brand. In a lot of ways, customer service is the most important kind of advertising. You can have the best ads, the most fantastic public relations, a wonderful spokesperson, incredible packaging, and a great product, but if you treat your customers badly one time, you'll never see them again. How important is it to keep that from happening? Very. American companies lose half their customers every five years. **I've seen estimates that reducing the customer defection rate by only 5 percent can actually *double* profits!** Pretty impressive. So why don't companies concentrate on that?

I have to do a little backtracking here. As hard as it is to pin down exactly what makes for good customer service, there are four characteristics that are almost universally shared by companies that consistently rate highest in customer service:

1. They develop a new vocabulary that changes the way employees view and treat customers.
2. They continuously try to improve the quality of their products or services.
3. They set clear and consistent expectations, and they always deliver on them.
4. They set up a system that encourages customers to give them feedback, in effect turning the customers into beta testers.

Let me give you a few short examples of companies that do an incredible job of integrating these four points into their advertising strategy and their brand DNA:

• **Lands' End promises quality, affordable prices, and top-notch service—and they deliver.** Because about 85 percent of the company's orders come in by phone, operators are a critical ingredient. Lines are open 24 hours a day and the company tries to keep staffing levels high enough so that 90 percent of calls get answered within 10 seconds, day or night. In the rare times when they're understaffed, overflow calls are routed to stand-by operators who work from home!

Service is important on the company's relatively new website, too. If you're lost on the site or can't find exactly what you're looking for, click a button and you'll get a call from a Lands' End operator within a few minutes. The company never misses an opportunity to ask customers for feedback. Those comments get combined into a 3-inch-high printout every month that managers use to adjust product offerings and training, ensuring that they're delivering on customers' expectations. Maybe that's what attracted Sears to buy the company.

• **Disney has one of the most amazing customer service records anywhere.** I think part of the reason is their corporate vocabulary. At Disneyland and Disney World, for example, park visitors are called "guests," and the employees themselves are referred to as "cast members." That may not seem like a big deal, but I think it emphasizes in customers' minds that they should expect to be pampered and in employees' minds that they play a critical role in keeping customers happy. Apparently it works: Close to 70 percent of Disney's guests are repeats.

- **The Ritz-Carlton hotels have an even more impressive retention rate: Their goal is 100 percent and they come pretty darn close!** Ninety-nine percent of the Ritz's guest say they were satisfied with their experience. Over 80 percent were extremely satisfied. What's good for the customers is good for the company, too: Since 1995, pretax earnings have nearly doubled.
- **No one exemplifies the what's-good-for-the-customer-is-good-for-the-company idea better than Southwest Airlines.** They've turned a profit every year for the past 30 years, which is unheard of in the airline industry, and they've led the Department of Transportation's list of fewest customer complaints for 11 years running. Unlike their huge rivals, Southwest has never had layoffs.

PASSING THE BUCK

More and more companies are putting their customers in charge of their own service. In a lot of ways this has been a good thing: It's let companies trim their staff and keep their customers happy at the same time. Think about ATMs, for example, bag-it-yourself grocery stores, and self-service gas stations. In these situations, consumers don't need a lot of help. All they want is to get in and out as quickly as possible, so letting them take care of themselves is great for them and for the company.

Other times, though, turning over responsibility to customers might save you a little money in the short term but could cost a lot in the long term. Take airline websites. On the surface they seem like a great idea: They're easy, they're fast, they put the customer in control, plus they let the company cut its customer service payroll. They also save millions in commissions by squeezing travel agents out of the picture. But those savings come at a cost: thousands of ticked-off customers who can't get the help they need with special requests or problems and who have to wait 45 minutes on hold to talk to someone just so that they can order a kosher meal because the airline doesn't have enough people to take all the calls.

Every once in a while, someone comes up with a great idea that completely redefines service. I'm sure that the last time you traveled you checked gate arrival and departure info on the airline's website and used flight notification on your cell phone or PDA. You didn't? Wow, I guess that means that the airlines are keeping a fantastic service (that actually exists, by the way) to themselves. How's that going to help anyone? The airlines should be hitting us over the head over and over with the idea that we can take control by using a service they provide. Doing that would be a lot more effective in getting our business than trying to convince us that one airline has more legroom or another has better meals, none of which is believable, anyway.

It's kind of similar with rental cars. It used to be that you arrived at the airport and had to stand in a long line to deal with surly employees who were cooped up all day behind a tiny counter. Then you got packed into a bus and taken to a huge parking lot where you'd have to schlep your suitcase up and down every aisle looking for your car. By the time you finally found it, you had a sore back and were annoyed as hell.

Eventually, the big rental companies had to deal with this customer service disaster. They started to automate things and streamlined their entire system, got rid of a lot of employees, and put in self-service counters. All of this got people to their cars a lot more efficiently, especially their top customers. National started Emerald Isle, Avis has Wizard, Hertz has the #1 Gold Club. Customer satisfaction went way up almost overnight.

So here's the irony. The rental companies improved customer satisfaction (and maybe even customer service) and saved some money on personnel, but they ended up hurting their own revenues because without employees—even surly ones—there wasn't anyone around to push upgrades, sell collision damage waiver, or rent out cell phones. The problem is that they were thinking of the event, not the strategy. The event was about saving money and reducing airport congestion. The strategy would have been about establishing a relationship with the customer over the long haul.

Some companies have gone in the other direction, giving customers more control and *adding* employees at the same time. Not all that long ago, buying a computer was a one-size-fits-all kind of thing—you went to the store and bought whatever they had from an incredibly limited set of options. Then, along came Dell, saying, "Hey, I'll build you a computer any way you want it." Really and truly, building computers to order isn't all that complicated. But it made buyers feel important and gave them a lot more control than they'd ever had before. Dell's customer service was and still is spectacular. People flocked to Dell (and some of the other toll-free-only vendors that cropped up later) and basically forced IBM out of the

retail business. Gateway took their commitment to customer service a little further, actually opening brick-and-mortar stores.

LESS COMPETITION EQUALS LESS CUSTOMER SERVICE: DUMB, DUMB, DUMB

If you're old enough to remember Lily Tomlin, you probably remember her
great sketches as Ernestine the telephone operator, where Ernestine says,
"We don't care. We don't have to. We're the phone company." I don't
know that there's a better way to sum up what happens to companies when
they don't have a lot of competition.

Despite deregulation, phone companies are still in about the same
place they've always been. Walk into one of their stores to buy a phone
and you'll have to beat the salespeople off with a stick. But come back a
few weeks later to replace that same phone with one that actually works
and you'll get the runaround for days. Why? Because they can. They know
that your phone options are limited (especially since you're only a few
weeks into a two-year contract), and chances are, no matter how badly
they treat you, you probably want to keep the phone number you have
now, so you'll be back for more.

These guys win the award, hands down, for the worst customer service
in the world. Their slogans say they don't sell phones, they sell solutions,
but the clowns they hire to work in their stores either don't know that or
don't care, and I can prove it. Maybe that's why AT&T is in so much
trouble.

On a couple of occasions, I've had to call the phone company that provides service (if you call it that) to my home because I haven't had a dial
tone. They listen, then tell me that someone will have to come out to look
at the wiring and the first appointment they have is three days later. This
is the 21st century! Who the hell ever heard of having to go two days
without phone service?

More amazing than that, the person who answers the phone says,
"Good morning, my name is Jennifer. How can I provide you with excellent service?" Then, before I can explain the problem, Jennifer puts me on
hold where I have to listen to some idiotic recorded sales pitch for 15 minutes before she comes back to tell me that she has to transfer me to a different department. Excellent service? Who are they kidding? Remember

that everything communicates. And it doesn't take much to see what this experience communicates: "We know that people like to hear about customer service these days, so we're training our people to pay lip service to the idea. But we really don't care."

Look, what I'm talking about is not brain surgery. It's about defining and delivering great service in terms you can live with. It's really more about an attitude than anything else. The guy who runs the gas station on the northeast corner of Main and First knows that the other three stations at that intersection have pretty much the same gas at the same price. But if he gets out there and provides old-time full service ("May I clean your windshield? Your tires are low, would you like me to fill them up and check your spare?"), he'll be offering something that the other guys aren't. He knows that without differentiating himself in that way he's out of business. Maybe the airlines need to hire people who've worked in industries where they die without customer service.

In all fairness, some of the blame sits squarely on our shoulders. After all, we go to a restaurant, get crappy service, and still give the waitress a 15 percent tip. Maybe if we stopped rewarding rotten service, the people who provide the rotten service and the companies who hire them would have some incentive to change.

Fortunately, not everyone who operates without competition acts the part. In Vail, Colorado, you have to renew your auto plates every year. They send you a bill, you send them a check, and they mail you back a little sticker. Last year, my stickers didn't show up, so I called the city to ask what was up. Having a pretty dim view of city government, I was expecting to get transferred to 16 different departments, leave voicemails for 38 people, get disconnected 7 times, then have to send another check. Instead, I reached someone on my first call who told me that the stickers they'd mailed me had been returned for some reason, and I had three choices: Come in and get them, send someone else to get them, or have them mailed out again. I'm still in shock.

COMMUNICATE WITH THEM

Nothing infuriates someone with a problem more than being told No without a decent reason or having some clerk refuse to do something because "that's not our policy" when it would be almost no effort at all to resolve the issue. People don't give a damn about your policies or your rules. They hate feeling helpless. All they want are solutions. Of course, you're not going to be able to resolve everyone's problems to their satisfaction. But in most cases you can make them feel a lot better by simply telling them the rules *before* something happens.

A few hours after you call the *New York Times* to subscribe, you get a very nicely written email that lays out the terms of your relationship. It tells you how to reach them if you have billing questions or didn't get your paper or want to put your subscription on hold while you're on vacation. And it tells you exactly how they'll be billing you: They'll charge your credit card every month unless you tell them otherwise. Even though the result is the same whether you know the rules up front or not, knowing them makes you feel more like a partner and less likely to be screwed over.

Think of all those times you've waited on hold with some annoying recording telling you over and over and over and over how important your call is and how the next available customer service person will be with you as soon as he or she is available. Part of what is so infuriating about that is the uncertainty: You have no idea how long you'll be on hold—could be a minute, could be an hour. They keep telling you how much they value your business, but they aren't doing much to show it.

On the other hand, when you get stuck on hold and the computer voice tells you that you're third in the queue or that your wait time will be approximately 17 minutes, you've got a lot more control over the situation. You know how long you'll be there and you can choose to wait or to call back later. The choice is yours, not the company's.

Sometimes otherwise well-meaning attempts to communicate with customers backfire. When United's San Francisco-to-Sacramento flights land, the flight attendants come on the overhead and say, "We know you have a choice and we appreciate your choosing United." Unfortunately, everyone on the plane already knows that they don't have a choice (United is the only carrier that flies this route); having someone say they do just rubs it in.

If you fly Delta, you'll notice that on a lot of their routes their flight times are 20 minutes longer than everyone else's. Well, it's not because they're taking a different route. The real reason is that they wanted to improve their on-time statistics and they figured out that adding an extra 20 minutes to each flight would increase their odds. The problem is that their customers figured it out pretty quickly and resent being treated like idiots.

And what is your independent service provider telling you when you call their tech support line because you can't get online and the recording says, "If you're having trouble logging on, check our website for common fixes to common problems." How dumb is that? If you can't log on, how can you possibly get to their website? The moral of the story? If you don't have anything to say, shut up.

Communicating with customers and consumers isn't a one-way street with you doing all the talking. Communicating with customers and consumers—just like communicating with your spouse—involves plenty of listening, too. If you listen carefully enough, you just might learn something. **If you're not absolutely sure what it takes to keep your existing customers happy or what it would take to convert an ordinary consumer or infrequent customer into a regular customer, ask.** Ask questions at the cash register. Print your toll-free phone number on all your packaging so that customers can contact you. Ask current customers what they like about their experience with you, what they don't like, and where you could improve. Find people who aren't buying your product and ask them why not. Call up people who've sent you nasty letters about some horrible experience they had with your company and ask them what you'd need to do to get them to come back again. Keep track of every answer to every question and use the information to design a strategy that will make things better.

In the early 1990s, Ford asked car buyers about the features that consumers felt were most important to them. The company integrated a lot of the information they collected and came up with the Taurus, which set all sorts of sales records. The first time I stayed at a Ritz hotel, I asked for some extra bedding. Now, every time I go back, there's an extra pillow and blanket on the bed. And personal shoppers at Nordstrom's and Macy's keep track of customers' purchases and will let you know when they get a new line of handkerchiefs that match the suspenders you bought last year. Amazon.com tracks the books you buy and uses that information to offer you books they think (or their computers think) you'll find interesting. So if you bought a book from them on van Gogh, you may get an email telling you about other books on artists who cut off their ear and mailed it to their girlfriend.

I'm not going to get into permission marketing here. There are dozens of good books on the subject. But let me say that the purpose of communicating with consumers and customers is to build and maintain your relationship with them. Asking them to tell you what they like and don't like about your brand or to help you design your products is great, but whatever goodwill and loyalty you develop can be lost in an instant if you misuse the information you're collecting. Customers will only spend the time answering your questions if they feel they can trust you. Selling customer data without their permission or bombarding them with offers for stuff they don't need is the best way to show them that they can't trust you.

CH, CH, CH, CHANGING INTO A
CUSTOMER-CENTERED ORGANIZATION

If you know or even suspect that your customer service efforts aren't everything they should be, I have three words for you: *Fix them fast.* If your problems have just started or they're not really out of control, you need a two-pronged approach: (1) Immediately do whatever you need to do to take care of the problem quickly and efficiently, and (2) when the dust has settled, figure out what went wrong and make sure it doesn't happen again. I don't mean to be flip about this, but it's really that simple.

There's no shortage of proof that a company's customer service levels correlate directly with business success and profits. But what really puzzles me is why most companies out there—including a pretty good-sized majority of the ones that come to Zyman Marketing for consulting—pay so little attention to customer service. I've spent a long time analyzing this and I've come to the conclusion that the problem is companies just can't get themselves out of the rut of doing things the way they always have.

Customers' needs are always changing, and in this environment, management can't rely on the same bag of tricks. It's more important than ever to be *externally* focused on consumers, customers, and trends. The table below shows how things are today and where they need to be to ensure success.

Very, very few companies have restructured themselves along these lines. Microsoft is an exception and uses a four-step process to satisfy their customers' needs:

1. **Find out what consumers need and want and find solutions.**
2. **Translate solutions into code.**
3. **Integrate solutions into a global standard (MS-DOS, Windows, etc.)**

4. **Package solutions into a friendly user interface and deliver them in consumer-driven applications.**

Of course, remaking your company into a customer-centered organization won't be easy, especially since in most cases it's going to require a complete top-to-bottom corporate overhaul. You're going to have to change the way your entire company thinks, researches, responds, creates, and implements strategies, advertises, and everything else. The specific

TABLE 8.1   SUCCEEDING WITH FOCUS AND RESULT

	FOCUS	ROLE OF ADVERTISING	RESULT
The way things are today	Focus is internal, on the business' needs instead of the customers' needs.	Advertising is a support function designed to facilitate communication. It's easily copied, reactive not proactive, and overall doesn't do much more than promote awareness.	There's no sustainable value proposition. There's no relationship with the customers and no customer loyalty because they don't clearly get how the brand benefits them.
The way things need to be to succeed	Focus is on the customers. Understand their needs and wants. Who are the people willing to buy? What do they want? What are they thinking about?	Advertising is a strategic function that communicates the brand's assets and how they meet customers' needs and wants.	A sustainable, differentiated value proposition. Customers understand how the brand delivers benefits that meet their needs and wants. Relationships with customers are built.

steps are different for every company, but keep these three rules in mind as you go through the process:

1. **Take it easy.** No matter how committed you are or how much money you have to blow, you're not going to change your organization's complete structure overnight. Appointing a VP of customer service or creating a task force to deal with the issue won't magically solve your problems. They're good first steps, but it'll take a while before things filter through to the entire company.

2. **Think first, talk later.** Most corporate execs I know are action oriented, which means when they see a problem they try to take care of it immediately. In the case of customer service problems, the temptation is to put the PR people on the case right away, to send out press releases and buy full-page ads in all the papers announcing a "renewed commitment to their customers." Sounds like a great idea, but it's not—at least not this way.

I have no objection to doing everything you can to improve your company and promote your brand, but there's a timing problem here, which gets back to my point about overpromising on expectations. Chances are that telling the public that you're going to transform your company into some kind of customer service Mecca will only raise their hopes and get them all excited. But in most cases, customer service problems are so systemic that a few new policies and procedures won't do the job. So if you happen to be a little off the mark—say you improve customer service by only 300 percent instead of 500 percent—you'll dash those hopes and the public will never forgive you.

This is sort of what happened when Saturn first came out. Part of Saturn's value proposition was that they cared about what customers had to say and that customer interaction and feedback were important parts of the brand. In the early days, this was true, and people started flocking to Saturn in droves. From the moment they walked in the door, expectations were high and Saturn delivered. But after a while, Saturn lost their grip on their customer service premise and customers abandoned the brand as fast as they could. Remember when Eastern Airlines was dying? They promised excellent service, on-time performance, and a bunch of other stuff they didn't (or couldn't) deliver on. None of that kept them from disappearing.

The moral of the story is fix your problems first, then start running your mouth.

On the other hand, if you've got it, flaunt it. Do you offer 100 percent satisfaction or your money back? Would 97 percent of your customers recommend your company to their friends? Do you have the shortest wait times in the industry? If you're offering good service—however you define it—let everyone know.

3. **Make sure everyone in the company knows how important customer service is.** And I mean *everyone*, because you, your board of directors, the guy who cleans the toilets, that temp who's helping out in the mailroom for a week, and everyone in between are all in a position to influence consumers. This point is so important that I'm going to spend the rest of the chapter talking about it.

SELLING FROM THE INSIDE OUT

I've spent a lot of time talking about how important it is to understand your customers and their wants and needs before you can sell them anything, and how important it is to communicate with them in a way that establishes trust and builds relationships between them and your brand. But I've left out a group of consumers who should be the very first group of people you focus on when you start thinking about selling your brand: your employees. I know this sounds a little crazy, but if you think about it for a minute, you'll agree.

Whenever I give a speech to a bunch of business execs or do a presentation on customer service to a consulting client, it doesn't take long to convince them of the exact importance of a commitment to great customer service. They get all inspired to make their companies customer service centered and they can hardly wait for me to stop talking so that they can rush back to their offices and get started. But sometimes I almost have to physically grab them and drag them back to their seats to listen to the most important point of all: **Before you can even think of selling your brand to consumers and customers, you have to sell it to your employees.**

Employees are the link between all those brand-new, wonderful-sounding, customer-centered corporate philosophies and those real-life, credit-card-carrying customers. How a brand is positioned in the consumers' and customers' mind is nearly 100 percent dependent on employees.

Actually, this link between customers and employees is more like a circle: Employees who treat customers well create loyal customers; loyal customers bring in more profits for the company, which often leads to better compensation for employees, which makes them happier, which means they treat customers better, which makes for more loyal customers, and on and on. Unfortunately, too few companies understand this basic point and even fewer take the time to do anything about it. The result is horrible customer service problems.

STARTING ALL OVER FROM SQUARE ONE

We talked earlier about how a consumer's experience of a product or service is usually more important than the actual product or service itself. Okay, so you know that. Your customers know it, too, although whether they can articulate it is a different thing. But do your employees know it? Do they understand their role in creating that all-important experience? Not if you haven't told them.

Most companies make the dangerous assumption that employees automatically know that their job is to keep customers happy and that they instinctively know how to do it. But I can guarantee you this: The biggest reason customer service isn't what it should be in most companies is that employees don't know what their job is or what their employers expect from them. If you don't make those things crystal clear, your employees won't have a clue. When Delta says, "Ready when you are," they need to explain what that means not only to consumers but to employees. When Carl's Junior runs ads that promise, "In and out in three minutes," they're telling customers that they understand how rushed their lives are and that they're going to do whatever they can to help. But ads don't serve hamburgers; people do. At the W Hotel—and every other hotel—beds are the centerpiece of the experience. If you advertise that you have the best beds in town but your local property manager decided to save a few bucks by buying cheap ones, you've got a problem.

My company helped design a strategy that resulted in a special marketing campaign for Aspen called "Aspen Day and Night." But we didn't just drop the plan in their laps and take off. We briefed every resort employee we could get hold of—ski school instructors, waiters, lift operators, limo drivers—on exactly what "Aspen Day and Night" meant: top-of-the-line customer service 24 hours a day. We let every one of them know that the success or failure of the program was up to them.

In short, make sure that the strategies you develop are understood, appreciated, and acted upon by your employees. If you can do this, you can transform your employees into a powerful force for building brand equity. On the other hand, any miscommunication between you and them about what your goals are can completely undermine your other advertising and branding messages.

Sears, for example, advertises "complete satisfaction or your money back"—always a good marketing message. Unfortunately, that idea wasn't communicated to employees in the return departments, whose performance evaluations were based in part on how few items they took back—a policy that made customers looking for guaranteed satisfaction think twice about shopping at Sears again.

For the next few pages I want to give you a bunch more examples of companies that get it and those that don't.

I had a problem with my home DSL line, so AT&T sent a guy out to the house to fix it. I invited him in, but before he stepped inside he put on slippers so that he wouldn't mess up my carpet. Obviously, this guy knew that keeping customers happy was an important part of his job. Fixing the DSL would have been enough, but for an additional cost of 29 cents for the booties, he showed me that they'd keep me happy in other ways, too. On the other hand, a few days after the installer left, I called AT&T to ask them a DSL-related question. I had to go through 16 layers of voicemail before I got a live person! And that doesn't even include the "for Spanish, press 8" that they threw in there after I'd already responded to 8 or 9 English-language commands.

On international flights, customers tend to rate their satisfaction with the trip based on how many hot towels they get and how many times the flight attendants call them by name and remember their drink orders. Bumpy ride? So-so food? Who cares? Singapore airlines gets this, which is why they're consistently rated the top international airline. China Airlines, which flies many of the same routes and competes head to head with Singapore, doesn't. They haven't figured out that there's a difference between serving 120 meals and serving 120 people. They serve meals; Singapore serves people.

If you ever go to La Scala in Rome, you know from the moment you walk in the door that you're in opera heaven. Everyone who works there—from the ticket takers to the guys who pour the Perrier at intermission—is an opera buff. They can talk intelligently about opera in general and take you through the one you've come to see scene by scene. They understand that they're there to enhance your experience.

At Walt Disney, everyone in the company, from the busboys in their hotels to the captains on their cruise line, knows that the whole reason they're there is to make your Disney experience fun. You may not like Disney's politics, but one thing's for sure: They understand the message and they get it right every time.

My co-author had an experience with Dell that highlights this philosophy. He'd ordered a new laptop a week before flying to Atlanta to meet with me about this book. Dell had promised him that the computer would arrive two days before he left town, but the day he was supposed to leave, the computer still hadn't arrived. He was understandably furious. He called Dell's customer service people, and after a few minutes of yelling at the first person who answered the phone, he got a supervisor who fell all over himself apologizing and immediately offered a $300 rebate. The delivery problem was actually UPS's fault, not Dell's, but this supervisor recognized that Armin didn't really care whose fault it was—he just wanted his laptop. The supervisor had a chance to turn a potential terrorist into an evangelist, and that's exactly what he did. Armin has recommended Dell to everyone he knows. The situation could just as easily have gone the other way if that customer service supervisor hadn't clearly understood his role in providing excellent customer service and had tried to blame the problem on UPS.

Because I fly a few hundred thousand miles a year, United gave me Big Kahuna status. I got a fancy brochure with a list of all the perks, which they claim are reserved exclusively for their most valued customers. Great. But a few months ago, I was in the airport and saw that they'd printed my wife's name on my ticket by mistake. So I stopped by the customer service center and asked for some help straightening out the problem. The woman sitting behind the desk took a quick look at the ticket and announced that there was nothing she could do. I argued with her for a bit, but she wouldn't budge. All that warm and fuzzy feeling I had about being a Big Kahuna member disappeared. What's the sense of telling me that I'm a valued customer when they didn't bother to let their employees know?

Something very similar happened to me at two different Hertz locations in Mexico. Both times I arrived at the airport and was told that they didn't have a car for me. And both times I got pissed and told the clerk behind the desk that I wanted a ride to my hotel, I wanted them to drop a car off there later, and I wanted a big discount. One guy knew what his role was and agreed right away (maybe he used to work at Dell). The other guy just shrugged his shoulders and told me that wasn't their policy. The incredible thing is that in the United States, as a platinum member I'm treated like royalty, and I wouldn't rent from anyone but Hertz. But in Mexico, never again.

It all starts with educating your employees on what your brand's message is and never letting them forget that everything communicates—your storefront, your lobby, your delivery vans, even the font on your faxes and invoices. Everything that your customers, clients, vendors, and even your competitors see has to reinforce your message.

Your receptionist is often the very first point of contact for new and prospective customers—either in person or on the phone. If this person doesn't have at least a basic understanding of your products and services, he or she will look like a fool (and so will you) when a caller asks for some information about your company. I went on a tour of one of Miller's bottling plants and asked the guide why they put Miller Lite in clear bottles. Instead of saying "to show how pure it is," or even "I don't know, but I'll find out for you," the guide got very defensive and insisted that "there's absolutely nothing wrong with clear bottles."

And what about the people who arrange the furniture in your lobby or who lay out your store or restaurant? What about the graphic designer who created your logo and your stationery, or the temp who's helping out in the mailroom? What about the people who clean the bathrooms, do the invoicing, pay your bills, and drive the trucks that deliver your products? Every one of them plays an important role in establishing in consumers' minds who you are, what your brand stands for, and how it can benefit the people who use it. Every one of them is part of your product.

If your employees understand your goals and their role in achieving them, they'll be a lot more likely to support them. Think about what happened during the Vietnam War. Our soldiers never understood why they were there ("beating the Commies" wasn't terribly specific). They had no idea how they fit into the picture, what was expected of them, or what rewards they (or the country) would see if they were victorious. The three

administrations that ran the war—Kennedy, Johnson, and Nixon—didn't
seem to have any firmer grasp on any of those things. Congress was split
on the issue and so was the public, which never really got behind the
troops. Not surprisingly, morale sucked and the war dragged on and on.
When the soldiers finally came home, they were pretty much ignored.

But the Gulf War was a completely different thing. Everyone knew
exactly what the goal was: to kick Saddam Hussein's butt out of Kuwait. It
was announced from the very start and conveyed to everyone right down
the line. Congress backed the plan 100 percent and so did the top brass.
Each soldier knew what was expected and how he or she fit into the overall plan. Plus, the first Bush administration did an excellent job of selling
Desert Storm to the public, which in turn supported the troops, who were
treated as heroes when they came home.

NEVER STOP PREACHING TO THE CHOIR

Fortunately, there's an easy way to solve all these problems: **Talk to your
employees—but in a very special way. Really and truly, they're
another group of consumers, so when you're thinking about communicating with them, pretend you're designing an ad campaign.** This
means asking yourself the same questions about your employees that
you'd ask about any other group of consumers you're trying to reach:
What's important to them? What do you want them to know about your
brand? What do you want them to do? It also means that what I've said
over and over about dealing with other consumers applies here, too: Tell
them what you want them to do, why they should do it, and what's in it
for them, or they won't do it.

When *The End of Marketing As We Know It* first came out, Pat Robert-
son had me on his show. I arrived at the studio a little early and was surprised that Pat wasn't there yet—most anchors are there before the guests.
I asked where he was, and one of his assistants said he was "preaching to the
operators." Every week, she said, Pat gets together with the operators to
talk to them about the role they play in the company. The goal of Robert-
son's brand is to collect money from people. And since the operators are
callers' first contact and the ones who will be taking down the credit-card
numbers or giving out the mailing address, it's critical that they always
know what their mission is and just how important it is to the company.

Politicians do the same kind of thing all the time. They know that the people who work for them are essential to getting the brand's message out, and if they can't get those people to buy the message, they haven't got a prayer of getting anyone else to buy it, either. So they have special events for the volunteers who staff their offices and make those get-out-to-vote calls, and the college kids who stand in supermarket parking lots trying to register voters, and even the folks who roam neighborhoods hanging those last-minute campaign flyers on doorknobs. They shake hands, kiss babies, and ask about the family cat, because they know that if they don't win over the people who work for them, they'll never get their campaign off the ground.

HOW TO REACH THEM

There are dozens of different ways to get your message across to your employees: group or face-to-face meetings, company Intranet, bulletin boards, newsletters, or even specially designed promotional or advertising campaigns aimed solely at your own people, kind of like a pregame speech a coach might give his players. When we launched "Coke Is It!" we put together a film that we showed our drivers every morning before they went out on their routes. It was of two guys driving a Coke truck straight at a 20-foot-high wall of Pepsi cases that was blocking the road. As the truck slammed through the wall, sending Pepsi debris everywhere, the voiceover said, "Momentum. When you have it, nobody can take it away from you." It was incredibly effective in letting the drivers know exactly what we wanted from them. It made them feel strong, proud, and like important members of the team.

You can also use your more traditional advertising to communicate with your employees. DirecTV, for example, has a series of wonderful ads that show an installer standing on a customer's roof while the customer keeps asking him questions: Can I really get 10 football channels? Can I really get 7 movie channels? The installer answers, "Yes, sir," to every question, and when he comes down, the customer is delighted. In another ad, a couple has just moved to a new house and is unpacking. When they open up their dish-in-a-box, the installer jumps out. The message to customers from both these ads is "we're a company that fulfills your dreams and we'll be there when you need us." The message to DirecTV employees is "delivering superior service to our customers, anytime they need it, is what we're all about."

AND WHILE YOU'RE AT IT, DO SOME LISTENING

My mother always told me that the reason people have two ears and only one mouth is that listening is more important than talking. I don't always agree with everything my mother said, but when it comes to dealing with employees (and customers, for that matter), she was absolutely right. Employees are the ones who are in contact with your customers. They see how the customers react to your brand; they see the look on their faces and hear the tone in their voices. They can tell you what your customers are *really* saying and what they *really* believe, in a way that the customers themselves might never be able to tell you. Employees can also tell you what they need to do their job better.

Listening to your employees and going out of your way to solicit their input is more than just a way to augment and refine your customer research efforts. It's also a very important way of letting your employees know how important they are to you and how much you value them.

THE BIGGEST COMMUNICATION CHALLENGE:
WHEN THINGS GET TOUGH

Sometimes, for whatever the reason, something happens that changes your business in a huge way. The most common scenarios are mergers, Chapter 11, and layoffs. When something like this happens, most companies' instinctive reaction is to clamp down on the flow of information. But that's exactly the wrong thing to do. When your employees' world is being turned upside down, communicating with them is more important than ever, and silence is absolutely not your friend. In these times people's most pressing question is whether they have a job, and you have to be able to answer that question. Not knowing makes them feel helpless. It impacts their job performance as well as their commitment to the company. How do you think they'll perform when they read in the newspaper that profits are off 17 percent and that their stock options are underwater?

The simple solution is to do the same thing I suggested you do when managing any other kind of public relations problem: Tell the truth, tell it all (or at least as much as you legally can), and tell it fast. When employees don't hear from you, they assume the worst, and they'll look to the media to give them the scoop on what's happening. Anything they don't get from media, they'll fill in with speculation and rumor. Keeping your employees representing your company positively during tough times can be a real challenge, which is why it's especially important to remember that your employees are consumers and that everything you do communicates.

A few years ago, when 7-11 was going through a leveraged buyout, times were tough and the company understandably needed to cut costs. Unfortunately, they started in a particularly dumb place. I happened to be chatting with a flight attendant a while ago and she told me that she used to work at 7-11 but had quit when the company cut out the Christmas turkeys they used to give employees and dropped the employee softball team. To you, a few birds and baseball bats might sound insignificant, but to 7-11's employees they weren't. Getting rid of them destroyed their sense of community.

If you're unfortunate enough to be in Chapter 11, the only real way to get out is to sell more stuff to more people. And you'll never be able to do that unless you can give your employees a reason to work harder.

I know that's going to be tough, especially if you've gotten to the point where you have to cut some jobs. But before you start swinging your ax, keep in mind that the decision to lay people off affects a lot more people than you think. Sure, there are the ones who get laid off. But if the employees who stay worry that they're next, they'll spend all day reading the help-wanted ads online instead of paying attention to the customers.

Employees who don't get laid off are very concerned with why you're doing what you're doing and whether you're being fair. Are you laying people off because you really have to or because you want to pad your shareholders' (and your own) pockets? Employees don't trust companies that cut low-level jobs but keep paying their executives telephone number–size salaries. When Cisco Systems had to downsize, the CEO cut his salary to zero and had the company pay for some pretty liberal retraining for the people he let go.

Are you planning to offer a severance package to people you let go? If not, the ones who don't get laid off will worry that you'll treat them just as badly when their time comes. On the other hand, if you treat departing employees respectfully and nicely—some severance, maybe some out-placement counseling or retraining—your remaining employees will see you as a caring employer and they'll be happy to help you over the hump.

Your customers are affected by layoffs, too. If people hear, for example, that an express delivery service is laying off drivers, they may get concerned that fewer drivers will lead to package delivery delays, which could prompt them to switch to another company.

Fortunately, not every rough spot is going to be as dramatic as a bankruptcy or a merger. When we introduced New Coke in 1985, we didn't spend enough time getting the word out to our employees about what we were doing and why. Big mistake. (Of course, we didn't have a lot of time—the whole thing lasted only 77 days—but there's no question we blew it by not moving faster.) The media was murdering us and our employees felt as if the whole world were laughing at them. If they had to travel on company business, they took their Coke baggage tags off their suitcases, they stopped telling people where they worked, and their commitment to the company slipped. There's no way in the world that their job performance wasn't affected.

For some reason, we had done a much better job a few years earlier when we introduced Diet Coke. We sent hundreds of employees a six-pack by FedEx so that they could have it in time for the huge launch we did at Radio City Music Hall. We billed it as a big thing and our people were proud to be a part of it.

KEEPING YOUR EMPLOYEES HAPPY

If you think that doing all these somersaults to keep your employees happy and in the loop is going to be expensive and time-consuming, you're right. So why bother? Because it'll make you money, or at least save you a lot, which is basically the same thing.

I talked earlier about how important customer retention is and how even a 5 percent reduction in the defection rate can really boost profits. Well, the same goes for employee defections. Replacing employees costs somewhere between 25 and 200 percent of their annual salary. A 5 percent increase in retention can increase your profits by 25 percent or more. Obviously, it's cheaper to keep employees than to let them walk away.

And since American companies turn over half their employees every four years or so, you have plenty of opportunities to bank a few bucks.

There's also a clear connection between employee retention, customer satisfaction, and corporate profitability. A few years ago, Sears analyzed data collected over two decades from 800 of their stores. They found that a 5 percent increase in employee satisfaction generated a 1.4 percent increase in customer satisfaction, which in turn yielded a 1 percent increase in profitability. I don't know about you, but that says something to me: Happy employees make for happy customers.

What do you have to do to retain your people? The first thing is to recognize that there's a difference between satisfied employees and loyal ones. In the same way that satisfied customers can abandon your brand at any time, having satisfied employees is no guarantee of anything.

In 2000, a couple of big international consulting firms surveyed close to 10,000 workers in 32 countries and came up with some pretty horrifying results. It seems that no matter where they are in the world, employees fit into one of four categories:

1. **Truly loyal** (34 percent): These are the dream employees. They come in early, stay late, bend over backward to make customers happy, and recruit their friends to come work for you.
2. **Accessible** (8 percent): These guys are pretty much like the Truly Loyal types, but they'll probably leave within a year or two, most likely for family reasons rather than a lapse of commitment to you.
3. **Trapped** (31 percent): They hate their jobs and would like to leave but can't. They might need the money or the prestige, or maybe they're afraid they won't be able to get another job.
4. **High Risk** (27 percent): They hardly do any productive work at all and are halfway out the door, anyway.

What this means is that only a third of your employees are truly loyal, are committed to your brand, and are planning to stick with you. The rest are satisfied but they just work there. They're not committed to the success of the company. They're also just killing time until something better comes along. If you think that these satisfied employees care about your company and are going to go out of their way to do anything to help you, think again. I hope you find this as depressing as I do.

MAKING EMPLOYEES INTO BRAND AMBASSADORS

What turns a satisfied employee into a loyal one? Well, except at the very bottom of the wage scale, people leave jobs for all sorts of reasons, most of which don't have anything to do with money. Take-your-ferret-to-work Tuesdays and free Snapple in the refrigerator may satisfy employees' desires for rodents and iced tea, but it won't make them loyal.

What they really want is to be treated well. If they feel mistreated in any way, they'll take out their frustrations and anger on you and your customers, doing anything they can to get revenge. They'll make personal phone calls while they should be working, and they'll steal your pencils and paper clips. They'll charge personal expenses to company credit cards and pad their expense reports. They won't pass on important messages from vendors, they'll be surly to your customers, and they'll bad-mouth the company to everyone they see. Petty, vindictive, and childish? Absolutely. But also incredibly common. **Employees can be either positive or negative evangelists: Treat them badly and they'll take you down; treat them well and they can really grow your business.**

Do you remember Eastern Airlines? The employees absolutely hated the management and thought they weren't being treated fairly. When the company started having problems, the employees took it out on passengers. The result? No more Eastern Airlines.

Contrast that with Continental. Continental was in Chapter 11 not that long ago and now they're the top airline in terms of customer satisfaction. Was it the management? Nope. New planes? Wrong again. It was top-quality customer service, which, in case you haven't noticed, is delivered by employees. Gordon Bethune, the CEO, really gets the importance of treating people right and so do his employees.

Of course, "treat them well" is a phrase that means different things to different people. To me it's about giving employees recognition, appreciation, opportunities for growth and development, a chance to be part of a team, some degree of control over their environment, independence, and the right tools to do the job.

Train Them

One of the best ways of all to retain employees is to invest in them (yes, I'm going to talk about getting a return on your investment in a minute). And the best way to do that is through training and education, which will allow them to grow, develop, and learn new skills. It's actually one of the very best investments your company can make to have direct bottom-line impact.

Every single cast member at any of Disney's theme parks gets at least a few days of training in how to treat every customer as a valued guest, the park layout, and delivering on the company's four major promises: safety, courtesy, efficiency, and entertainment. When Disney found that guests were asking sweepers, cleaners, and other janitorial staff all sorts of questions, they started training them, making sure they know where the rest rooms are, how to get from one ride to the next, what time the parade starts, and anything else a guest might want to know.

Lands' End gets about 14 million calls a year at their various call centers, but new operators and customer service people aren't allowed to take a single call until they've received 75 hours of training. And at the Ritz-Carlton hotels, first-year managers and employees receive 250 to 310 hours of training.

Unfortunately, a lot of companies I know have actually cut training programs because they're tired of spending money giving employees skills to put on their resume so that they can get a job with the competition. I see the point, but I think money spent training employees and improving their skill base is well worth it. Sure, you'll have some jerks who will take advantage of you. But most of the time employees see training as a sign that you're interested in them and committed to them, which will make them more loyal. Even if someone you trained does leave before you have a chance to recoup your investment, chances are that she'll be so delighted with the way you treated her that she'll tell her friends how great it was to work for you. Southwest Airlines, for example, has a great reputation in the industry for the way it treats employees. Turnover is far lower than the industry average, and the company is consistently rated as one of the best places to work. I think it's no coincidence that *Forbes* says the company is one of the most admired in the country.

Okay, here's the return-on-investment part: The American Society of Training and Development found that spending money on training actually improves companies' shareholder return and gross profits. In a recent survey they did, ASTD found that companies that spent about $1,500 per employee on training every year saw a 24 percent increase in profits and a 218 percent increase in income per employee.

Empower Them

Giving employees some control over their environment and the authority to make decisions goes a long way. After being trained, Disney's cast members are given the authority to do whatever's required on the spot to deal with problems and keep guests happy. They're actually discouraged from getting management involved. And at the Ritz-Carlton, any employee can spend up to $2,000 to handle a customer complaint or rectify a problem.

Quit Giving Them Bonuses

Well, sort of. If you do give bonuses, at least tie them to customer satisfaction and not some other useless measures. You can't reward your in-house sales reps for achieving calls-per-hour and sales-per-call goals and still expect them to establish rapport with your customers and build relationships with them.

Your employees need to understand and have respect for what you're doing. Not long ago, MCI did a study of seven telephone customer service centers. They found a significant link between employees' perceptions of the quality of MCI's service and how satisfied their employees were. The more satisfied employees were, the more satisfied customers were, and the more likely they were to keep using MCI.

One big consulting firm surveyed tons of employees at different companies and asked whether their employers deserved their loyalty. Less than half of them felt that their company stood for anything that was worth making a commitment to. That's a dangerous place for you to be.

The final piece of the puzzle is that you're going to have to learn to quickly adapt to a constantly evolving environment. As the economy and political situation change, customers will insist on better service. This means you'll have to provide your employees with extra training in how to deal with customers' demands.

At the same time, employees' quality-of-life and work-life balance issues are going to gain importance, and they'll put a higher value on intangible benefits such as flexibility and telecommuting. Some may decide that life's too short to be stuck doing things they don't like, which may make them more likely to leave jobs if they aren't happy. Others who are more risk averse may be more inclined in uncertain times to stay with employers who provide them a safe haven and give them a chance to increase their value in the marketplace.

CHAPTER 9

The Proof Is in the Pudding

I've given you dozens of examples of mistakes that companies in every country in the world make when it comes to their advertising. And I've tried to drill home the point that companies will fail if they don't stop making those mistakes. We need to broaden their definition of advertising to include more than 30-second television commercials or well-designed print ads. We need to stop resting on our laurels and stop acting as though a big brand name is enough to get customers to walk through the door. We need to figure out who our customers are and what they want, and we all need to constantly give those customers reasons to buy. We need to demand concrete results from every dollar we spend and stay focused on selling more stuff more often to more people for more money. **Finally, we need to never, ever forget that *everything* communicates.**

In this chapter, I give you two case studies that do an excellent job of illustrating exactly what happens when companies don't follow my advice. You've heard of both these companies. One became famous because of a dog, the other because of a number: Chapter 11.

Feeling a little skeptical? Don't be embarrassed; you're certainly not alone. Most businesspeople feel the same way. But let me put it this way: A lot of the companies I currently consult for are run by executives who just a few years ago were telling me I was nuts and were making all sorts of excuses for why they had to keep doing what they'd always done. Eventually they came around, and if you keep paying attention, so will you.

Oh, one other thing: Although some of the information I'm talking about in these cases came from my talks with company execs and Zyman Marketing Group's proprietary research, most of it came from trade journals (including *Advertising Age*, *Chain Store Age*, *Brand Week*, and *Restaurant News*), newspapers (including the *Wall Street Journal*, *New York Times*, *Chicago Tribune*, and *Los Angeles Times*), magazines (including *The*

Economist), analyst reports (*Dow Jones Corporate Filings Alerts* and others), and other public sources, which in a way makes these cases even sadder than they already are. After all, by the time news about how badly a company is screwing up gets into a place where anyone with a computer can get to it, the company itself has known—and not acted on—the same information for a long, long time.

KMART

If Kmart has such a well-known brand, what's it doing in bankruptcy? Simple: Kmart forgot about positioning. It was once the low-price leader, but when the competition forced a change from promotion-based pricing to everyday low pricing, Kmart couldn't—or at least didn't—make the shift. Remember what I said about positioning yourself or someone else will do it for you? Instead of vigorously defending its position or trying to reposition its core brand to keep it current, the company moved into specialty retailing—a big mistake for a generalist. It couldn't keep up with changing demographics and let its stores fall apart. The result, as Dustin Hoffman's character said in *Rain Man*, is that "Kmart sucks."

Almost no one remembers anymore, but Kmart actually created the concept of discount retailing in America in 1962. It was such a success that it quickly overshadowed its parent company, Kresge, which had been around since 1897 and was one of the largest general merchandise retailers in the country. Kmart was the absolute change leader. They defined a whole new way of shopping, offering a low-price alternative and focusing on understanding consumers and their behavior.

Growth was phenomenal. In the 1970s, Kmart doubled their annual sales and decimated the competition (which at this point included Wal-Mart) by opening as many as 250 stores a year. Then it seems that they got a little cocky and kicked back, thinking that the incredibly powerful and well-known Kmart brand would be enough to keep discount shoppers streaming in the doors.

It reminds me of when the Pepsi Challenge rolled into the first Texas market. It created a lot of buzz and Coke's sales actually grew! Top management's immediate response was "See? No problem. They can't touch us." Others of us, which would include me, said, "Better watch out— they're stealing our future." But no one paid any attention. Apparently the same thing happened to Kmart. Competitors were quietly copying all or part of their positioning. I can just imagine someone in the company saying, "Hey, they're ripping us off left and right out there." And I can imagine some dumb manager answering, "Nah, they're not the same. They can try, but they can't be us." Famous last words.

By the 1980s, Wal-Mart was still playing the part of the tortoise to Kmart's hare. They and Kmart's other competitors continually upgraded their merchandise and inventory systems and modernized the look of their stores to keep up with current trends. Kmart kept napping. In 1990, Wal-Mart had used the straight-to-the-point slogan, "We Sell for Less," to completely reposition Kmart right out of their own niche. Wal-Mart overtook Kmart as the biggest discount retailer.

When Kmart finally woke up, it was too late. They thrashed around looking for some way to get back in the business and settled on trying to attract a more affluent clientele. Their plan was to keep using Blue Light specials and deep discounts on a few items to entice customers into the stores, then get them to buy more expensive, high-markup, designer-label products, such as Martha Stewart.

If Kmart would have done even the most basic market research, they would have found what just about anyone in the country could have told them: The Kmart brand meant low-cost merchandise. Shoppers looking for Martha Stewart wouldn't think of going to Kmart, and current Kmart shoppers couldn't have afforded Martha even if they'd wanted her.

Kmart was chasing after two completely different demographics, and the results were predictable, just as they would be if Southwest Airlines were to all of a sudden install expensive first-class seats and dress their flight attendants in ball gowns. People fly Southwest because it's cheap and fun. People shopped Kmart because it was cheap, period. Eventually, Kmart was repositioned by both Wal-Mart, which outdiscounted Kmart, and by Target, which went for the cool-stuff-for-less market in their modern, architect-designed stores.

As if that weren't bad enough, Kmart had relied for years on an outdated (although pretty successful) way of reaching customers: They used huge numbers of newspaper supplements and advertising circulars to announce massive reductions on the loss leaders that they hoped would lure customers over to the designer section. Besides being phenomenally expensive, this kind of advertising put a strain on the company's merchandising and distribution systems because orders for those loss leaders came in huge waves. This kind of erratic order cycle also made it impossible for Kmart's suppliers to predict manufacturing runs, which ultimately raised Kmart's prices.

If nothing else, this last point illustrates what I've been saying about needing to see a return on every expenditure. Because Kmart's advertising methods ended up increasing their costs, there was no way they could compete head-to-head with Wal-Mart on price. (Wal-Mart's "everyday low pricing" strategy completely eliminated blips in their supply chain and almost completely eliminated the need for advertising, since they rarely had any sales to announce.)

In 2000, Kmart's new CEO, Charles Conway, tried to stop the hemorrhaging by upgrading the company's computer systems and supply chain. But the patient was practically dead.

Okay, let's talk about packaging, which, as I hope you remember, goes beyond the actual carton that something comes in. When it comes to Kmart, the packaging I'm talking about is the store itself.

During their big growth period in the 1970s, Kmart built most of their stores in cities. As people began relocating from the cities to the suburbs, Kmart was left with a declining customer base. Wal-Mart and Target, on the other hand, who had built stores in the suburbs from the start, were having a field day. To top it off, Kmart spent hardly anything on upgrading stores or on employee training. Along the way, they earned themselves a reputation for having dingy, old-looking, outdated stores staffed by people who couldn't get jobs anywhere else. After a while, Kmart became a cliche for low rent and low class. **Everything communicates.**

And it only gets worse. Apparently things weren't bad enough for Kmart, so starting in about 1984 they went on a buying binge, snapping up Walden Book Co., Payless drugstores, Office Max, Borders bookstores, and Builder's Square—businesses that had little or nothing to do with Kmart's core brand. I don't know how many times I've said this, but if you're increasing your revenues through acquisitions, it's going to catch up with you eventually. By 1994, that's exactly what happened, and the company nearly went bankrupt. They ended up having to sell almost all of their recent acquisitions, plus they closed about 200 of their own stores.

Then Kmart did perhaps the worst thing of all. They started cutting advertising, which naturally put the nail in their coffin. All they would have had to do was keep defining what the Kmart brand was all about. If you're having trouble getting people to buy your brand, you need to give them a reason to buy, right? But if you don't advertise, how can consumers possibly know what you want them to do?

Let me give you some hard numbers that might illustrate for you the exact financial ramifications of Kmart's packaging, positioning, strategy, branding, market research, and advertising failures, and their refusal to demand a return on their investment:

- From 1990 to 2000, Kmart's market share dropped from 30 to 17 percent. Wal-Mart's went up from 30 to 55 percent on sales of $218 billion, up from $33 billion, and Target's rose from 10 to 13 percent on sales of $39 billion, up from only $15 billion in 1990.
- Kmart seems to do pretty well in places where they aren't competing head-to-head with Wal-Mart or Target. Unfortunately, according to some estimates I've seen, there's a Wal-Mart or a Target within seven driving minutes of 80 percent of Kmart's stores. Too bad.
- Since 1987, Kmart's sales were up 52 percent. Sounds pretty good, until you hear that Target's were up 600 percent and Wal-Mart's were up 1,800 percent over the same period.
- Over the last 14 years or so, Kmart has earned less than $4 billion. That's what Wal-Mart earns in 6 months.

TACO BELL

The Taco Bell story is similar to the Kmart story in a number of ways: Both created powerful brands that defined their category, both rode a wave of incredible growth, both sat back and did nothing while their competitors responded to the market's needs and overtook them, both lost touch with their core customers and got repositioned by the competition, both tried to be all things to all people, and both had to deal with serious quality, customer service, and packaging issues. But what really makes Taco Bell so interesting is that they had one of the most popular ad campaigns of the late 20th century.

The company got started in the early 1950s in San Bernardino, California at the same time and in the same town as the McDonald brothers opened their first restaurant. The idea of good-quality, inexpensive, quickly served Mexican food was a hit. The company grew rapidly, and by 1977, when they were bought by Pepsico, they had about 900 stores and sales of $108 million (essentially a rounding error next to McDonald's $3.7 billion).

But Taco Bell wasn't worried about McDonald's because they'd done a fine job of differentiating themselves from the burger chains with their adobe-looking buildings, sombreros, and Mexican-sounding menu. By 1984, they'd become so successful that they decided to move out of the Mexican fast-food sector and into the mainstream.

That meant taking on McDonald's and Burger King and the others, which they did by remodeling their stores, making their uniforms less ethnic looking, adding drive-thrus, and including some gourmet items on the menu—in other words, getting rid of most of the things that had differentiated them from their competitors in the first place. At the same time, though, they created new differences: "We have all the same stuff as the burger guys," they said, "meat, cheese, lettuce, tomatoes—it just looks a little different. Plus, we make your order fresh for you right on the spot, so it doesn't have to sit around under a heat lamp for hours." All in all, a fantastic example of how a company can reinvent and reposition itself in response to changing trends. The new identity gave people a reason to buy and sales kept rising.

In 1988, though, growth stalled and Taco Bell snapped into action. They did some consumer research and introduced the 49-cent taco—a move clearly aimed at attracting 18–34-year-old guys, daily users who actually ate some kind of fast food 17 times a week. Really. They identified a group of consumers, found out what they wanted, and gave it to them— great stuff. They developed a huge following among college-age students and budget shoppers and sales took off again. Later, they added a three-tiered pricing structure and business just kept getting better and better. Pretty soon Taco Bell had a 70% share of the Mexican sector and a 3% share of the overall fast food category. Not bad.

But then a whole bunch of things happened that turned the tide. First, there were reports that in order to keep their prices low, the company had cut corners on quality, including their beef, which was obviously a main ingredient. Second, they neglected to take into consideration that their core market—broke college students—were growing up, getting jobs, having kids, and watching in horror as the fried tacos of their youth started to build up around their guts. Third, by the mid-1990s, everyone in fast food had some kind of value pricing, which meant that cheap tacos weren't enough to grab anyone's attention anymore, and Taco Bell couldn't come up with any other compelling reasons to get people to buy Mexican instead of a burger and fries.

When sales flattened out, Taco Bell did exactly the right thing by firing their ad agency: If the ads aren't selling the product, dump them. But then, in some kind of misguided attempt to reduce expenses, they stupidly cut their ad budget from 8% of sales down to 5%.

And then they got hit with something completely beyond their control: The press started going on and on about how unhealthy fast food (and Mexican fast food in particular) was—too much fat and cholesterol. Taco Bell responded immediately, coming up with "Border Lights," a line of lower-calorie, lower-fat items. "Border Lights" must have seemed like a good idea at the time (their CEO even announced to the press that they'd sell $5 billion worth of "Border Lights" over the next 5 years) but they really should have done some more research.

The fact that they came up with a low-cal, low-fat menu at all seemed to a lot of people almost like an admission that Taco Bell had been selling unhealthy food. And the fact that they left the high-cal, high-fat items on the menu and charged less for them seemed (to me, anyway) like a sign that they didn't care. Also, by announcing such an optimistic sales goal, they set a target that they couldn't possibly hit—a violation of my rule about making changes first, shooting your mouth off later. Worst of all, they abandoned their core customers. Male college students think they're indestructible and don't care about fat or calories. Women do. Another rule broken: Work on keeping the customers you have before you go out and chase down new ones. No big surprise that same-store sales immediately tanked, dropping 4% in 1995 and another 2% the next year.

As you can see, what started off as a responsive, well-run marketing organization had started to fray around the edges. In 1997 Taco Bell started a completely new ad campaign featuring talking Chihuahuas and wrestlers wearing pink tights. The wrestlers disappeared fairly quickly, but people loved the dogs, and by the end of 1997, Taco Bell had introduced the phrase "Yo quiero Taco Bell," which doubled the amount of Spanish most people knew. The dog went on to become the most recognized—and most awarded—spokesanimal of the decade.

Immediately after the first Chihuahua commercial aired, sales took off. People—especially teens—stopped what they were doing, took a new look at the company, thought "Hey, cool," and went to Taco Bell and bought something. But when the next dog ad and the one after that never went beyond the humor and didn't give customers any reason to go back to Taco Bell, they said, "So what?" and went to Pizza Hut instead.

One of the main reasons to hire spokespeople (or spokesanimals) is to borrow some of their imagery. Can you tell me what kind of image a talking dog that looks more like a long-legged rat could have for a restaurant? Personally, I don't think the connection could possibly do a restaurant any good.

Sales slipped and kept on slipping for the next two years. Eventually, the company realized that winning ad industry awards wasn't selling any enchiladas, so they dumped the dog, who was followed pretty quickly by the CEO, who'd agreed to keep the campaign running long after it was obvious that it was a disaster.

The board brought in a new CEO, Emil Brolick, who used to run Wendy's. He figured that the way to turn things around was to introduce some higher-priced items, just like Wendy's had done. But instead of helping, that just made things worse: Was Taco Bell going after more affluent customers by offering upscale fresh-Mex, or were they going after the Gen-X-ers with low-priced bulk food? While Taco Bell was trying to get a prescription for corporate schizophrenia drugs, other Mexican fast-food chains (like El Pollo Loco, Rubio's, Del Taco, and Baja Fresh) that knew their customers were delighted to step in and pick up some market share.

Taco Bell's more upscale menu generated slightly more revenues but also reduced transaction volume. So they flip-flopped again and tried to get back into value pricing with some new 99-cent selections. But by then it was almost hopeless: The company that had created value pricing in the first place and had completely defined its category had completely lost track of who its customers were. To make things worse, they'd let their packaging go to hell, too: Consumers were tired of the watery beef the company had been using to cut costs, and they were bored with a menu that hadn't changed much in years. The restaurants were dirty, service was slow, and the employees had a lot to learn about customer service.

Taco Bell has started taking steps to rebuild. They're cleaning up stores, improving customer service, and trying to make up their mind about which customers to go after. They've already started to see results:

Earnings from the second half of 2001 through the first quarter of 2002 were up a little. But given where they were before, they've still got a long way to go.

Still, Taco Bell doesn't give up easily. They fought back before and they can do it again. They just need to stick to what they know and remember that people need reasons to buy, and they need them over and over and over again.

CHAPTER 10

Never Miss Another Opportunity

I've been in marketing and advertising for about 30 years, and I still marvel at the number of companies that never seem to miss an opportunity to miss an opportunity. I know that I've pointed out dozens of ways that businesses of all sizes screw up their advertising either by refusing to recognize that **everything they do communicates** and that **everything is advertising** or by simply mismanaging their existing advertising efforts. At the same time, I've given a lot of real-life examples of companies that do their advertising right, and there are plenty more that I didn't talk about. But it is puzzling that very few companies ever try to apply to their business what has been successful for others.

As you were reading the previous chapters, you may have occasionally muttered to yourself that you already knew what I was talking about and you may have wondered what kind of return you'd be getting on the money you spent on this book. I have two things to say about that: (1) If you already know or have seen or have thought of all these things, why haven't you acted on them? (2) The fact that you thought about the investment you made in this book is a sign that you've already absorbed one of my biggest points: Get a return on every nickel you spend. I'll bet you weren't doing that before.

Finding learning opportunities isn't hard—they're all over the place. All it takes is a bit of looking and some creativity. So I'm going to leave you with a whole bunch of questions that I've thought about over the years—questions that I think will show you just how many opportunities there are out there that most people miss.

The object here isn't to get you to answer all these questions. My goal for this chapter (and for the whole book, really) is to have it be like yoga for your brain—a tool that can help you limber up those synapses and stretch your limits a little. At the end of the workout, you'll be able to look at things in a different way, and you'll never have to miss another opportunity to deepen your relationships with your customers, grow your brand, and increase your sales.

• Have you ever wondered why in-flight airline magazines don't sell airline tickets? Those magazines have actually become independent profit centers that generate their own income stream. Typically, they always have a letter from the president of the airline talking about some award the airline won or the newest employee of the quarter. Then they move on to a series of ads for credit cards and exercise machines and executive book clubs and speed reading programs and everything but the most important thing: airline tickets.

What a missed opportunity! Here they are with a captive audience. They've got a guy sitting in front of their magazine for an hour or two or five or eleven. The fact that he's on the plane reading the magazine in the first place is a pretty good indication that he flies once in a while and that he flies that airline. So why don't they try to sell him more tickets? The simple answer is that airlines—and most other businesses—suffer from the same disease: an insistence that it's more important to go after the customers they don't have than to try to sell more stuff to the ones they do have. If you've been paying attention, you know where I'm going with this: Acquiring new customers is a hell of a lot more expensive than retaining existing customers.

You saw what happened after September 11: People stopped traveling, at least for a while. Swissair went out of business and so did Sabena. And most of the airlines that were left posted record losses and cut routes left and right. But there are still plenty of people flying. All the airlines would have to do is devote a little space in their own magazines to helping current passengers plan their next vacation, or explain how flying to places they normally drive to can save them time and money. If every regular passenger took just one more trip a year, the airlines would be back in the black in no time.

• How many times have you sat in a movie theater watching the previews and decided months before the movie has even been released that you're going to see a particular film? So why don't other companies in other businesses copy the coming attraction model? Microsoft does, but they're pretty much alone. They announce that they're coming out with a new version of XP or Office or whatever; they tell us how they've developed the program, what's new about it, how it responds to customers' concerns, and how it's going to change our lives. The result is a lot of buzz, a lot of publicity, and a lot of people making purchase decisions well in advance. Chances are that you can do the same kind of thing, maybe on a different scale, in your own business. Hey, if George Lucas can have people camping out in front of movie theaters three months before he releases the latest *Star Wars* installment, why can't you?

• Why do retailers spend so much of their money and time trying to increase store traffic and so little to convert the traffic that's already there into sales? Back when I was just starting out in marketing, I remember some more senior people talking about how supermarkets engineered their stores. They figured out that consumers tend to walk into a store and mosey along the inside perimeter. So the grocery traffic engineers set things up so that the biggest impulse buys and the products that had the most velocity—which, coincidentally, happened to be the biggest margin products—were arranged right where the most customers would be.

Why don't more companies do that? The Limited is a pretty typical case, redesigning their store layouts every week for the past twenty years. If very many companies are taking a cue from the grocers, I haven't heard about it. And even if they are, why is it that only about 20% of people who go into retail stores actually buy something?

A few companies try to convert their existing customers. Ikea does it in the most infuriating way, by making their stores into mazes and practically imprisoning their customers. Wal-Mart, however, has done a great job. They know they have to talk to consumers in every possible way. They not only greet each one at the door, but channel them through to different places and manage the interaction between them and the merchandise in a very proactive way.

• Why don't very many companies know exactly who their heavy users are? When I worked for the Coca-Cola Company, our business grew because we understood the daily drinkers, the heavy users. If all we could get is all the people that drank every day, we'd have been perfectly happy. Wouldn't Pearle Vision Centers be thrilled to have customers who buy new glasses or contacts every year? (They probably have the information right in their computers and could print up a list anytime they wanted—assuming they'd think to do so.) Wouldn't McDonald's like to serve only the people who buy a Happy Meal or some kind of combo every day instead of trying to get Pizza Hut customers to make a change? Wouldn't the airlines like to have people who travel more often—not necessarily the business traveler, but people who pay those full fares? And shouldn't the auto makers know which people buy a new car every year and target them? Why are so many companies leaving so much money on the table when all they'd have to do is reach right out and grab it?

• Why don't businesses pay attention to what politicians do? Politicians know how to win customers, and the reason they're so successful is that they have a drop dead date. In business we don't have drop dead dates. There's always some excuse for why we aren't selling as much as we should be or making as much as we should be: a bad quarter, the economy, the weather, the cat ate my homework, whatever. Politicians who have bad quarters go back home and can't attract customers for four years. Can you imagine what would happen if companies that didn't make what they should have had to close a plant for a year? Don't you think that having a sword like that hanging over their heads might make them just a touch more aggressive and might get them to create ads that sell instead of ads that entertain and win awards?

• How come insurers don't think of the total consumer capture? I have a different insurer for my cars than for my houses. And none of the agents I deal with have bothered to call me with an offer to consolidate all my coverage. Why aren't these agents being trained to see a massive opportunity to get existing customers to buy something from them that customers are paying more to get from someone else? How come we haven't been able to figure out that advertising and communication in general is intended to build relationships that will create customers for life? Whenever I give a speech, I ask people how many of them are customers for life. No one raises their hand. Then I ask them how long they've been patronizing the same neighborhood restaurants or gas station or grocery store or cleaners. It's amazing that even though so many of us *are* someone's customer for life, we don't recognize it and do what it would take to get our own customers into the same position.

• How come we didn't learn anything from the dot-coms about the stupidity of capturing any eyeballs they could instead of targeting the ones with the wallets?

• We're all probably members of some "reward and recognition" program, such as a Hertz #1 or United Airlines Mileage Plus. So why don't more of us understand that *recognition* is more important than *reward*? We feel special when we get to board the plane first. And we feel special when the maid at the hotel drops a *USA Today* or the local newspaper outside our room. And we feel special when the desk clerk tells us when we're checking in that she's upgrading us—at no charge—to a room on the VIP floor. Those neatly arranged little bottles of shampoo in the bathroom, which cost the hotel almost nothing, say "I care." The broken ice machine down the hall says "I don't." Why don't more companies get this?

I spent some time talking in several earlier chapters about how what happened on September 11, 2001 changed the business landscape. I don't want to rehash those discussions here, but I want you to get a sense of how profound those changes have been.

Imagine taking a glass of water and just shaking it a bit. When the water stops sloshing around it'll look pretty much the same as it did. But the water you're looking at after the shakeup is fundamentally different. There's not a single hydrogen or oxygen molecule that's in the same place it was. The molecules that were there still are, just in a completely different place. This may seem like a silly analogy, but it really isn't.

Too many companies made the mistake of just wrapping themselves in the flag and hoping that the impact of September 11 would blow over and that everything would get back to normal soon. They were wrong. Sure, at this point things may have settled down, and they may even look the same as they used to, but *everything* is different.

September 11 gave us an excuse to center ourselves, to rethink exactly where our values are and to figure out what we want to do with our lives in the future. It also brought us out of the closet and made it okay to say that the economic situation in the United States and the rest of the world wasn't quite as rosy as we'd have liked. And it allowed us to rethink a lot of the value propositions we live by, to figure out what kind of capacity we truly have for action and how we're going to utilize our assets.

All this has turned the ad business on its head. Our consumers may look the same, but the molecules in their brains have shifted. Asking *what* isn't enough anymore; we also have to ask *why*. And knowing how people *think* isn't enough, either; we have to know what they *feel*. But one thing hasn't changed: If all that knowledge about your consumers doesn't make them buy your product or service, you're pouring your advertising money down the drain.

I could write another 500 pages and still not hit all the sales-increasing advertising opportunities that businesses miss every day. Even if I could list them all, I'm not sure it would help you. But you can help yourself by learning to think critically about what's going on around you. Whenever you buy something, ask yourself why you bought that product instead of the alternative. And whenever you find yourself patronizing someone else's business and saying, "Hey, that was a good idea," think about whether there's some way for you to adapt that idea to your own business.

If you pay attention, you'll see that I've been right all along: *Everything communicates*. Advertising opportunities are everywhere, and just being aware of this will help you get more out of your existing programs and will enable you to develop broader, more effective strategies. With that under your belt, you'll be better able to do what you really wanted to learn to do when you picked up this book in the first place: Sell more stuff more often to more people for more money.

One last thing: Microsoft has their proprietary code, Kentucky Fried Chicken has their patented combination of 11 herbs and spices, and McDonald's has their secret sauce. And then, of course, there's Coca-Cola's closely guarded secret formula. All that mystery and mystique makes for great advertising slogans, but the *real* secret behind the success of these companies and many others has nothing to do with Java script or food and chemical ingredients. Instead, it all comes down to hiring the right people for your organization and giving them the leadership and skills they need to succeed. If you can't do that, you're doomed to fail.

Most corporate CEOs will agree with me. Whether they're heading up a huge multinational or a small start-up, they'll tell you all day long that their people are their most important asset. Too bad so few of them actually act that way. The truth is that when it comes to people, most companies have no idea what they're doing. They don't know how to find the best people, they don't know how to lead them, they don't know how to manage and teach them, and they don't know when to get rid of them.

But I do. I'm the guy with the secret formula. Hey, maybe I'll write a book about it. . . .

INDEX